I Eat, Therefore I Think

I Eat, Therefore I Think

Food and Philosophy

Raymond D. Boisvert

FAIRLEIGH DICKINSON UNIVERSITY PRESS
Madison • Teaneck

Published by Fairleigh Dickinson University Press
Copublished by The Rowman & Littlefield Publishing Group, Inc.
4501 Forbes Boulevard, Suite 200, Lanham, Maryland 20706
www.rowman.com

16 Carlisle Street, London W1D 3BT, United Kingdom

Copyright © 2014 by Raymond D. Boisvert

All rights reserved. No part of this book may be reproduced in any form or by any electronic or mechanical means, including information storage and retrieval systems, without written permission from the publisher, except by a reviewer who may quote passages in a review.

British Library Cataloguing in Publication Information Available

Library of Congress Cataloging-in-Publication Data
Boisvert, Raymond D.
I eat, therefore I think : food and philosophy / Raymond Boisvert.
pages cm
Includes bibliographical references and index.
ISBN 978-1-61147-686-6 (cloth : alk. paper)—ISBN 978-1-61147-687-3 (electronic)
1. Food. 2. Philosophy. I. Title.
B105.F66B65 2014
100—dc23
                              2014007094

ISBN 978-1-61147-712-2 (pbk : alk paper)

∞™ The paper used in this publication meets the minimum requirements of American National Standard for Information Sciences Permanence of Paper for Printed Library Materials, ANSI/NISO Z39.48-1992.

Printed in the United States of America

For the next generation:
Alex, Lorène, Daniel, Heike

Contents

Acknowledgments ix

Introduction 1

1. Ceres Disrupts Philosophy as Usual 9
2. Hospitality: The Elemental Virtue 21
3. Hungry Being: The Parasite 37
4. Knowledge: Carnal, Personal, Convivial 55
5. Art as Invitation 73
6. Clock Time/Stomach Time 93
7. Fraternity as a Political Ideal 105
8. Religion, Recipes, Negligence 119

Conclusion 135

Bibliography 149

Index 161

About the Author 165

Acknowledgments

Books like this identify a single author, but that person could not possibly have produced the work alone. My Siena College colleagues in the philosophy department have read and listened to various versions of this manuscript and provided helpful commentaries. For that I am grateful to Julian Davies, Paul Santilli, John Burkey, Jennifer McErlean, Pablo Muchnik, Joshua Alexander, and Fanny Söderbäck. The same is true for two helpful colleagues in Siena's political science department, Laurie Naranch and Vera Eccarius-Kelly. In the wider world of philosophy I have gained invaluably from conversations with and criticism from Lisa Heldke. Without the help of librarians, many hours would have been lost trying to find sources. For their assistance I am indebted to Sean Maloney, Catherine Crohan, John Vallely, Pat Markley, Sean Conley, Bill Kanalley, and Gary Thompson.

Physically putting together a manuscript is time-consuming. I was much helped by the secretaries in the faculty support office at Siena College. In that regard I wish to express my gratitude to Ellen Johnson, Sue Kuebler, and Yana Usyatinskaya.

Several chapters are based on earlier essays. For permission to use material originally published elsewhere I am grateful to the following:

- The Pennsylvania State University Press for use of material from "Diversity as Fraternity Lite," *Journal of Speculative Philosophy* 19, no. 2 (2005): 120–128.
- The University of California Press for use of material from "Clock Time/Stomach Time," *Gastronomica* 6, no. 2 (2006): 40–46.
- The Philosophy Documentation Center for use of material from "Ethics is Hospitality," *Proceedings of the American Catholic Philosophical Association*, 78 (2004): 289–300.

- The University of Illinois Press for use of material from "What is Religion? A Pragmatist Response," in Stuart Rosenbaum, ed. *Pragmatism and Religion: Classical Sources and Original Essays*, 209–228. Copyright 2003 by the Board of Trustees of the University of Illinois.
- The Southern Illinois University Press for permission to use, as an epigraph, a passage from John Dewey, *Art as Experience*, in *The Later Works*, vol. 10, 1925–1953: 1934.

As I wrote these pages the memory of my grandfather Josaphat Deslauriers, a good cook as well as a kind and gentle man, kept me company. My entire interest in the philosophy/food intersection would never have arisen at all were it not for my wife Jayne who made me appreciate the many interlocking levels of beauty and meaning associated with eating.

Latham, NY
Five Islands, ME

Introduction

Essen und Trinken hält Leib und Seele zusammen.[1]

—German proverb

UN-FORGETTING THE STOMACH

Herman Melville's narrator, Ishmael, thought he knew the direct relationship between philosophy and the stomach. They were incompatible. He described "a man who gives himself out for a philosopher" as someone who "must have 'broken his digester'" (Melville, 59). Boris Pasternak also used food-related imagery when he had Lara, in *Dr. Zhivago*, complain: "I think a little philosophy should be added to life and art by way of seasoning, but to make it one's specialty seems to me as strange as eating nothing but horseradish" (Pasternak, 339). One novelist tells us that philosophers have defective stomachs. The other that they settle for a monotonous, marginal diet. As we shall see in this book, there is much to vindicate the two indictments. Academic philosophy too often ignores the stomach and embraces the "we only deal with horseradish and we are proud of it" isolation from ordinary life. This book is an attempt to show how philosophers can be better served if they appreciate in their professional lives what they take for granted in their ordinary lives: good "digesters" and well-balanced meals.

The roots of the philosophy/stomach incompatibility run deep. Plato, the great fountainhead of all Western philosophy, set the tone early. Our "need for nurture," he complained, only obstructs the attainment of truth (Plato 1977, 15, 66b). In that regard, Plato remains emblematic of the "broken digester" attitude of philosophers. Plato's greatness, however, is that just about everything in philosophy is already contained somewhere in his works. It is not surprising then, that he also provides a crucial hint that will allow us to move beyond the incompatibility identified by Ishmael. When he wrote about how we gain knowledge, Plato's analyses took a surprising turn. Instead of stressing novelty, breakthroughs, or heretofore unknown material of any kind, he spoke of "remembering" or "recollection." For him, this was linked to a story about the preexistent soul and knowledge it already contained.[2] Even without this background, the term remains significant. His word was *anamnesis*, literally "not forgetting." This emphasis on "re-collecting," or if we use the Greek root, "de-amnesia-ing," can serve as an important reminder (anamnesis again) for us.

Much coming to awareness is, in fact, recovering what has been forgotten, neglected or relegated to the margins. No individual or culture can hold all important concerns at the center of attention all the time. A botanist and a geologist on a hike will pay attention to different aspects of their surroundings. As certain dimensions become focal, others, of necessity, move to the periphery. Similarly, if a political community wishes to privilege equality, all sorts of good things follow. Individuals from the lower and middle classes, women, along with racial, ethnic and religious outsiders, can now take their rightful places based on talent, not birth. When equality is overemphasized, however, when it is too focal, then, as Kurt Vonnegut's "Harrison Bergeron" made clear, other important ideals, freedom, justice, prosperity, development of talent, tend to be diminished.

Recognizing this focal/marginal interplay, and taking a clue from Plato, we can define an important task for philosophers. Their work is that of revisiting the margins, examining the forgotten, and advocating for some re-collection of them as part of a reorganized focal mix. They engage in such activity realizing its never-ending character. Each newly established central cluster will occasion a penumbra of its own. This, in turn will necessitate a renewal of the entire process. Such alternating perchings and flights, to use a metaphor from William James, define the philosophical life cycle (James 1890, 243).

The book that follows is an exercise in *an-amnesis*. It does not seek, as Descartes did when he set the pattern for Modern philosophy, to sweep away inherited wisdom and begin from radically new foundations. It aims, more humbly, to alter the mix that has become dominant in much contemporary philosophy. Its goal is un-forgetting, or phrased positively, retrieval. We shall see, however, that although this is a simple goal, its ramifications are not simple at all. They provoke important reorientations in how we understand ourselves, our fellow human beings, and the natural world. In this regard my analysis seeks to restore an older understanding of philosophy as a "way of life," in the expression of Pierre Hadot.[3]

Because philosophers engage in thinking, logic, reflection, and contemplation, they are tempted to overlook how philosophy is a "way of life." In this regard, they are reinforced by a special forgetfulness. Biologically, this neglect is surprising. It involves discounting something that is as obvious as it is necessary: the human being's recurring cry for food. Professional philosophers can hardly deny that they are embodied, stomach-equipped creatures. Still, when it comes to engaging in the work of philosophy, this aspect quickly disappears. As we will see in chapter 1, with very few exceptions, philosophers have, even if their digesters were not literally broken, kept their spotlight away from stomach and resolutely focused on mind. This has led to a disregard for what is manifest, omnipresent, and, although overlooked, philosophically significant.

EGGHEADS, NOT EGG EATERS

Literary satire has gone further than Melville and Pasternak in describing stereotypes. On one of his adventures, Gulliver visits a land populated by mind-dominated individuals, the "Laputans." Their effort is directed at those most nonmaterial of subject matters: mathematics and music. Still, being physiological creatures, they need food. As eggheads, they can't be bothered growing it. Since they live on an island suspended above the earth, "wine and victuals" have to be "drawn up by pulleys" from the land below (Swift, 161). To make them palatable, these victuals must undergo an initial transformation. For us, this might mean using grandmother's recipes, a favorite cookbook, new ingredients. Not so for the Laputans. Preparing food means sculpting it into shapes that reinforce their two areas of interest. They will only eat what resembles food as little as possible. Gulliver is stunned to find on his plate "a shoulder of mutton, cut into an equilateral triangle" along with a pudding shaped "into a cycloid." The second course offers "two ducks, trussed up into the form of fiddles," sausages that resemble flutes, and pieces of bread cut "into cones, cylinders, parallelograms, and several other mathematical figures" (Swift, 159).

While we might not appreciate much about how the Laputans approach food, their tables remain places where something partially recognizable as a meal is served. The next step in the rationalization of eating would be to find someone who eliminated this connection altogether. Another delightful storyteller, L. Frank Baum, has given us just such a character in *The Magic of Oz*. He is, of course, a "professor." His name: Wogglebug. Wogglebug revels in his wonderful invention, the meal-in-a-tablet. This is a time-saving, efficiency-enhancing device. It provides the equivalent of "a bowl of soup, a portion of fried fish, a roast, a salad and a dessert, all of which gave the same nourishment as a square meal" (Baum, ch. 21). Here is the highest ideal for abstract, instrumental rationality: provide nutrition in the most time-saving manner. Who could complain? Well, the intended beneficiaries, for one. Wogglebug's students were not at all impressed. He, proud inventor, was stunned by their ingratitude. They longed for tasty food. "It was no fun at all to swallow a tablet, with a glass of water, and call it a dinner; so they refused to eat the Square-Meal Tablets" (Baum, ch. 21). When Wogglebug insisted, the students, rambunctious, disrespectful, food-loving bunch that they were, "threw him into the river—clothes and all" (Baum, ch. 21).

Thankfully, real philosophers are neither Laputans nor Wogglebugs. Still, an overemphasis on mind situates them in the Laputan/Wogglebug trajectory. Setting out on a different path, this book examines what it means to welcome our status as stomach-endowed. As we shall see, this is not a matter of simply adding one more element to the current synthesis. Taking the stomach seriously occasions a major rethinking of what has been the dominant philosophical perspective for several centuries. The chapters that follow develop a coherent grasp of things, a philosophy, in other words. They do so in a language that is direct and minimally technical. If the book succeeds, readers will be encouraged to reconsider certain basic assumptions that have, for a long time, provided the channels that guide the stream of ideas. By the book's end, readers should be able to think of philosophers without imagining them as either Laputans or Wogglebugs.

RETHINKING PHILOSOPHY

Plenty of preliminary work has been done by other philosophers but with an important difference. Most reflection that takes food seriously has been in the realm of applied philosophy. This has been especially true with regard to questions of ethics. World hunger, the treatment of animals, gender questions, vegetarianism, agricultural practices, and genetically modified foods have all been subjects of important studies. Famous names like Peter Singer, Mary Midgley, and Tom Regan have made contributions here, along with newer thinkers like Susan Bordo, Lisa Heldke, Erin McKenna, Andrew Light, Paul Thompson, and Michiel Korthals. There is an ample bibliography of works on these topics.[4] In another area, aesthetics, Carolyn Korsmeyer has almost single-handedly reacquainted the two contexts for "taste": that of the table and that of the creative arts. Her groundbreaking *Making Sense of Taste* gives a good indication of how traditional philosophical approaches come in for broad revalorizations when taste in its primary biological sense is taken seriously.

By contrast to these more targeted explorations, my own investigations address the nature of philosophy itself. This is a book about how philosophy, along with its subfields, would undergo important transformations if a new point of departure were adopted. What point of departure? That of embracing the concrete blend of stomach and mind that after all identifies us, the beings who engage in philosophizing. Lisa Heldke has identified a four-level taxonomy to classify how philosophers deal with food. The most prominent involves applying philosophical categories "to new or uncustomary food-related topics," addressing hunger from the perspective of Aristotelian or Kantian ethics, for example. Another has to do with switching contexts for ongoing deliberations, treating vegetarianism, say, as an issue about food and eating rather than one simply about animals. The third results from textual research that rediscovers what philosophers in the tradition have explicitly said about food. The fourth she describes this way: "rephrasing/recasting familiar philosophical questions in new ways prompted by analyses of food." My undertaking falls within this fourth category. Such a project, Heldke goes on, can encourage substantial alterations in the philosophical grasp of things. It can "disrupt or transform longstanding features of our philosophical map." It can also "reveal unacknowledged philosophical presuppositions" and allow for "fundamentally new ways of philosophical thinking" (Heldke 2006, 207–208).

To develop a philosophical touch that can "transform longstanding features of our philosophical map" and encourage "fundamentally new ways of philosophical thinking," the chapters that follow unfold in a particular order. Chapter 1 explores the standard philosophical focus on the mind and the kinds of mind-exclusive approaches typically developed by philosophers. It retrieves a more concrete starting point for philosophy: everyday lived experience. The new originating center brings with it an important shift in at least two key areas. First, typical textbook questions such as "How can I know anything?" or "Is the world really there?" move from center to periphery. Second, the language of subject and object, dominant for so long, comes to be displaced. In its stead the human being, reviving an older term, is recognized as a "convive." The convive is literally the one who "lives with" others but is also the table guest, the one who finds continuity between the biological, the social, the ethical, and the esthetic. The revision of philosophy's originating questions takes us back, most fundamentally, to a world where *dealings* with things, not wondering about their reality, set the context for philosophizing.

Chapter 2 extends the moral question by exploring hospitality. Here is a virtue closely associated with food, and, perhaps for that reason, neglected by philosophers. Since philosophical reflections on this topic are scarce, the chapter draws on religious and literary sources. Hospitality's older meanings are recovered in a way that moves beyond the current understanding, mostly reduced to "entertaining one's friends." Getting a more comprehensive grasp on hospitality requires thinking of hosts and guests in a wider context, that of dealing with strangers, outsiders, those who are different from us. The difficult question "Who is my neighbor?" drives the discussion.

Chapter 3 continues this line of thinking by exploring a pejorative food-related term, "parasite." Once again, we are confronted with an important memory loss. What has been forgotten is how the term was once honorific. The original "parasites" (literally, "fellow-eaters") worked the sacred grain fields in ancient Greece. They were given, as a reward, a place at the communal dining table. When the multiple meanings (honorific, pejorative, biological, sociological) of "para-site" are recollected, their very complexity allows "parasite" to serve as root metaphor for understanding some generic traits of existence. This is especially true in terms of revalorizing two terms dismissed in older philosophical orientations: dependence and neediness. Rehabilitating dependence and neediness makes us suspicious of campaigns that privilege social purity by identifying "parasites" whose annihilation is deemed a necessary step toward preserving self-enclosed purity.

Purity along with certainty have typically been praised as defining traits of knowledge in the most honorific sense. Chapter 4 challenges this praise. Here, the path of un-forgetting takes us all the way back to Genesis. The Hebrew term for "knowledge" has several concrete senses, including that which has come down to us quaintly as "carnal knowledge." Philosophers have tended to privilege, by contrast, a detached, impersonal, spectator stance for achieving certitude. A stomach-sensitive perspective, taking shared meals seriously, will move "personal" knowledge back to the center. Growing familiarity over time becomes, once again, the model for knowing. The risk, vagueness, approximations, and fallibility that accompany this model are embraced as key ingredients if the aim is seeking truths rather than certitude.

The general theme of moving beyond the spectator self-image occasions important reconsiderations of our relationship to the arts. This is the subject of chapter 5. Dismissing our self-imposed amnesia about the stomach allows a renewed appreciation for the many ways we are participants rather than spectators. The stomach, after all, necessitates active dealings with the world. Drawing on both the American philosopher John Dewey and Yanagi Soetsu, the Japanese champion of what he called *mingei*, "arts of the people," chapter 5 explores how participation, community, and involvement now become central to art "works" (art "objects" being no longer a suitable label). Instead of the spectator-friendly painting as the exemplary art, the participant-friendly tea ceremony comes to occupy a prototypical position. Art is now thought of in terms of invitation and gathering, an approach that helps make sense of Heidegger's claim that art is the "becoming and happening of truth" (Heidegger 1971, 71).

Tea ceremonies, along with the biological rhythms of tea plants, provide the opening images for chapter 6, dealing with time. Time was a major preoccupation of twentieth-century philosophers. Martin Heidegger, Henri Bergson, Alfred North Whitehead, and William James were insistent that we are beings-in-time, not creatures outside of it. But how exactly are we to think of time? Typically, we turn immediately to clocks. In doing so, we marginalize that aspect of time associated with lived experience. When we bring attention back to the stomach, we find ourselves in the presence of one of nature's great rhythmic timekeepers. An efficiency-dominated world will want abstract, absolutely predictable, perfectly coordinated timekeeping. This is clock time, uniform, linear, neutral with regard to natural occurrences, and one source of our harried condition. Our stomachs and their recurrent calls for nutrition remind us of another time, one that is inextricably linked to natural occurrences, to repeating periods, to calls and responses, to consummations. It is a source of burgeoning possibilities, not fleeting moments. Reviving what the chapter calls "stomach time" allows us to confront "chronomania," the contemporary world's manic fear of unproductive lost moments.

One loss, when efficiency dominates, is simple conviviality. Chapter 7, taking a brief look at political philosophy, focuses on this loss. The great forgotten dimension here is *fraternity*, one component in the French Revolution's democratic slogan. *Liberty* and *equality*, the other two, remain central in both theoretical and policy considerations. Fraternity, though, has faded into obscurity. When democracy is more than just a formalistic set of procedures, when it is, as John Dewey put it, a "way of life," there is one key question for determining whether its promise is lived out in the practices of citizens: "Guess who's coming to dinner?" When that question can be answered generously, democracy flourishes in everyday life. When it cannot, the promise of democracy beyond its structural, procedural forms still leaves much to be desired (Dewey 1937, 217).

Religion, the subject of chapter 8, builds on the reminder of how we are involved with and implicated in our natural and social circumstances. Mind might have the luxury of dwelling on the fantasy of isolated, nondependent existence. Stomach does not. One etymological strand often associated with the word "religion," that it derives from *ligare* to tie or bind, provides a clue for my analysis. It helps retrieve a sense of religion as primarily the attitude that deeply feels the pervasiveness of interconnections and the responsibilities such an attitude brings with it. Religion is a great yea-and-amen saying to our condition as this kind of creature in this sort of world. Chapter 8 builds this case around a specific image: a little girl holds a handful of mashed potatoes. It's her birthday and the mashed potatoes are the best the inmates in the concentration camp can do to celebrate. In doing so, they also commemorate linkages that oppressive forces wish to drive into the ultimate forgetfulness, oblivion by extermination. "Recalling the ligatures" could be the shorthand definition of religion that results from this chapter.

RECIPES AND A LITERARY FRIEND

In the end, "recalling the ligatures" and Hadot's "way of life" could be thought of as two themes running through the entire text. Mind-exclusive philosophy can get away with emphasizing spectator-style, disinterested understandings of the human condition. Such a step is precisely what is blocked by a philosophy that remembers the stomach. In order to help keep the association of mind and stomach operative, each chapter includes an eating pause. Those pauses indicate a favorite recipe. Each is easy to make and amenable to customization for adapting to various tastes. The inclusion of recipes also serves to remind us how, instead of escaping into make-believe realms of pure reason or absolute certitude, a stomach-sensitive philosophy grows its analyses in the soil of ordinary lived experience.

Popular fiction has created a philosopher who understands this well. She is Isabel Dalhousie, editor of the *Review of Applied Ethics*, and protagonist in Alexander McCall Smith's detective series, The Sunday Philosophy Club. Isabel knows that some philosophers "think of nothing but consciousness" (Smith 2005, 93). Her own temperament has led her to acknowledge how "everyday life was exactly what philosophy was about" (Smith 2005, 150). She even asserts that "there is every reason why a philosopher should think about food" (Smith 2005, 203). As someone familiar with how philosophy is generally practiced and understood, she knows how such a statement requires explanation and justification. It "could be made only after a great deal of earlier ground had been covered and understood" (Smith 2005, 150). The chapters that follow aim at covering that very ground.

NOTES

1. "Eating and drinking keep the body and soul together." Tanslation by the author.
2. Plato's clearest statement is found in his dialogue entitled *Meno*.
3. Speaking of the ancient Greeks, Hadot put it this way: "Philosophy was a method of spiritual progress which demanded a radical conversion and transformation of the individual's way of being. Thus, philosophy was a way of life, both in its exercise and effort to achieve wisdom, and in its goal, wisdom itself. For real wisdom does not merely cause us to know: it makes us 'be' in a different way" (Hadot, 265).
4. See the bibliographical entries under Singer, Walters/Portmess, Regan, Aiken /LaFollette, Midgley, Mepham, Heldke/Curtin, Thompson, Bordo, McKenna/Light, Berry, and Korthals.

Chapter One

Ceres Disrupts Philosophy as Usual

> Among these latter, the Act of Eating which hath by several wise Men been considered as extremely mean and derogatory from the Philosophic dignity, must be in some Measure performed by the greatest Prince, Heroe, or Philosopher upon Earth
>
> —Henry Fielding

AN UNLIKELY BANQUET

The ample tables were ready. Appropriate decorations filled the hall. After all, this was to be a memorable feast. "Memorable" in a quite literal sense, since well-known names echoed throughout the room. The philosophy table featured Kant and several Hegels. Post-entrée servings included a Descartes cheese and a Leibniz dessert (Onfray 1995, 251). The feast unfolded as the brainchild of Daniel Spoerri to celebrate his induction to the Cologne Academy of Fine Arts. Spoerri had made food central to his work, going so far as to open a restaurant serving such delicacies as elephant trunk and bear meat (Onfray 1995, 248). A banquet marking his admission to the Academy seemed appropriate. But not just any celebratory meal. His would be a "homonym" banquet, which is why he had invited Mr. Kant and several Hegels to be his guests.

Following Spoerri's lead, but using our imagination, we can envision a feast for actual philosophers. The tables are situated around a central statue, that of Ceres, ancient Rome's version of Demeter, the goddess of agriculture. This is only fitting. The bounty to be shared is, after all, a gift from her. She also embodies several reminders of importance to this particular group. First, her presence signals dependency. The diners are dependent on factors not of their making, especially soil and weather. A second reminder derives from the Indo-European root for her name. "Ceres" can be traced to *ker, to grow (Klein, 261). In this way she helps philosophers recall how their task involves seeds and growth. As Michel Serres points out, what good is a philosophy if it does not give birth to new worlds? (Serres 1992, 120). Finally, Ceres urges the guests to keep their attention focused on those concerns identified by the label "concrete" (from *concrescere* to "grow with," another derivative of *ker). Her presence is crucial, since rootedness in lived experience, what should be the alpha and the omega of philosophical activity, tends too readily, with this group, to be neglected.

Limited neither by time nor by the requirement of homonyms, we can gather people from a wide range of places and times. Leibniz, Descartes, Voltaire, and Rousseau can represent continental pre-Enlightenment and Enlightenment thought. There are places for Confucius from ancient China, as well as for Democritus, Plato, Aristotle, from the land that gave us the original story of Demeter/Ceres. The British Enlightenment will be represented by Locke, Hume and Berkeley. To Schopenhauer, Nietzsche, and Kierkegaard goes the task of representing the nineteenth century. Important figures from the turn of the twentieth century, William James, Henri Bergson, Bertrand Russell, Charles Peirce, and Gabriel Marcel, will be there.

Because of his importance, a place will also be set for Jean-Paul Sartre. This is a controversial choice. He tended to be a rather difficult dining companion. Those unfortunate enough to be seated at his table would notice immediately what has come out in stories of his life: personal hygiene was not a high priority. They might also be troubled by his dining demeanor. Unlike his Gallic compatriots, Sartre was annoyed by the body's regular cry for nutrition (Onfray 1989, 135–136). An inveterate city-dweller temperamentally uncomfortable with nature, he rarely ate vegetables or fruits unless disguised in pastry. Tomatoes revulsed him, as did seafood of all sorts. His preferences were for foods that had undergone the transformative effects of human hands. Sausages, sauerkraut, and chocolate cake were his favorites (Onfray 1989, 143). In deference to him, no crustaceans will be served. Not only did he detest anything from the sea, but once, in a post-mescaline state, he had imagined himself stalked by a lobster (Onfray 1989, 140).

Such a dinner, even without Sartre, seems not only fanciful but incongruous. It is not so much the mixed chronology of the guests. It is rather the oddness of the group and its setting. Three aspects stand out immediately: (a) Although they are all philosophers, most were not professional academics (James, Bergson, and Russell, for part of his career, are the only professors on the list); (b) every one of them is male; (c) there is also the incongruity of the setting. Picturing philosophers sitting around eating, "digesters" intact and being put to good use, will, as it did for Ishmael, strike most readers as strange.

We are used to Rodin's depiction of a thinker, solitary, introverted, occupied by deep ruminations (though not of the food sort).[1] The famous statue is naked, as if the philosopher in purest form could not be bothered at all with the goings on of normal, mundane life. The quotidian needs of food and food preparation, together with the appetite that drives them, have been at odds with "philosophical" interests since the ancient Greeks. Plato, we saw in the introduction, set the tone in his *Phaedo* by complaining that food was a distraction from higher things. He went so far as to write a dialogue, *The Symposium*, which is about a banquet where everything of interest begins only after the eating. Plato's disdain for appetite goes hand in hand, as feminists tend to remind us, with another sort of contempt. Not only is food missing from *The Symposium*, but women are banished as well. There is a central "female" in the dialogue, but she is an imaginary goddess who celebrates escaping the body as the best way to characterize love. Philosophy's towering early figure thus bequeathed his successors a triple exclusion: banquets without food, men without women, and love without the body. Women and embodied-ness made a real mark on late-twentieth-century philosophy. It is now time to redress the third exclusion, food.

A quick look at philosophy's history gives a sense of how challenging is this task. Plato's successor, Aristotle, needed no more than a comparison with cooking to dismiss music's role in education: "If they must learn music, on the same principle they should learn cookery, which is absurd" (McKeon, 1338a, 39–41). Such a harsh judgment was only reinforced by Aristotle's ranking of the five senses. He described the two "lowest" ones, touch and taste, as "slavish and brutish" (McKeon, 1118a, 26). Arthur Schopenhauer, although separated from the classical Greeks by some two thousand years, echoed the sentiment. Discussing art, he praised still-life paintings, unless they contained food. The exception, and it is a telling one, was fruit dangling on trees. These existed in a natural, pre-food state. What was Schopenhauer's objection? Food stimulates the appetite, incites desire, and draws us into entanglements with the world. It thus makes us prisoners of the object-enslaved will. Distracted in this way, we are far removed from the ideal of pure will-less contemplation (Schopenhauer I, 207–208).[2] The most important truth to be recognized, according to Schopenhauer, is the need for salvation attained by a "decided opposition to nature" (Schopenhauer II, 628).

Popular culture echoed this sentiment in a famous exchange. Early in the *African Queen*, Katharine Hepburn reacts in supercilious disgust to Humphrey Bogart with the phrase, "Nature, Mr. Allnut, is what we were put in this world to rise above." Such a sentiment, with regard to food at least, had a grip on one giant of twentieth-century philosophy. According to his biographer, Ludwig Wittgenstein "did not care what he ate so long as it was always the same" (Monk, 552). The tastes of another twentieth-century giant, Sartre, have already been discussed. He may have disdained the necessity of eating, but he considered his own mouth an organ to be kept occupied. A menu of the daily nonfoods that passed through his lips is instructive: two packages of especially strong cigarettes alternating with constant puffing on a pipe; at least a liter of various alcoholic beverages, especially beer, wine, distilled spirits; amphetamines, aspirin, and barbiturates; all bathed in cup after cup of tea and coffee (Onfray 1989, 136). Perhaps the most egregious case was that of Kurt Gödel, the mathematician-philosopher. Convinced that he was being poisoned, he stayed away from food altogether. The sad but inevitable result: he died of starvation.

Although they span two millennia, and hold sharply diverging views (they are philosophers after all), this Plato to Gödel sampling makes us aware that when it comes to dismissing food, there is cross-generational agreement. The great philosophical issues do call out to us, but it is a call best answered, according to these thinkers, by ignoring the annoying distractions associated with food and eating.

EATING PAUSE:
SIMPLE FISH IN WINE SAUCE

Surely, of the philosophers who ignored food in their theoretical life, some actually savored it in moments of relaxation. Since this is the first chapter, a delicious, yet easy-to-make recipe (yes, students, even you *can succeed with this one) seemed a good place to start. I borrow this from the household of Daniel (son), Heike (daughter-in-law), and Ben (grandchild). It is an adaptation of a recipe from Anthony Bourdain. Except for the sauce, it's a lot like sole meunière (miller's wife sole), so named because step one is to dredge the fish in what would have been abundant in the meunière's household, flour.* **Ingredients**: *about a pound of firm white fish; 1/2 cup flour; 4 tbsp butter in all; 1/2 to 1 tbsp capers (depending on personal taste); juice of 1/2 to 1 lemon (personal taste again); 1/2 cup of dry white wine.* **Preparation**: *Put flour in suitable container for dredging fish; season fish by adding salt and pepper; dredge fish in the flour.* **Cooking**: *Heat 2 tbsp butter over medium-high heat; cook fish until golden brown, about 2 minutes each side, depending on the thickness; remove the fish to a serving platter, keep warm; heat remaining 2 tbsp butter; add capers and heat through briefly (1/2 minute) and add lemon juice; add wine and heat through (about 1 minute). Cover fish with sauce and serve.*

A FEW STOMACH-FRIENDLY THINKERS

"To feed on books, for a philosopher or a poet," as George Santayana once said, "is still to starve" (Santayana 1931, 40). This is an incontrovertible datum. Even philosophers, in their moments of ordinary humanity, must admit its truth. A few have, bucking the trend described above. Having an *h* or a *u* in one's name seems to help. Combining both is even better. From ancient Greece, we get Heraclitus (*h* and *u* accounted for) who greeted visitors in an unusual place. Reacting to their surprise, he assured them that gods were present even in the kitchen (Freeman, 105). The next major exception is David Hume from eighteenth-century Scotland. With him it could well be more a matter of practice than theory. Late in life, he dedicated himself, as he put it, to "display my great Talent for Cookery." Hume's girth, Edward Gibbon referred to him as the "fattest of Epicurus's Hogs," may explain his positive food attitude (Mossner, 560, 561). He and Aristippus, a younger contemporary of Socrates, are the only two Western philosophers known to have been chefs.[3] The most famous phrase from a philosopher who embraced food came from someone whose first and last names included two *u*'s and one *h*, Ludwig Feuerbach (1807–1872). He is the source for the well-known "man is what he eats." The German pun ("der Mensch ist was er isst") is missed in translation. Feuerbach's claim is not to be taken literally. His phrase did not indicate support for a narrowly reductive materialism. He was simply and humorously providing a catchy phrase to make a point: the material dimension in life is important and must not be overlooked.[4] From Asia, we get other hints of a positive outlook. Lin Yutang, keeping the Confucian tradition alive in the twentieth century, referred to humans as "stomach-gifted" (Lin, 44). There is no trace of disdain for the material dimension of life in his description of the "Chinese spirit" that "glows over a good feast." Instead of body-spirit opposition, there is continuity. "From this well-filled stomach suffuses and radiates a happiness that is spiritual" (Lin, 46).

Overall, though, Hume, Heraclitus, Aristippus, Feuerbach, and Lin Yutang remain striking exceptions. In general, the philosophical community, whatever the epoch, either ignores or demeans one of humanity's central needs. Raising a challenge to this attitude, John Dewey, in the 1920s, urged philosophers to pay attention to that dimension of human experience concerned with "direct enjoyment" in "feasting and festivities." This was an area, Dewey claimed, that "hardly received the attention from philosophers that it demands" (Dewey 1925, 69). Here, presumably, was a good sign that the twentieth century would alter the philosophic penchant for either silence or disparagement when it came to food.

By and large this has not happened. The twentieth century ended with reflection on food almost as marginalized as ever. I say "almost" because as we enter the twenty-first century, there are some indications, small ones admittedly, of a change. In France, Michel Serres and Michel Onfray have taken reflection on food seriously. In England, Elizabeth Telfer has produced a book on philosophy and food. On this side of the Atlantic, the Deweyan challenge has also been taken up. Lisa Heldke, together with Deane Curtin, broke important ground with their anthology *Cooking, Eating, Thinking* in 1992. Susan Bordo's *Unbearable Weight* followed in 1993. Leon Kass produced *The Hungry Soul* in 1994. Carolyn Korsmeyer's *Making Sense of Taste: Food and Philosophy* appeared in 1999. In 2001 we saw the publication of Gregory Pence's *The Ethics of Food*. Heldke returned with *Exotic Appetites* in 2003. In 2004 Michiel Korthals published *Before Dinner: Philosophy and Ethics of Food*. The Open Court Press Popular Culture and Philosophy series joined the fray with a collection entitled *The Atkins Diet and Philosophy* in 2005. That same year Korsmeyer's important anthology *The Taste Culture Reader: Experiencing Food and Drink* was released. Other recent titles include *Food and Philosophy* (2007), edited by Fritz Allhof and Dave Monroe; Roger Scruton's *I Drink, Therefore I Am* (2010); and *The Philosophy of Food* (2012), edited by David Kaplan.

REDISCOVERING THE CONCRETE

Is this just a fad, or is it a trend that can move philosophical life forward? It is too early to tell, but these efforts do reflect the reawakening of an attitude that got off the ground with people like Dewey in the early 1900s, only to be lost by mid-century. One of philosophy's great intramural battles is between two antagonistic self-understandings. Philosophers wonder about everything including what the heck philosophy itself is. One self-understanding believes that philosophy is best done by and for specialists in highly technical analyses of arcane issues mostly involving "mind." Pasternak's Lara probably had people like this in mind when she complained about an unrelenting diet of horseradish. The other camp embraces philosophy as the thoughtful search for ways to live a good life, philosophy as continuous with the wisdom traditions of archaic societies. Midway through the twentieth century, Susanne Langer, fretting over the excesses of philosophy on the horseradish-only side (overspecialization, emphasis on "impractical puzzles" disconnected from the concerns of ordinary people), complained that the "springs of philosophical thought have run dry once more." The need, she said, was for a "whole world of new questions" (Langer, 13). Unfortunately, most of the questions that came to dominate English-speaking philosophy in the postwar period were associated with the "analytic philosophy" tidal wave that swamped American colleges and universities. This, as readers who have taken philosophy courses will realize, kept philosophy focused on technical issues relating to mind and language.

Such a focus reinforced rather than disrupted the asomatic tendencies that run deep in Western thought. With only two years left in the century, John Searle could still publish a work whose opening page asserted that "for a large number of philosophers the philosophy of mind is now first philosophy." Searle's book was to be a general introduction to the subject and carried the title *Mind, Language, and Society*, the last word suggesting perhaps a move (slight, given the title's two other terms) in the direction of philosophy as confronting issues dealt with in wisdom traditions. However, reflecting on his book after finishing it, Searle indicated that this move did not materialize. "I set out to write a book about mind, language, and society, and now that it is finished, I discover that a disproportionately large part of it is about the mind" (Searle, ix, x).

This was not the inexorable direction for philosophy to follow. In the opening decades of the twentieth century, there had been, besides Dewey, alternative inspirational springs to replace the ones identified by Langer as having run dry. Jean Wahl summarized these well by calling his 1932 study of Alfred North Whitehead (1861–1947), William James (1842–1910), and Gabriel Marcel (1889–1973), *Vers le Concret*. This "turn to the concrete," ignored in postwar English-speaking philosophy, is being resurrected by those works that take food seriously. The ramifications of rooting reflection in the concrete fullness of lived experience was discussed independently by William Barrett who was a sensitive reader of philosophy's history. Modern (roughly 1600–1900) philosophy, he noted, had effectively transformed embodied humans into dessicated "epistemological animals." "From Descartes to Kant, man was taken fundamentally as a perceiving-thinking animal, a mechanical body plus a conscious soul." Fortunately the period from the mid-nineteenth to the mid-twentieth centuries had seen a great "widening and enrichment of data." The older, simplified picture was gradually enhanced by "new sources of information, new regions of experience and feeling." At first, accumulation of the new data took place "within the old framework." As the accumulation mounted, however, it effected a "transformation of the whole." There was hope, in other words, for Langer's "world of new questions." Barrett's expression for the altered impetus both echoed Wahl and celebrated the linguistic association with Ceres: "I think we may baptize it as *The Search for the Concrete*" (Barrett 1964, 28, 29).

This search, in the United States, lost its most important guides when analytic philosophy marginalized the great American Pragmatists (William James, Charles Sanders Peirce, John Dewey), removing them for a generation from mandatory reading lists in philosophy classrooms. As we enter the twenty-first century there is hope that a growing number of philosophers will embark on a trek away from the world of "impractical puzzles," about which Langer complained. They can turn instead to what another great American early-twentieth-century thinker, George Santayana, called a "living philosophy." This would be one seeking to articulate "a distinct vision of the universe and definite convictions about human destiny" (Santayana 1913, 36). The details of this distinct vision and these definite convictions would depend on how philosophers undertook what Barrett called the "transformation of the whole." My aim in this book is to sketch what that transformation would look like if food and food practices were taken as worthy subjects of philosophical reflection. Some of those changes, as subsequent chapters will indicate, involve significant shifts in our basic understanding of things.

REAL HUNGER VERSUS PRETEND DOUBT

These initial comments are offered in the hope that readers will get a sense of how profoundly the whole atlas of philosophical maps would be altered if philosophers began to draw sustenance (so to speak) from an ever-present but overlooked source. The most immediate shift would reconnect philosophy to ordinary life. When thinkers choose a starting point far from the realm of Ceres, when they begin with detached minds, then judgments like that of David Pears make perfect sense: "Philosophy unlike religion, is not a part of ordinary life, but a kind of excursion from it" (Rorty 1982, 31). Such an attitude has not been with philosophy from the beginning. It rose to special dominance with the detour and new pathways that became dominant in Modern philosophy, pathways crystallized by Rene Descartes (1595–1650). The main direction for this detour led, eventually, to the place described by Searle: philosophy of mind as primary philosophy. In general, the rich landscape of philosophy came to be dominated by one feature. Epistemology, the theory of knowledge, a subfield, kept metastasizing. Eventually, philosophy came to mean, essentially, epistemology.

The route left behind by this detour was one championed by the "philosophy as a way of life" thinker Pierre Hadot. As a scholar of Greek philosophy, he emphasized a distinction highlighted within Stoicism, "a distinction between discourse about philosophy and philosophy itself" (Hadot, 266). Discourse, analyses of concepts, examination of language were important. They remained, however, not ends in themselves. They were subordinate to the ultimate goal of living a good life. The very word *philo-sophia*, love of wisdom, Hadot pointed out, "was enough to express this conception of philosophy." "For real wisdom does not merely cause us to know: it makes us 'be' in a different way" (Hadot, 265).

Instead of questions about how to be in the world, the post-Cartesian detour encouraged questions about whether the world could be said to be at all. When "first" philosophy is philosophy of mind, a particular set of questions moves to the center. Foremost among these are musings, like those undertaken by Descartes in the third of his *Meditations on First Philosophy*, about whether the world in general and even one's body in particular are actually there. Such questions have both frustrated undergraduates and given much ammunition to those who relish parody. As Bishop Berkeley described it, philosophers first throw dirt into their eyes then wonder why it is that they cannot see.[5] This is crudely put but touches an important issue. Points of departure, what we choose as the initial center out of which to work, are crucial. Philosophy is a reasonable, logically coherent enterprise. Having once chosen our starting points, we cannot simply declare how we wish those starting points to play themselves out. They have an inner dynamism and consistency of their own.

In the case of mind-centered philosophy, the dynamism leads directly that bane of entering philosophy students: "Is this table really there?" What seems most to puzzle authors of introductory textbooks is something ordinary people deal with effortlessly. The textbook philosopher asks whether the world is really there, and if it turns out really to be there, whether we can have any knowledge of it. Questions of this sort always sound odd to nonphilosophers. After all, they mostly think of themselves as part and parcel of a wider scheme of things through which they navigate fairly well. When they're hungry and reach for an apple, they aren't really led to wonder whether either their hand or the apple is really there. Philosophers, by contrast, have worked hard for several centuries to ring all the changes possible on what happens if we start by imagining we are not as we really are.

Descartes got all this "let's imagine we are not what we are" bandwagon going by starting his Third Meditation this way: "I will now shut my eyes, stop my ears, and withdraw all my senses" (Descartes 1641, 24). With this as an opening move, typical textbook questions seem inescapably urgent. One introduction by D. Z. Phillips, for example, gets right to the heart of the matter. For those puzzled about the sorts of problems broached in a book called *Introducing Philosophy*, the subtitle is ready with a distinct response: *The Challenge of Skepticism*. Phillips's text could more accurately, if long-windedly, be titled *Introducing something that still goes by the name philosophy but is really one sort of epistemology, that which assumes the Cartesian make-believe moment as a starting point*. The first three chapters give the game away: "Philosophers' Doubts," "Minds and the External World," "Primary and Secondary Qualities." Eventually the skeptical issue is dealt with and overcome. In the meantime, much ink has been spilled because of an initial move that is wholly artificial. First, dirt is thrown into the eyes. Then, a whole eyewash industry, academic philosophy, inc., emerges.

CONVIVES "R" US

The resulting edifice is an intellectual tour de force. It is widespread and entrenched. But it is based, here is where this book's theme comes into play, on an initial "make believe." Philosophers check their hungry selves at the office door. Saying "no" to ordinary life is the real wellspring of much current academic philosophy. Saying "yes" would change things dramatically. One particular "yes" is especially important: admitting the inseparable intermingling of psyche (mind), and gaster (stomach). This simple affirmation would change the nature of introductory textbooks. Stomachs can't waste time on universal doubt. They begin where they are. They have real concerns and aims, accompanied by real investigations about how to address them. Starting from scratch, setting aside inherited experience, shutting one's eyes, stopping one's ears, and withdrawing all one's senses, Descartes-style, could be deadly. Hungry selves have to deal with their ambient and depending on sense experience and traditional wisdom offer good places from which to begin. As hungry creatures, they do not pretend to be what they are not. They welcome having ears to hear, eyes to see, hands to grasp, and legs to move. They have to hunt, sow, harvest, process, store, cook, and, of course, eat. Plenty of real questions, concerns, and doubts present themselves. There is no need to invent artificial ones.

Charles Taylor is a Canadian philosopher who generously welcomes influences from a variety of traditions. He has succinctly critiqued the view that gives rise to artificial skepticism: "We can draw a neat line between my picture of an object and that object, but not between my dealing with that object and that object" (Taylor 1995, 12). Imagine, if it is not too difficult, that philosophers leave behind their self-image as pure thinkers spinning make-believe scenarios for themselves. They are now seated at the banquet imagined at the beginning of this chapter. They appreciate the role of Ceres and the human efforts needed to cooperate with her. The very way in which they identify themselves and their surroundings will have to change. For three centuries, philosophy has operated as an ellipse with two foci: "subject" and "object." Who were the subjects? Well, us. But not the whole us, certainly not the stomach-gifted us. Rather "subjects" were essentially humans-as-minds. As such, one of their main occupations was wondering about the connection between two separate realms set over against one another: the mind as a sort of container filled with ideas on one side and what came to be labeled "external" objects on the other. Subject and object thus came to prominence as two central components helping define the conceptual landscape of Modernity. They well suited what was an essentially spectatorial understanding of our place in the general scheme of things. We were minds with pictures of the external world in them. This led, naturally enough, to the reasonable (within this context) question about how the pictures in the mind were related to the objects in the world. But it is just this spectatorial context, the Modern conceptual landscape, that is put into question when we give up our make-believe illusions by admitting that we are stomach-gifted as well as mind-endowed. When Ceres and agriculture are brought back into the mix, it is dealings with things, not detached ideas about them, that take center stage.

Giving gaster its due, we can retrieve an old word. Such a move will allow us to replace the abstract, eliminative "subject" with the concrete, inclusive "convive." The convive, etymologically someone who shares a life with, literally, "lives with," is part of a nexus marked by interconnections and interdependencies. The convive is also, as its dictionary meaning indicates, someone who shares a table in enjoyment and celebration. The convive's life, by contrast with that of the subject, revolves around saying yes to its participational setting. It revels in consummatory experiences that emphasize body-spirit continuities. Such individuals, those who, in Taylor's terms, admit the primacy of *dealings* with the world, have a hard time drawing sharp barriers, whether between their minds and their bodies, themselves and the world, or the natural and the spiritual. With Santayana, the convive believes that "everything ideal has a natural basis and everything natural an ideal fulfillment" (Woodbridge, 4). Unlike the subject whose initial move is detachment, the convive is, from the beginning, immersed in dealings with both the natural world (gardening, hunting, gathering in order to guarantee sustenance) and the social world (cooking and eating with others, having learned from tradition which foods to prize and which to avoid). Those dealings, when accepted as the primary context for philosophizing, make it hard to highlight the skeptical questions prominent in introductory textbooks. We deal with things when we take for granted our interactions with them. Important questions are then raised, but they are those arising from the best ways to use intelligence for guiding those dealings toward their appropriate ideal consummations. The inspirational center for a stomach-sensitive philosophy thus moves away from the "can we know anything at all" approach of subject-centered thought. We begin, instead, with a question more consistent with that of Hadot's Stoics: How can we make our practices thoughtful?

Such a question embodies the first lesson associated with taking food seriously: the need to undertake a major shift in the very orientation of philosophy. The make-believe position of a spectator trapped within a mind can be jettisoned as the artifice it has always been. An individual, now a "convive" rather than a "subject," is someone "engaged in practices" and is a "being who acts in and on a world" (Taylor 1991, 308). Given this new, more concrete grasp of the human condition, what Charles Guignon describes as "our everyday, pretheoretical, practical lives" (Guignon, 83), we no longer need reveries of escape. In place of the fantasy that projects a disembodied subject, there is the convive, an embodied, social creature trying to make its way by engaging in well-considered practices. Once gaster is allied to psyche, the "philosophy as a way of life" ideal can be restored to its proper place. No longer is the activity to be thought of as David Pears's "excursion" from everyday life. Rather, it becomes the way of achieving thoughtful practice, the search for a wisdom that occasions a fruitful, flourishing life.

NOTES

1. That Rodin's thinker has become iconic in this sense is itself incongruous since, in its original setting, the sculpture had an altogether different purpose. It wasn't even called the "thinker." Composed as part of Rodin's "Gates of Hell," the reflective figure was called "the poet" and stood for Dante looking down on Rodin's doors filled with characters from *The Divine Comedy*.

2. Late in his work, supporting a pessimistic understanding of the human condition, Schopenhauer cites Luther: "In our bodies and circumstances, however, we are all subject to the devil and are strangers in this world, of which he is prince and lord. Hence everything is under his rule, the bread we eat, the beverage we drink, the clothes we use, even the air and everything by which we live in the flesh." *The World as Will and Representation*, Vol. II, p. 580.

3. That Aristippus was a chef is based on secondary evidence. Lucian, writing his satire *Philosophies for Sale*, referred to one individual on the auction block, probably Aristippus, this way: "Easy to live with, good company at parties, and a perfect companion for an amorous spendthrift out for a night on the town with a chorus girl. Besides, has a good knowledge of pastry and is an excellent chef—in short, a professor of soft living" (Lucian, 320).

4. See the article by Cherno in the bibliography.

5. Bishop Berkeley (1685–1753), after whom the California city is named, chastised fellow philosophers in this way: "Upon the whole, I am inclined to think that the far greater part, if not all, of those difficulties which have hitherto amused philosophers, and blocked the way to knowledge, are entirely owing to our selves. That we have first raised a dust, and then complain, we cannot see" (Berkeley, 90).

Chapter Two

Hospitality

The Elemental Virtue

> We took for a class motto the early Saxon word for lady, translated into bread-giver, and we took for our class color the poppy, because poppies grew among the wheat, as if Nature knew that wherever there was hunger that needed food there would be pain that needed relief.
>
> —Jane Addams

FEEDING STRANGERS

What delivers 2,300 calories, weighs just less than two pounds, comes fortified with vitamins, and is acceptable within the widest variety of cultural or religious dietary restrictions? It's life-saving fast food: the HDR, "humanitarian daily ration." HDRs, according to guidelines prepared by an interlocking group of acronym-friendly United Nations organizations, UNHCR, UNICEF, WFP, and WHO, have the advantages of a "long shelf life" and of being "convenient, fast and logistically easy to distribute" (*Food and Nutrition Needs*, 25). As far as the calorie total, the number 2,300 is a bit higher than the agreed upon 2,100 average for needy people with a "light physical activity level," aka PAL (*Food and Nutrition Needs*, 1). The acronym organizations are, by the way, the office of United Nations High Commissioner for Refugees, the United Nations Childrens' Fund, the World Food Program, and the World Health Organization.

When it comes to humanitarian aid, "fast food" takes on a different meaning from that associated with the drive-through. Victims of natural catastrophes or wars can often count on receiving HDRs within one day according to the website of the WFP. What they receive varies, but a typical menu goes like this: "Bean Salad, Barley Stew, Lentil Stew, Lentils and Vegetables, Rice and Vegetables in Sauce Herb Rice, Crackers, Vegetable Biscuits, Biscuit, Peanut Butter, Jam, Vegetable Crackers, Raisins, Fruit Bar, Flat Bread, Shortbread Cookie, Apple Fruit Bar, Fruit Pastry" along with an "Accessory Pack" containing "Red Pepper, Pepper, Salt, Sugar, Spoon, Matches (unprinted) and Towelette (alcohol free), Napkin" (Smith, 2004). This project of providing food prepared in one part of the world and delivered to complete strangers in another corner of the globe, rests on a commitment to the Universal Declaration of Human rights, "UDHR." In part, this declaration proclaims that "everyone has the right to a standard of living adequate for the health and well-being of himself and of his family, including food" (*Food and Nutrition Needs*, 1). Since rights without concomitant duties are empty, the United Nations agencies committed to the UDHR accept the duty of making the right a reality in practice, a practice whose success is enhanced by the provision of HDRs.

A quite different menu once greeted strangers at Manhattan's Broadway Presbyterian Church as described in a newspaper article. The meal might begin with a "light soup of savoy and napa cabbages." This would be followed by "endive salad" with a "basil vinaigrette." The entrée consists of New Jersey bison simmered "in wine and stock flavored with fennel and thickened with olive oil roux." Is it any wonder that a sign outside announced "The Four-Star Soup Kitchen"? For the homeless and the hungry who benefit from such a menu it's a lot better than other places that, as one diner put it, "give you slop and say it's better than nothing." Others, having preserved a discriminating palate even in times of hardship, are not beyond voicing criticism. One guest, for example, complained that sometimes "the experimentation gets in the way of good taste." The chef featured in the story was Michael Ennes, once a college English major, then chef for profit, and, subsequently, no longer "pampering the rich." Ennes claimed actually to appreciate the evaluative comments of his diners. "One thing we do here is listen to people and let them complain. Where else can a homeless person get someone to listen to them?" (Severson).

Whereas Ennes served five hundred meals a day, a character in Albert Camus's short story "The Guest" prepares food for only one stranger. Unlike HDRs delivered by airdrop, and unlike soup kitchen mass servings, the food is shared by only two people in the home of a teacher named Daru. Daru is a reluctant host. His "guest" is a prisoner foisted on him by the local law enforcement official. Arriving unannounced, the gendarme instructs Daru to take charge of the prisoner and deliver him the next day to a nearby town.

Left alone with the prisoner, Daru offers dinner. The meal is ultra-simple. A sort of flapjack (*galette*), an omelette, cheese, and dates (Camus 1957, 98–99). The prisoner, stunned, not at the simple food but rather at the ordinary act of kindness, asks, "Why do you eat with me?" The straightforward, albeit surprising, reply: "I'm hungry" (Camus 1957, 99). The situation, however, is not at all simple. At first, Daru carries a revolver in his pocket as protection. While preparing dinner "he knocked against the revolver stuck in his right pocket." As if to indicate how cooking and firearms are incompatible, he goes to the classroom and puts "the revolver in his desk drawer" (Camus 1957, 99). Having restored the proper host/guest relationship, Daru proceeds, first, to serve his guest, and then to serve himself. Other possible, and real, relationships, those of prisoner/guard, murderer/teacher, Arab/French Colonial, fade into the background, trumped by the decency accompanying the guest/host relationship.

Food is central to good hospitality. The next morning, teacher and prisoner, or rather, host and guest, share coffee and leftover flapjacks "seated together on the folding bed" (Camus 1957, 104). When Daru has accompanied the Arab partway to the mandated destination, he stops, indicates various routes, and lets the prisoner decide his own fate. On parting, Daru hands his guest some money and a package containing "dates, bread, and sugar" (Camus 1957, 107). This combination would not make it into an HDR, but, as Daru points out, "You can hold out for two days" (Camus 1957, 107). As if to indicate the universality of hospitality obligations, Daru points to one path leading to an encampment of nomads. "They'll take you in," says the teacher, "and shelter you according to their law" (Camus 1957, 108).

HDRs, soup kitchens, one-on-one hosting, these point to an underlying attitude that waxes and wanes, the admission to a stranger that, "you are a human being just like me, you are in need, and we humans help one another." HDRs, soup kitchens, and Daru all admit this, without taking the next step of saying, "we are really all identical." This may sound as if it is synonymous with "you are a human being just like me," but in significant ways it is not. The Arab is not a Frenchman, the Spanish-speaking guests who eat Michael Ennes's food have been shaped by different cultural forces than has he, and the denizens of rich northern industrialized countries supplying HDRs differ in many ways from those in need of emergency daily rations. Somehow, we need to provide assent both to "yes, you are a human being just as I am a human being" and "in many substantial ways we are very different."

Us and them

The historian David Hollinger has explored this issue in his provocative *Postethnic America*. "How wide is our circle of the 'we'?" he asks. The question had taken on special urgency because of an important twentieth-century shift. This was a move away from the Enlightenment paradigm of thinking universally, collecting all humans under the single rubric "rational animals." In this line of thinking "you are a human being just as I am a human being" had a simple connotation: strip away cultural differences and we are all alike. Unfortunately within the context of colonialism, "we are all alike" came to mean "I provide the standard and you should all be like me." The colonialist did not arrive in wonder and curiosity admitting much to learn. Rather the predominant attitude "we are all alike" translated readily into "we will all be alike when we have finished civilizing you."

Such a minimalist interpretation of shared humanity came to be challenged as studies like sociology and anthropology made cultural identity more and more a crucial datum. Politically, this research was reinforced as individuals resisted being lumped into a single all-encompassing category, especially one that denied full humanity to members of colonized civilizations. With the twentieth century came a tendency to think in terms of specific historically and culturally conditioned communities. Such a move, from "species to ethnos," in Hollinger's formulation, meant that the question of the "we" might just be "*the* great question in an age of ethnos-centered discourse" (Hollinger, 68). Neither imperialistic imposition of one cultural mode, nor its mirror opposite, a total sequestering of all cultural modes, reflects the complexities of the human situation. Translated into more old-fashioned terms, this question comes down to how the stranger, the one who is different, ought to be treated. Underlying this question is a key philosophical assumption about whether humans are "complete" or "needy."

Philosophers have had much to say about "ought" questions. They have debated meta-ethical discourse, divided over positions whose labels end in "ist," as with "absolutist," "consequentialist," or "situationist" ethics. Prescriptions and descriptions have fallen effortlessly from their lips. Virtues and values, they have defined, defended, contested. In all of this, however, a very old-fashioned virtue, one associated with food and germane to Hollinger's question, has been conspicuous by its absence: hospitality. Here is a virtue that is not only important for living a virtuous life but one that allows for a more fluid option than whether cultural imperialism or multicultural relativism would allow. It also defines a basic attitude that has wide repercussions for the kind of philosophy (in its original sense of "love of wisdom") we embrace.

Hospitality once held pride of place as a mode of acting in traditional societies. It has been championed and celebrated in religion and literature. Ceres herself tested the hospitality of those she encountered while searching for her missing daughter. When she found it wanting, swift retribution was her response. Somehow, perhaps because meal-sharing is central to its exemplary functioning, philosophy tended to ignore it. When we take eating and its associated practices seriously, such an oversight must be corrected. The best way to address it is to ignore academic provincialism and, acting hospitably, welcome perspectives from outside of philosophy. We have already looked at places often ignored by philosophers: refugee food packets, soup kitchen menus, simple homes where old-fashioned behaviors survive. The soup kitchens are often associated with religious communities. This gives us a hint for looking to religion for help. Camus, as a literary writer, provides another clue for resources, the testimony of literary works.

EATING PAUSE:
FAMILY MEAT LOAF

When our sons went off to college they were stunned that their new friends had only contempt for meat loaf. True, the cafeterias' versions were not that great, but they remembered their mother's version fondly. Since hospitality need not involve fancy fare, here is Jayne's meat loaf. **Ingredients**: *1/2 cup bread crumbs; 1 lb ground beef; 1/2 cup ketchup; 1 egg; 1/2 cup chopped onion; 1/2 cup chopped green pepper; about 1/2 tsp each of salt, pepper, and oregano; 1 tbsp parsley.* **Preparation**: *Mix ingredients together. Form into loaf shape. Place in loaf pan. Top with more ketchup and parmesan cheese.* **Cooking**: *Bake at 350 degrees for 40 minutes.*

HOSPITALITY IN RELIGION AND LITERATURE

Religion, sometimes friend, sometimes foe to philosophy, offers an important opportunity to learn. First, though, we must assume a hospitable attitude and allow ourselves to welcome contributions from areas far different from our own, areas that often engage in different modes of discourse. Exaggeration to make a point, for example, is a stock rhetorical move, one found even in foundational religious texts.[1] Take Lot, upright citizen of Sodom and Gomorrah. Two strangers arrive. Lot insists they stay with him, transforming them from *strangers* to *guests*. Soon, the townspeople, having heard of the newcomers' arrival, gather in a mob. Corrupt to the core, they want the visitors for sexual sport. "Bring them out to us so that we many know them," says the quaint language of Genesis. Appalled, Lot refuses. Welcoming these men into his home means accepting responsibility for safeguarding them. So strong is his commitment that he makes a desperate offer: "I've got two virgin daughters, take them instead." Fortunately, the visitors turn out to be angels whose powers bring the nonsense to an end. They restore a temporary order by blinding the troublesome crowd (Genesis 19:3–26).

Lot's cavalier offer to sacrifice his daughters stuns contemporary readers. But the very horror of that offering allows something else to stand out: his absolute commitment to hospitality. Just as the biblical language of "knowing" echoes a time long past, so, too, does the absolute demand of hospitality seem not only antiquated but downright misguided. Lot's extreme response helps highlight an important lesson: hospitality is to be taken seriously. It is not, for him at least, an expendable, minor virtue.

For us, welcoming strangers, real strangers, does not fall under the heading "moral obligation." We tend, rather, to consider hospitality as a private, discretionary act. We speak of hospitality and entertainment in the same breath. Both are considered branches of etiquette. Hospitality as entertainment depends on temperament, desire for company, and sufficient wealth. Such entertainment might help make life enjoyable, but it is not one of the central "oughts" required for a life judged morally admirable. The "rational animal" of philosophy need not make of hospitality a central obligation.

As the story of Lot indicates, things have not always been so. In the biblical context, an appropriate label for the human being can be "the hospitable animal." The experience of the Torah, Emmanuel Levinas claimed, can be encapsulated in three concepts: *fraternity*, *humanity*, and *hospitality* (Derrida 1999, 67). When Job wanted to prove his worth as a good man, he spoke of generosity to outsiders. "I was a father to the needy, and I championed the cause of the stranger" (Job 29:16). When the supporters of the soup kitchen at Broadway Presbyterian want to explain why they do what they do, they can cite the Gospel of Matthew. He describes Jesus as saying that salvation will come to those who feed the hungry, relieve the thirsty, and welcome the stranger (Matthew: 25:34–35). For traditional India, a land with lots of pilgrims but no hotels or restaurants (taking money for food was a great failing), wayfarers could always count on receiving food and shelter.[2] Bedouin hospitality, as Daru indicated, is legendary. "A stranger traveling in the desert," the *Encyclopedia of Islam* points out, "is offered lodging and the best food available." "It was a point of honour to protect the djār (suppliant) as effectively as one protected one's own kin" (article Idjāra). The "Rule of St. Benedict" is categorical: "Let all guests who arrive be received as Christ" (ch. 53).

The literary roots of hospitality, themselves woven together with religious themes, go back, not surprisingly, to the Greeks. An early play, Aeschylus's *The Suppliants*, explores the generous welcome given to a group of endangered women. They have neither the wealth nor the power to return the favor. For their act of welcome, the hospitable prince and his people place themselves in grave danger. In *The Odyssey*, hospitality is so central that each of its twenty-four books explores it in some way or another. Hospitality's paramount importance is signaled by the god who takes a special interest in strangers, none other than Zeus himself. Steve Reece's careful study of hospitality in *The Odyssey* indicates how "the most powerful god oversees this most vital institution of human civilization—Zeus Xeinios, protector of suppliants and strangers" (Reece, 65). Hospitality, considered in this context, takes on a significance way beyond simple domestic etiquette. It is celebrated as a major virtue, the hallmark of a civilized, humane life. Such a centrality is highlighted by a recurring story line: any visit can be a theoxeny, the outsider being a god in disguise.[3]

Homer's fascination with hospitality led him to create the prototype of anti-hospitality and thus of uncivilized, inhumane behavior: Polyphemus the Cylops. Food is important here, too, albeit in an inverted way. Here is someone who, instead of feeding guests, eats them. With Polyphemus and his fellow Cyclops, Homer provides the philosophical anthropology inimical to hospitality. Cyclops thinks of himself as self-sufficient. The primacy of self-sufficiency means, spiritually, he does not fear the gods and, temporally, does not meet with others for political deliberation. Because he has no need to engage in agriculture (the land provides ample goods), Cyclops has little sense of dependency or vulnerability. Curiosity about others is nonexistent. He and his compatriots have no ships. They remain self-satisfied as a stationary, non-journeying people. Homer's description draws an important dividing line. Who are the least civilized? Those who do not fear the gods, have no deliberative assemblies, need not engage in agriculture, and fail to travel. They are neither bread eaters nor wine drinkers, activities that demand cooperative, intermediate steps between natural bounty and its transformation into "food" and "drink."

Ordinary humans are not at all like Cyclopes. Our lives are marked by interdependence and the need to toil for our sustenance. Even in technologically advanced societies, the vulnerability to unpredictable natural forces remains ever present. We live in communities, accept reciprocal responsibilities, deliberate together, cultivate food, develop cuisines, and travel. Many factors, positive and negative, conspire to make us wanderers: the lure of the unknown, famine, the desire to learn, war, economic cupidity, persecution. In several languages the word for "guest" is ambiguous, indicating not only the unknown status of the stranger but also how today's host can become tomorrow's stranger in need. The Arabic word *djār* means both "the one seeking protection" and the "protector." Latin and French use the same word to identify both host and guest, *hospes* and *hôte*.

What philosophers have to say

Were philosophers to welcome literary and religious figures in their homes, they would find themselves mostly tongue-tied when the subject of hospitality was raised. Their heritage offers merely scattered and peripheral treatments. "Rational animal" clearly trumps "hospitable animal" in their analyses. Plato makes the "stranger" a major character in some dialogues (*The Sophist*, *The Statesman*) but with little emphasis on hospitality. Only in *The Laws* do we find a reiteration of the Homeric attitude. Plato there claims that strangers, lacking the supportive webs of friends and kinsmen, deserve special consideration (V, 729e). Aristotle offers even less. He identifies "generosity" or "liberality" as a virtue appropriate for the free citizen. This generosity is linked to friendship (*Nicomachean Ethics*, 1128a, 20–22), and its exercise is limited to those who have sufficient wealth (1178a, 29–30). No mention is made of hospitality as either a subcategory of generosity or as a wider, more encompassing virtue.

For an explicit embrace of hospitality as central, we must fast-forward to the eighteenth century when the universalist "species *not* ethnos" approach was on the ascendancy. Kant's *To Perpetual Peace: A Philosophical Sketch* includes a late section that lists the following as the "Third Definitive Article for A Perpetual Peace": "Cosmopolitan right shall be limited to conditions of universal hospitality" (Kant 1795, 118). This notion of hospitality, is, however, sharply attenuated. No longer is the stranger considered as a possible theoxeny, with the positive obligations thereby implied. For Kant, hospitality does not involve transforming strangers into "guests," that is, welcoming them, as did Daru, with food and shelter. It signifies something negative: not treating them as enemies. Kant's demand, while universal, remains nonetheless minimal: "If it can be done without destroying him, he can be turned away; but as long as he behaves peaceably he cannot be treated as an enemy" (Kant, 1795, 118).

Among contemporaries, one thinker willing to address the topic is Elizabeth Telfer. Her book *Food for Thought* was a pioneer in linking food and philosophy. "Hospitableness," she declares, deserves to be labeled a virtue. However it remains a minor virtue, one that is mostly "optional" (Telfer, 82, 96). Telfer's breaking of new ground by devoting an entire chapter to hospitality is to be welcomed. The limitations of her approach emerge when she engages in a categorization of hospitableness. She identifies three types: (i) hospitality to one's circle (this is sort of "official" hospitality, that extended to people with whom we are in certain formal relations, either of work, family, or some other linkage of common interest); (ii) "Good Samaritan" hospitality (extending food, shelter, kindness to those in need, regardless of their relation to us); and (iii) hospitality to friends (entertaining those whose company we prize and cherish outside of any formal relationships).

The first two, she considers "optional." "One cannot," as she points out, "try to be every kind of good person" (Telfer, 96). While there may be a general duty to help "those in need," circumstances permit flexibility about "which needy people to help and how to help them" (Telfer, 96). In general, behavior labeled "virtuous" is not optional. After all, "virtuous" as a term of approbation, brings with it a kind of "ought to do" attitude. Telfer reminds us that great needs run up against limited abilities and resources. Such constraints mean, in the case of hospitableness, that the "ought" aspect cannot be interpreted as an ethical absolute. Otherwise there would be a self-contradiction: the absolute demand negated by the inability to exercise it in practice. Still, there is one type of hospitableness that comes close to being a duty of this sort, the third one, hospitableness to one's friends. Because the bonds of friendship are stronger than those to "one's circle" or to strangers in need, and because the circle is limited, Telfer considers hospitableness to one's friends to be much less flexible and, thus, to stand as a moral virtue without the qualifier "optional" (Telfer, 97–98). It avoids the category of "optional" because in this case we find an equilibrium between level of obligation and availability of resources.

Although Telfer goes a long way to rehabilitating hospitality, her analysis is limited in several ways. First of all, her label "optional" is unfortunate. We can certainly, as Telfer does, envision situations in which we are called upon to provide hospitality but are circumscribed by various limitations in our ability to provide it. Here prudential judgments come into play. Telfer rightly emphasizes the gap between obligation and resources. She properly identifies the straited circumstances that allow no perfect overlap between an absolute demand and the ability to satisfy that demand. However, instead of introducing the qualifier "optional," which can readily be interpreted self-servingly, it might be better simply to embrace the absolute demand/limited resources tension and accept the special responsibilities it imposes on us. Recognizing the obligation as a real obligation can motivate us to work toward finding the necessary resources to carry out virtuous action. At the very least, a sense of apathy, which uses lack of resources as an easy excuse for inaction, can be blocked by identifying hospitality as a central virtue/important obligation.

This is the tack taken by the twentieth-century philosopher who did the most to rehabilitate hospitality, Jacques Derrida. To block self-serving quiescence and emphasize the strong motivational impulse associated with a virtue, Derrida wishes us to hold together in a sort of creative tension both "unconditional hospitality" and "hospitality circumscribed by law and duty" (Derrida 2000, 135). We could add, thinking of Telfer, that the contrast can also be articulated as that between "unconditional hospitality" and the limitations of circumstance. Both the unconditional and the conditioned hospitality, taken by themselves, can undermine what is best in hospitality. "One of them," as Derrida points out, "can always corrupt the other, and this capacity for perversion remains irreducible. It *must* remain so" (Derrida 2000, 135). An important shift in philosophical assumptions comes into play here. It makes no sense to seek a single, ultimate, unitary grounding for action. In human life, pluralism rules and there will always be a tension resonating at the base of things. Unconditional hospitality, besides being unrealistic, would bankrupt the host, making future hospitality impossible. Conditioned hospitality, without the impetus of an unconditional duty behind it, would be easily reduced to a self-satisfied charity easily restricted in extent. Instead of labeling this hospitality as "optional," a label that can lead us to avoid facing difficult decisions about strangers, better would it be to go the Derrida route. This offers a path that at least drives us out of self-interested passivity and forces us to make prudential choices in the full awareness that we are falling short of what the virtue demands. The tension comes with the awareness that no sooner have we made one attempt at acting in accordance with the virtue, than other calls come to us, calls that, in turn, require further responses. The temptation to minimize the importance of the call as "optional" is diminished.

Besides its unfortunate use of "optional," much of Telfer's analysis is also framed within specifically modern assumptions, assumptions inimical to recognizing the importance accorded to hospitality in traditions outside of philosophy. Philosophers do not work in a vacuum. Beyond the explicit rigor of analysis and the turgidity of prose, there are often a set of root metaphors that shape the direction of and provide contours for conceptual work. In Telfer's case, the root metaphor, one typical in Modern European thought, is that of humans as completed selves. Such a philosophical anthropology, emphasizing sedentary, atomistic, autonomous individuals, tends to think (1) of all obligations arising only from consciously engaged contracts, and (2) of growth and change resulting from external satisfactions rather than from inner transformations. (Why should there be such transformation when, for all intents and purposes, we are already completed entities?)

If, instead, we think of ourselves as constantly growing selves, we can admit to multiple, diverse, and changing interests. Our desires are not fixed, but educable. Interests, the large cluster of impulses that allow personal and social transformation, unfortunately get made over into "self-interests" when we think of ourselves as fixed, completed entities. John Dewey pointed out how "many good words get spoiled when the word self is prefixed to them." His list included "pity," "confidence," "control," and "love" (Dewey 1922, 96). We could easily add "interest" to this list. Limitations emerge when we (a) substitute the singular "interest" for the more generous and accurate "interests," and (b) attach the prefix "self" to the singular term. Such a double move channels the main lines of our activity along an axis of covetousness that can be served via purely external satisfactions.

In short, within the Modern paradigm, the adult's self-understanding is that, as Dewey puts it, of "one ready-made self behind activities" (Dewey 1922, 96). Such a self is not needy or "hungry" in any primal way. Its covetings have nothing to do with its status as an incomplete, developing creature. Ennobling growth is not a primary concern. Accumulation along with multiplications of opportunities for enhancing pleasure and avoiding pain become the primary concerns. Hospitality, given such a context, becomes mainly the self-centered drive for pleasant company or the self-satisfaction involved with donations to charity. Telfer's formulations tend to situate hospitality completely within this perspective. Once again, there is an unfortunate choice of synonyms. "Hospitality" comes to be a term almost interchangeable with "entertaining." "A hospitable person, I suggest, is someone who entertains often, attentively and out of motives appropriate to hospitality" (Telfer, 86).

Homo viator/Homo sedentarius

While it is true that "hospitality" and "entertaining" overlap (providing food and good company are prominent in both), their connotations differ sharply. In the paradigmatic sense, "entertaining" signifies sharing food and good companionship with friends. To Hollinger's question "Who is the 'we'?" there is a straightforward, ready-made answer: those like us. "Hospitality," by contrast, connotes, in its prototypical case, care for the stranger. HDR's, Ennes's four-star soup kitchen, and Camus's schoolteacher are exemplary in this way. To understand fully the entertainment/hospitality contrast requires examining root metaphors associated with the human condition. One starts with the self as homebody, the autonomous self, well situated, autonomous, and secure. Around this image was built the philosophical anthropology of the Modern era.

Things were not always so. Here is where the Spanish-born American philosopher George Santayana becomes helpful. An almost a throwaway line in his "The Genteel Tradition at Bay" helps us grasp a major shift in self-understanding that occurred between the medieval and the post-Renaissance, that is, Modern, world. "The mind of the Renaissance," he asserted, "was not a pilgrim mind, but a sedentary city mind, like that of the ancients" (Santayana 1931, 130).

Santayana's use of "pilgrim" rather than "wanderer" leads him to an unfortunate exaggeration about the ancients. Socrates may have been an inveterate city dweller, but as we have seen, Odysseus certainly was not. The important point is how hospitality takes on a central importance for those cultures in which the "humans as wanderers" metaphor remains central to self-understanding. Gabriel Marcel, the earliest French existentialist, rehabilitated the outmoded metaphor in a book he appropriately entitled *Homo Viator*, man the wayfarer.[4] So long as humans considered themselves as in the condition of *Homo viator*, as engaged on a journey, so long would hospitality, and not just entertaining, be prized as central to human life. It is not surprising in this regard that the injunction to Moses that he establish "cities of refuge" comes in what we know as the book of Numbers but whose Hebrew title, translated "In the Wilderness," better describes the wanderings therein depicted (Numbers 35:9–15).

Homo viator, humans as wanderers, though, is itself partial and incomplete. Santayana has identified a basic orientational difference in human self-understanding. It needs to be complemented by a Derrida-like embrace of resonating tensions. Instead of the either-or option, better it is to emphasize a correlative pairing. One term would be what Santayana finds as dominant in the post-Renaissance world. I would call it *Homo sedentarius*. It isolates the sedentary, settled homebody as prototypical. The other, summarized by Marcel's *Homo viator,* describes humans as wayfarers or wanderers.

With regard to hospitality, the gap separating *Homo sedentarius* from *Homo viator* seems, at first, to be immense. For *Homo sedentarius*, hospitality can be understood in terms of entertaining and is, as such, optional. For *Homo viator* hospitality is a defining characteristic of civilized life itself. Wanderers, after all, feel deep in their bones, not to mention their stomachs, the importance of being welcomed. But is the opposition so stark? Santayana's division would be misleading if, ignoring the Derrida-inspired lesson to think in terms of resonating tensions, it considered humans as *either* sedentary *or* wanderers. After all, history provides ample examples of peoples, once settled, who were forced to become people without a home: Amerindians, European Jews, the Acadians, West Africans, Tibetans, Armenians, the Irish, Palestinians, Bosnians, Vietnamese boat people.

The etymological traces indicating the two-fold nature of words like *hospes* and *hôte* suggest the importance of a complementary rather than a contradictory approach. They help us focus, not on a single dominating image, but rather on a resonating tension at the very heart of the human condition. When we imagine ourselves as both *Homo sedentarius* and *Homo viator*, our attitude toward hospitality takes a 180-degree turn from that of traditional philosophy. Telfer, still rooted in *Homo sedentarius*, took a major step in making hospitableness a suitable subject for philosophical reflection. Such an analysis, however, simply introduced hospitality within a preexisting context. This context remain unchallenged and, thus, unchanged. To occasion a change that does more than append hospitality to preexisting philosophical orientations, Derrida offers a more fecund alternative. Drawing inspiration from Emmanuel Levinas (1906–1995), Derrida became a famous exponent of making hospitality as prominent in philosophy as it once was in literature. He went so far as to declare that "hospitality is culture itself and not simply one ethic amongst others" (Derrida 2001, 16). In doing so, he suggested ways in which thinking of hospitality encourages a fundamental philosophical reorientation.

That Derrida would draw on Levinas is significant. Here was someone working at the axis of several influences. What the axes have in common is a move away from some dominant Modern (1600–1900) ways of thinking. There was, first of all, the influence of Martin Heidegger who sought to shift philosophy away from its Modern paradigms. There were also pre-Modern sources of inspiration, the sacred texts of Judaism. Levinas contrasts Odysseus, the wanderer who returns home, with Abraham, the more fully wandering wanderer who "leaves his fatherland forever for a yet unknown land" (Derrida 1999, 129, note 12). By contrast, the prototypical manifestation of *Homo sedentarius* was, as we have seen, Polyphemus the Cyclops. For him the fundamental relationship to others is, in the word Derrida draws from Levinas, an "allergic" one (Derrida 1999, 95). The stranger, even prior to being given a chance, is considered hostile and dangerous. Although the

Greek term *xeinos* was ambiguous, indicating both "guest-friend from a foreign country" or "potentially hostile stranger" (Reece, 19), such ambiguity is lost on the Cyclopes who think of the outsider strictly in terms of hostility.

Humility + wonder = *fecunditas*

Rampant allophobia (*allo* is the Greek prefix for "other") can best be combated by a self-reinforcing triad that cannot be encompassed under the rubric of entertaining: humility, wonder, and the hospitableness that results. *Homo sedentarius*, too often characterized by self-satisfied complacency, tends not to manifest much humility or wonder. This is devastating for hospitality, whose importance cannot be appreciated without humility, a preliminary recognition of our limitations. Absent such recognition, there is little motivation for wonder, seeking out and learning from what is unfamiliar. The residents of settlement communities, wrote Jane Addams, "must be content to live quietly side by side with their neighbors, until they *grow into a sense of relationship and mutual interests*" (Addams, 98). The italics, which I have added, indicate an important aspect of hospitality. Benefits do not move in one direction only, from the givers to the receivers. Those who have come to share in the lives of others also benefit by growth and change. A new "we" results. It is a "we" identified by relationships and mutual interests that might not have been antecedently in existence, at least not in the exact forms that they have taken after the contact and interaction.

Here is where the bidirectional arrow of hospitality comes into prominence: both guest and host benefit. We can now appreciate more fully how the ambiguity of terms meaning "guest" *and* "host," the French *hôte*, for example, is a rich one. Either "guest" or "host" can be substituted at the points of ambiguity in the following formulations: The *hôte* is always receptive to learn from the *hôte*; the *hôte* is awakened and enriched by contact with the *hôte*. The ennoblement of the human condition can occur in both directions. The host benefits as surely as does the guest. The French title of Camus's story, *L'hôte*, exploits this ambiguity. Who is host and who is guest? Daru, host in one sense, is, in another, an outsider, a Frenchman living in Algeria. The prisoner, guest in one sense, is someone at home in his own country. So long as both are categorized under one dimension only, important aspects of who they are remain occluded.

Humans, typically, have more to offer than is grasped in any initial impression. "Modesty" as the French personalist philosopher Emmanuel Mounier explained, has nothing primarily to do with fear of sexuality. Modesty, rather, recognizes how much more any individual is than the accumulation of her (for it is usually a her in question) physical attributes, when those are the object of a single-minded gaze (Mounier, 79). Instead of being limited, easily definable individuals fitted into a prearranged category, humans "overflow" their initial presentation. The prisoner in Camus's story is just a "murderer" initially. Shared meals and shared time together, even though brief, provide hints of a more complicated character. Modesty, properly understood, encourages others not to judge prematurely, to allow the individual to exhibit an overabundance (Mounier, 79). Hospitality and shared meals provide the situations and time in which that overabundance can be made manifest.

Absent the humility and wonder associated with a genuine welcome, self-satisfied home dwellers remain blind to this overabundance. If we are already completed selves, discrete units whose characters, for all intents and purposes, are fixed and finished, our relations to others fall into certain channels. These others are not, cannot be, opportunities for an enlarged understanding, a reshaping of desires and needs. There is no question of educating or modifying desires, of restoring, in other words, a wide cluster of interests. Relations with others can only promote or frustrate preset self-interests. Strangers and outsiders fall into limited channels. They may be pleasant company or occasions for manipulation or obstacles to be overcome. In the more formal Levinasian language this describes the contrast between "hospitality" and "thematization" (Derrida 1999, 21–22). To "thematize" is to confine. It is to work in terms of categorizations, of placing a single instance into ready-made classifications. Thematization blocks access to the overabundance that is the other.

From a different religious tradition, that associated with St. Francis, comes an analogous emphasis on overabundance. St. Francis favored maternal metaphors, and one in particular is important here: *fecunditas*. This provides a way of describing the divinity and, subsequently, of identifying a fecundity in which all creatures share.[5] Having not been university educated, St. Francis avoided the intellectually dominant neo-Platonic current that dismissed the material world and sought refuge in a One that was above being.[6] There is one God, but to say that God is One unduly limits the ontological fullness of what is the source of all. The problem, though, is not simply a theological one of oversimplifying the divine. There is an important practical ramification. Emphasis on the oneness of divinity can readily translate into a sorting out of "us" (who have the one God) from "them" (who do not). William James was working within the more generous tradition when he entitled his book on religion *The Varieties of Religious Experience*. He title is instructive in two ways. It indicates the importance and necessity of embracing a diversity that well reflects divine fecundity. It also helps avoid the temptation toward a self-satisfied *Unity* of religious experience, a unity that can easily become a tool for power and domination. Imagining humans in particular and beings in general, through the *fecunditas* prism carries important implications. Since each of us, in several ways, reflects the *fecunditas* out of which we come: (a) we are always more complex (overabundant) than we seem to any thematizing (stereotyping) figure; (b) we are, in the deepest sense, incomplete and needy, that is, precisely not gods, but rather people who can learn, grow, develop only by entering into contact with what is different from us. Hospitality, in other words, is not optional. It is elemental.

NOTES

1. For a discussion of biblical hyperbole, see Caird, especially pp. 110–117.
2. "Consideration for a guest is enjoined in the sacred Law-Books of India as an important part of the duty of a householder" ("Hospitality," *Encyclopaedia of Religion and Ethics*, 1913).
3. *The Odyssey* opens with just such a situation. The stranger, apparently "Mentes, lord of the Taphians" is actually Athena (I, 121–123). Nausicaa, well brought up and virtuous, states it directly: "Every stranger and beggar comes from Zeus, and whatever scraps we give him he'll be glad to get. So, quick, my girls, give our newfound friend some food and drink and bathe the man in the river, wherever you find some shelter from the wind" (VI, 226–232).
4. See Gabriel Marcel, *Homo Viator*.
5. "The triune God is the firstness (*primitas*) and fecundity (*fecunditas*) of all that is, including the inner being of God" (Osborne, 55).
6. "Francis had a basic education in reading and writing in the local church school of Assisi. Since he had not been trained as an intellectual in his youth, he never absorbed the Christian Neoplatonic attitude toward creation. . . . The Neoplatonic ladder of ascent presented a movement away from, and rising above, natural, sensible things, as if they were inferior and, in some sense, not truly real" (Delio, 6).

Chapter Three

Hungry Being

The Parasite

> One result of our analysis has been to make a sharp separation, in the social realm, between the closed and the open. The closed society is one whose members cling to each other, indifferent to the rest of humanity, always predisposed to attack or defend, constrained, in the end, to a combat mode of life.[1]
>
> —Henri Bergson

BAD HOSTS, BAD GUESTS

The previous chapter restores hospitality as a central virtue for living a humane life. It could be read as overly optimistic about how things will turn out when strangers are invited to share our tables and homes. Camus, whose moving portrayal of simple and absolute hospitality makes "The Guest" a classic text in this regard, also provides a cautionary tale. His play "The Misunderstanding" (*Le Malentendu*) inverts the prodigal son parable. As told in Luke, a generous and compassionate father welcomes back a ne'er do well offspring who made a mess of his life. The welcome involves a majestic feast involving a special treat, eating meat. Full of joy and forgiveness, the father orders his slaves to "get the fatted calf and kill it, and let us eat and celebrate" (Luke 15:23). Not surprisingly, the returnee's elder brother is miffed. He complains about all the fuss made over someone "who has devoured your property with prostitutes." He, the loyal, hardworking one, has never gotten so much as a "goat" to "celebrate with my friends" (Luke 15:29). Allowing the brother back into the family fold is bad enough, but what adds insult to injury is preparing a feast, killing "the fatted calf for him" (Luke 15:30).

Camus inverts the story, turning the lost son into a success story. After a long absence he returns to reconnect with his sister and widowed mother. Not only to reconnect, but to share his bounty with them. He hopes to ease their difficult lives and compensate for years of absence. Unsure how to proceed, he decides to hide his identity and simply stay as a guest at the inn run by his mother and sister. They, meanwhile, have grown bitter and mercenary. Although hosts at a guesthouse, their hospitality is limited. It starts and stops within the boundaries of an economic transaction. When Jan, the brother, tries to engage his sister in conversation, she interrupts brusquely: "Coming here you are entitled to the rights of a client. . . . Take on the role of a client, that is your right. But do not take on any more" (Camus 1958, 37). Their philosophy, to use an expression from Fielding's *Tom Jones*, is that of the "Exchange Alley" school. All transactions are reduced to those of exchange for profit (Fielding, 211).

Nowhere is this better exemplified than in one of the two scenes involving drink in the play (there are no food scenes). The son has in mind the Gospel parable and imagines himself being greeted by the feast for the prodigal son (Camus 1958, 22, 63). Instead, his disguised identity, together with the exchange-alley attitude of his sibling, creates a very different atmosphere. One can imagine a happy reunion involving food and drink. There would be tears, joy, and laughter all around. Instead the scene is of a lone individual nursing a beer obtained only because he is a paying customer. The second scene involving drink seems to follow the interpersonal rather than the exchange model. Without having ordered any, Jan is brought some tea by Martha, his sister. But this is a special tea. Following their customary pattern, mother and daughter identify a guest as a special source of extra funds. Not that the guest has any choice. He is drugged, robbed, and then unceremoniously dumped into the river.

Here are bad hosts if ever there were ones. They rank down there with Macbeth, murderer of his royal guest.[2] In the cold-blooded mother-daughter pair, Camus has provided a warning. Things don't always work out well in the hospitality relation. The previous chapter, with its favorable take on hospitality could come off as somewhat Pollyanna-ish. This would be misleading. Even "The Guest" ended on a dissonant note. Daru, the school teacher, returning home after his kindness to the prisoner, is greeted by a sign scrawled on the wall: "You handed over our brother. You will pay for this" (Camus 1957, 109).

It is not only hosts that can turn a virtue into its opposite. Literary works also offer us guests who, once allowed inside, abuse the generosity of their hosts. In *The Odyssey* that role is taken up by unwelcomed suitors seeking to marry Penelope. As is often the case with bad guests, their abuse involves a one-way relation in regard to food: take, take, take; never give. Penelope, generous-spirited though she is, cannot help complaining about the "guests" whose "own stores, their bread and seasoned wine lie intact at home." Meanwhile, they "infect our palace day and night, they butcher our cattle, our sheep, our fat goats, feasting themselves sick, swilling our glowing wine as if there's no tomorrow—all of it, squandered" (Homer, XVII, 592–597).

The comic playwright Molière has provided another example. He is Tartuffe who insinuates himself into a household and proceeds to undertake various schemes: seduction of the daughter, seduction of the mother, manipulation of the husband such that all wealth and property would be transferred to him. Quite naturally, he eats and eats. The family maid, having viewed how Tartuffe gorges himself, can't believe how her master has been fooled. "He pets and spoils him with such tenderness, A mistress would be satisfied with less; Gives him the place of honor when they dine, And beams to see him eat enough for nine. He saves the choicest bits for that man's part, And when he belches, he says "Bless your heart!" (Moliere, I, 2, 189–194). Having been away for a while, the husband inquires about his wife. The maid responds by informing him about her illness, but Orgon shows concern only for Tartuffe, even though the latter is not at all described as being in bad straits.

Dorine: Madame had a bad fever, two days ago,

And a headache that really brought her low.

Orgon: Yes. And Tartuffe?

Dorine: Tartuffe? Fit as a fiddle:

Red mouth, pink cheeks, and bulging at the middle.

Orgon: Poor fellow!

Dorine: Then she had no appetite,

And therefore couldn't eat a thing that night.

Her headache still was just too much to bear.

Orgon: Yes, And Tartuffe?

Dorine: Piously, with her there,

He ate a brace of partridge like a flash,

Then half a leg of mutton in a hash (Molière, I, 4, ll. 231–240).

Well fed from his host's pantry, Tartuffe's plan is simple. Control everything, be the guest that forces out the host. He is, following ordinary usage, your classic "parasite." The parasite only takes and never gives; it knows neither propriety nor limits. Welcomed, initially, the parasite blocks all future welcomings. Instead of E. M. Forster's "only connect," the parasite's motto is a simple: always exclude. At least that is how the "parasite" is ordinarily understood. A careful examination of this creature closely associated with food ("para-site" means, literally, the "one who eats next to another") complicates things. It does so to such a degree that, properly understood, the parasite can serve as an appropriate root metaphor for exploring a difficult subfield of philosophy, its general theory of reality: metaphysics.

SUBSTANCE AND AUTONOMY

Traditional articulations of metaphysics have not been friendly to hospitality. Lacks of welcome, accusation, and even banishment have been constant temptations. Too often, philosophers have preferred the role of exclusion-oriented gatekeeper over that of generous-spirited host. Plato voiced such a closed-door approach when he made specific suggestions about a community's poets. Poets and dramatists, he complained, lead away from the path of truth. They distract and distort. What to do? Book X of his *Republic* gives the answer. Admit that there is a quarrel between philosophy and poetry. Then embrace the former while discarding the latter. As the seventeenth century opened, Rene Descartes, seeking certitude, looked around at traditional ways of learning. He found them all wanting. History, literature, older philosophies, and travel do not get us certitude. Just the opposite, these interlopers confuse the mind. They should no longer be welcomed. Direct access to truth, Cartesian-style, is best gained by keeping such intermediaries at bay. Most notorious, from a police-state perspective, were the early-twentieth-century positivists. They purged with great abandon. Their one big idea, "if it's not verifiable it's meaningless" transformed a rich and varied philosophical garden into a sparse desert. Guests coming to dinner uttering words like "justice" and "beauty" were ruthlessly driven away.[3]

Too often triumph in argument is valued over truths in attainment. Such thinkers have embraced the drive for domination, *philo-nike*, love of victory, over *philo-sophia*, love of wisdom. Despite the Levinas- and Derrida-inspired signs of change, a prosecutorial, attack-and-sequester penchant remains a lingering presence. Part of the explanation lies with the exclusive attention given to mind. This comes at the expense of other dimensions of human life. Specifically neglected is the stomach, the organ that insists that we embrace what is outside of ourselves.

When Levinas complained that Heidegger's *Dasein* "was never hungry" he hinted at a shift that would cause a major upheaval in the philosophical tradition. The subfield at issue has had a varied career. Its name, "metaphysics," was a misnomer from the beginning. Aristotle had produced a series of texts dealing with what he called "primary" or "fundamental" philosophy.[4] An editor of his works, placing these texts after those collected together as the "physics," called them "metaphysics," those that "come after the physics." This name then took on a life of its own. "Metaphysics" came to mean the study that sought access to a realm beyond the physical, an understanding still evident today in bookstores where the "metaphysical" shelves are filled with titles exploring the occult.

Aristotelian-style thinkers, recovering the earlier sense of "fundamental" philosophy, continued to welcome the discipline because it dealt with the most concretely immediate of questions, the generic traits of existence, or, in more formal language, the nature of "being *qua* being." More specialized studies provided analyses from specific perspectives, for example, looking at chemical composition, cellular activity, properties of material things. Metaphysics, by contrast, sought to provide some general mode of approach for understanding the way things are. This grasp would be rooted in ordinary experience, not in the specialized studies. It would allow humans to situate themselves, get their bearings, as they made their ways through life. Jose Ortega y Gasset stated the need for "metaphysics" succinctly: "man engages in metaphysics when he seeks a basic orientation in his situation" (Ortega 1969, 26).[5]

Articulating such a basic orientation has often taken the form of locating a root metaphor. Thought is analogical, understanding the unfamiliar in terms of what is more familiar. Wine writers, for example, cannot articulate what their taste buds are perceiving except by using a vocabulary that, literally, is foreign to the grape: "cherry," "vanilla," "mushroom," "earthiness." Philosophers, like other people, also think this way. They work with some fruitful analogue, which, by extension, opens paths for getting a grasp on the real.[6] Aristotle, at the beginning of metaphysics, had highlighted *ousia* and gave as example of the primary sense "an individual man or horse" (*Categories*, 2a13, McKeon, 9). The term *ousia*, often rendered now as "being," might better be translated, one prominent scholar suggested, by the word "entity."[7] Latin authors translated it as "substance." This word, like "metaphysics" then took on a life of its own. "Substance" became the basal term and gave metaphysics a particular trajectory. "Substance" came to be characterized first and foremost by nondependence. It was that which needed nothing else. We are now in a presence of the combination (substance-centered metaphysics and "substance" considered primarily as nondependent) that provided fertile soil for the anti-hospitality dimensions of European metaphysics to thrive.

Rene Descartes set the stage. When he got around to defining "substance" in his *Principles of Philosophy*, he characterized it this way: "By *substance* we can understand nothing other than a thing which exists in such a way as to depend on no other thing for its existence" (Descartes 1985, 210). Given so stringent a definition, only God, strictly speaking, fits the bill.[8] After all, total nondependence is kind of scarce in our world. Descartes, however, was a great intellectual bellwether. He had a knack for crystallizing ideas that were on the ascendancy. The notion of substance as self-sufficiency was one whose ramifications would spill over from the divine to the human realm for many centuries to come.

"Substance," identified with the highest being of all and characterized as absolute nondependence, can't help but suggest a scale of evaluation. Self-sufficiency, never fully possible for us, nonetheless becomes the key metric. It is what determines whether one is approximating or is distant from the highest Being. Given such a background, it is not surprising that the new scale for authentic existence, a scale consistent with the metaphysics of substance, placed autosufficiency at the high end. Dependency and neediness became traits associated with inauthenticity, a distorted, immature, deficient status. Within this value scheme, the need for food becomes automatically problematic. What is best and most "substantial" in us would never be hungry. Hunger identifies a flaw and a flawed state. It defines an entity as needy and dependent, two traits now treated as irrevocably negative.

The seventeenth through the nineteenth centuries can sort of be categorized by the predominance of "never hungry," "never needy" aspirations. Several thinkers from early in the period indicate how pervasive this theme was. John Locke, different as he may have been from Descartes, nonetheless formulated his own variation on the substance-as-self-sufficiency theme. In Locke's handling, substance becomes a sort of "I don't know what." Yet, this "I don't know what" must be acknowledged as real. We know that qualities always inhere in some substance. They are qualities of something. Colors, for example, are definitely dependent, incapable of separate, stand-alone subsistence. This means, Locke argues, that, beyond them, even though not given in direct perception, "we accustom ourselves to suppose some *substratum* wherein they do subsist." This is "substance" (Locke 1690a, 245). In plain English, Locke says, the "true import of the word" is "*standing under* or *upholding*" (Locke, 245). Locke may not be sure exactly what it is, but he is certain that something self-sufficient must be there.

At the beginning of the eighteenth century in Germany, one thinker seemed poised to challenge the dominating theme. Gottfried Wilhelm Leibniz developed what he called a "monadology." His substances were "monads," the "true atoms of nature and, in brief, the elements of things" (Leibniz, 68, par. 3). Leibniz emphasized how composite entities had to be made up of these monads. He spoke of relations and the unfolding of properties, both of which, one might think, would result from interdependent interactions. He even used the stomach-friendly words "appetite" and "appetition" to indicate drives for change (Leibniz, 70, par. 15). His whole scheme indeed, as we read it today, suggests a cellular model in which the component parts interact with each other, respond, alter, send out signals of their own, thereby providing the networks that give rise to a composite organism. This is the very point, though, where Leibniz felt the limitations of his age. Unlike communicating cells, the monads must be self-enclosed. They "have no windows," as he put it (Leibniz, 69, par. 7). Monads cannot be needy. They have to contain, already from the beginning, all that they will be.

Mid-seventeenth-century English had witnessed the first introduction of a Greek-derived term that was demanded by substance metaphysics. This was "autarchy," complete sovereignty over the self. Leibniz uses this very word in his *Monadology*. Describing the monads, he says "they have a sufficiency (*autarkeia*) that makes them sources of their internal actions" (Leibniz, 70, par. 18). Outsiders of all sorts need not apply. They are not required for the full unfolding of a monad's inner self. So taken for granted was the self-sufficiency theme, that David Hume, later in the eighteenth century, could make this sweeping pronouncement: "All beings in the universe in themselves" (i.e., prior to the accretions of subjective experience) "appear entirely loose and independent of each other" (Hume, 466).

Each of these positions typifies a dominant strain in Modern (1600–1900) thought. They all identified a privileged ultimate something characterized by a high degree of "autonomy," to use another word that entered English in the 1600s. If autonomy in the sense of nondependence most crucially characterized "substance," then whatever was dependent, needy, "hungry," or "heteronomous" became, by definition, deficient. Today, informed by the science of ecology, such a one-sided emphasis on self-enclosure seems itself partial and misguided. We tend to take our bearings more from biologists who embrace interconnection, like Darwin who was fascinated his entire life by earthworms. We can marvel with him at our dependence on the lowly creatures who "prepare the ground in an excellent manner for the growth of fibrous-rooted plants and for seedlings of all kinds" (Phillips 2000, 56). There is a wonderful link, as Darwin knew, between the work of earthworms and the bounty on human tables.

Even without a Darwin to confirm it, ordinary experience, recognizing how important is division of labor, testifies to the ways in which neediness, interdependence, and interconnection define our situation. How then, did the modern notion of self-sufficiency come to reign supreme? A conjunction of factors played an important role. The new notion of "substance" was, first of all, reinforced by the understanding of metaphysics as "going beyond." If truth could only be found by escaping the here and now, then a philosophically inclined truth seeker could safely marginalize the here and now. This helped remove (albeit by artificial decree) a certain messiness associated with the world of concrete experience.

Second, it was also due, in part, to social and political considerations. The metaphysics of nondependence emerged in concert with an ethics of *anti*-dependence. This is the sort of ethics that helped marginalize hospitality. Humans, feeling trapped, formerly by Church and now by State, sought a philosophy of liberation. Who could identify a more sweeping tool for liberation than the claim that self-sufficiency represents the deepest, most authentic truth about reality? John Locke and Jean-Jacques Rousseau provided explicitly political statements of this attitude. They both projected the nondependent ideal into an imaginary original state of nature. In that state, authentic and uncorrupted, freedom was understood as nondependence or insulation from the demands of others.[9] The positive drive for democratic institutions was thus, from the beginning, mingled with a bias in favor of defining freedom as nondependence.

PARASITES REHABILITATED

Such a one-sided neglect of life's interdependent dimensions was bound to occasion a correction. Madrid, in the 1930s, provided one. Delivering a series of lectures as holder of the Chair in Metaphysics, Jose Ortega y Gasset made a shocking pronouncement. Undermining the Modern theme entirely, he declared that being is "needy." His formulations could not have provided a sharper contrast with traditional substance-centered thought: "It is a mutual need which defines beings. To be is to be in need; I need things, things need me" (Ortega 1960, 209).

For those of us who live in a post-Darwinian, post-ecology age, admitting interdependence as a characteristic of existence comes as no big shock. What proves more shocking is a move made by the contemporary philosopher Michel Serres in his book *Le parasite*: introducing the parasite as a prime analogue for thinking through what this interdependence really means. Here, surely is an odd choice. "Okay," we might say, "parasites, by definition, are not able to exist autonomously, but why pick such an inherently unappealing creature?" First of all because the parasites are a lot more prevalent than most of us like to think. "When you preserve a deer," one biologist told science writer Carl Zimmer, "you're preserving twenty species of parasites from four kingdoms" (Zimmer, 238). Indeed, so prevalent are parasites that they make up the "majority of species on Earth." The study of life, says Zimmer, "is, for the most part, parasitology" (Zimmer, xxi). Second, the parasite has gotten a bad rap. Parasitologists, as we shall soon see, bristle at the one-sided, distorted view of the creatures they study. Indeed, historically, "parasite" meant someone with an official and honorific function in ancient Greece.

Such scientific and cultural observations are mostly overlooked and forgotten. If philosophers have, as indicated in the introduction, an interest in reexamining the peripheries that house the overlooked and the forgotten, then the overlooked and the forgotten with regard to the parasite offer an area for exploration. The philosophical side of this project even has a high-powered name, the "hermeneutics of recovery." We will be recovering and rehabilitating positive meanings for terms that, within substance metaphysics, had been tainted. If successful, the analysis will reveal that parasites need not be thought exclusively on the model of the insatiable interloper seeking always to destroy its host.

We can begin the hermeneutics of recovery by examining the word "parasite." In itself it is innocent enough. It literally means the one who eats (*sitos*) next to (*para*) another.[10] A "parasite" could then be considered a "tablemate" a "co-eater," even a "companion." It is anyone or anything showing up and insinuating itself beside others. For the ancient Greeks, the "parasite" was initially the title for a respected position. It indicated someone "who gathered, stored and distributed the sacred grain" (Zaidman, 198). The office involved what was "both a privilege and an obligation," receiving a special portion of the meat from a ritual sacrifice (Zaidman, 198).[11] "Parasiting," joining in at ritual meals, eventually became a general communal obligation.[12] It served as a ritual encouraging social solidarity. Such communal meals were held in the *Prytaneum*, the community dining hall that housed the sacred hearth of the city. This locale was also where the "city's permanent honoured guests" ate, "the beneficiaries of *sitesis*, a privileged limited in the fifth century to a small number of citizens who embody all the values of the past aristocratic city" (Zaidman, 200). Readers familiar with the *Apology* of Plato will recall that in the second address to the jury, where his task is to suggest a fitting punishment, he asserts that, for his services to the city, he deserves "free food in the Prytaneum" (*Apology*, 37a).[13] Socrates, beloved model philosopher that he is, culminates his career by asking to become a parasite.

As those who were granted privileged access to free meals began to abuse their status, the newer, pejorative connotation emerged. Ordinarily, when we speak of parasite, we think of a Tartuffe, someone who takes but never gives, the guest who is never a host, the intruder who ruins a host and then departs.[14] Given such a context, rehabilitating the parasite requires recovering the many layers of alternative meanings associated with the term. The payoff for taking such a step: recognizing how a multilayered grasp of parasiting helps explicate the full dimensions of Ortega's "needy-being" metaphysics. Not only can this new root metaphor help us rethink metaphysics but it provides us, in a paradoxical twist, with a grasp of things more congenial to hospitality than to banishment. As an orthographic aid in developing this line of thought, I will often insert a hyphen as a reminder that "para-sites" may or may not deserve the wholly negative connotation usually accorded to "parasites."

Implication 1: Neediness

Why does Serres focus on the parasite? Three elements stand out. First, the Ortega valorization of neediness. We have seen how Leibniz highlighted "autarchy." It makes perfect sense that this word, together with its cognate "autonomy," would come to dominate in conjunction with a metaphysics of substance, one privileging nondependence. In our post-Ortega and post-ecology era, there is need for a different prime analogue. This one would replace autarchy, now recognized as exception rather than rule, with neediness and dependence. The biological para-site fits this bill well. It cannot be envisioned as having its own separate, self-enclosed status. By its very nature, it must enter into relationships. It cannot survive unless inserted into ongoing situations.

Traditional philosophical terms, their meanings coordinated with substance metaphysics, words like "thing," "entity," "subject," or "object," readily lend themselves to "surface and depth" sorts of analyses. There is a fundamental, authentic being, "substance," accompanied by a secondary set of add-ons: relations, interactions, interconnections. Hume's claim, with some italicized help, well encapsulates this position: "All beings in the universe, *considered in themselves*, appear entirely *loose* and *independent* of each other." The shift to a parasite model allows us to grasp how Hume's "considered in themselves" does not really mean "considered in themselves" at all. It means "considered as an artificially isolated projection which specifically ignores the concrete interminglings that characterize their existence."

Implication 2: Value goes all the way down

The second helpful dimension of "parasite" is analogous to the first. Once again, mixture replaces separation. Terms favored within substance metaphysics, terms like "thing," for example, can suggest a primitive, ethically neutral status, that is, a status prior to valuations. This makes sense, given a semantic landscape dominated by the self-sufficiency ideal. If, like Hume, we arbitrarily eliminate all the interrelationships into which a thing enters, then our construct, in its unreal, abstract condition, can indeed be considered value-neutral. The same cannot be said of "parasite." Just because its very being *is* its intertwinings with other entities, its being is at the same time a valuing. It is always selecting and choosing the contexts that are most appropriate for it to enter. It is also always having an impact, for good or ill, on those it affects.

This unavoidable interloper status has led, quite understandably, to the negative connotation typically associated with the term. Parasitologists, however, offer a corrective. Parasitic relations providing mutual benefits, it turns out, are more dominant in nature than is usually assumed.[15] Serres, in line with this, wants to emphasize the dual possibilities for good and evil resulting from the same source. Is the neighbor-eater who has just joined us good or bad? Good, possibly good, at least. The prisoner sharing a meal with the teacher in Camus's "The Guest" turns out to have been trustworthy. But also bad, possibly bad. Tartuffe, stuffing himself on Orgon's food as he plots the family's demise, turns out to be an evil, destructive force. Para-sites may become destructive parasites. They may also develop into helpful symbionts.

What is at work here is a kind of concurrence of opposites. This concurrence must be recognized and emphasized in any metaphysics that aims at doing justice to concrete existence. Take, for example, Venus, goddess of love. Is she a good or bad force in human life? Obviously good say those influenced by Cole Porter songs, happy marriages, contented families. Not so fast, say those who have lived heartbreak, jealousy, rape, divorce, pedophilia, or untimely death of a child or spouse. The Stoics, faced with such a predicament, and ignoring the correlativity of opposites, offered a closed rather than open solution: fence Venus in.

Don't let things get to you, warned Epictetus. Avoid love, if love means being overly dependent on a particular object of affection. This applies to possessions like a favored piece of pottery. Treat it as interchangeable with other pieces. Diminish the level of attachment and, presto, you also diminish the pain that comes with loss. Pottery and artifacts, though, were not the only objects of affection that concerned Epictetus. He also had his sights set on avoiding human heartbreak: "If you kiss your child or your wife, say to yourself that you are kissing a human being" he begins, suggesting the move to generic interchangeability. The stage is then set for absence of pain should things go awry. "For then," Epictetus continues, "if death strikes it" (this particular individual, your child or spouse) "you will not be disturbed" (Oates, 469). Such harsh closing off of affection would seem to most of us, not worth it. We who instinctively embrace the law of opposites are too often without a general grasp of existence that is consistent with this embrace. "Needy being" metaphysics offers an alternative more consistent with ordinary experience.

Implication 3: Avoid purity, get the mixture right

Substituting the root metaphor of parasite for that of substance also helps in a third way. It encourages us to alter how we phrase communal goals. "Ideal," when woven into the fabric of the "substance-as-self-sufficiency" orientation, valorizes purity, that is, elimination of what is other. Whatever interferes with authentic nonrelational existence is, for it, a contaminant. Here is the attitude characterized by Derrida, following Levinas, as "allergic." Valorizing purity leads in practice to excisions. Excisions and exclusions become prerequisites for achieving the ideal. In human life, the banish-and-exterminate tendency has manifested itself most appallingly in genocidal projects. An illustration from the Nazi era is typical in this regard. It shows a microscope exposing various "bacteria." We could just as well substitute "parasites."[16] The lens reveals stars of David (Jews), triangles (homosexuals), dollar signs, and British pound symbols (corrupting influence of English-speaking money), and the hammer and sickle (communists). These represent the interlopers contaminating the race. Keeping the blood pure, goes the accompanying text, is the only way to stay healthy (Proctor, 162).

Within the context of a metaphysics that admits that *to be is to be needy* and for whom the necessarily dependent para-site is a root metaphor, "ideal" and "purity" no longer have pride of place. The sociologist Mary Douglas once wrote a book dealing with food and entitled it *Purity and Danger*. Within the realm of "needy being" metaphysics, purity *is* the danger. Combinations, blends, and mixtures now move to the evaluative center. "Optimal" and "harmonious" tend to be its preferred adjectives. The end sought is no longer that of eliminating contaminants in order to purify. It is, rather, to optimize the various blends: of components, of order and interruption, of repetition and novelty, sameness and otherness, connection and dissolution. There is little fervor for maximizing one particular dimension at the expense of all others. Such eliminative fervor endangers the "optimal" blend, always characterized by mixture and marked, when successful, by "harmony," which is not to be confused with "unity."

Here is an important implication of "hungry" or "needy being" metaphysics. Good comes to be understood in terms of proper blendings and mixings. If the parasite is the basal entity, then whatever is, already involves mixture. After all, the parasite cannot exist on its own. Evil derives not simply from the presence of a factor, say Venus, but from deficiencies and excesses. Because the coincidence of opposites is recognized, it is harder to justify blanket condemnations. Now the trick is to work toward achieving the right mix of components, a mix that recognizes the "contaminants" as possible sources of good as well as of evil.

INTROMITTERS "R" US

All "contaminants" are intruders, but, if the para-site model is taken seriously, not all intruders are contaminants. This is important. After all, within "needy being" metaphysics, the status of interloper is a universal one. Neediness drives the para-site to insinuate itself in the midst of ongoing activities.

It cannot survive apart. It is always "beside," "next to," "between" others. This is what defines its modus vivendi. The parasite, and by extension, each of us, is, to use an old Scottish law term, an "intromitter" (Smith 2005, 239).[17] The intromitter insinuates itself "between," a preposition that takes on special significance within "needy being" metaphysics. Substance-centered philosophy tended to gravitate around a particular grammatical form, the noun. Two of the most prominent nouns were conceived of as standing over against one another: subject and object. The trajectory most consistent with "needy being" metaphysics looks instead toward indicators of positionings and relationships, the prepositions.[18] The real action takes place *between* subject and object, *between* subject and subject, and *between* object and object.[19]

If this new orientation seems to valorize interlopers, well, it does. It recognizes, to be more specific, that *to be* always involves intromittance. *Esse est inter* (to be is to be between) might be the appropriate Latin formulation. The parasite must, this is a matter of life or death, find a midst into which it positions itself. No less an exemplary figure than Socrates, offers a perfect example. How does Socrates proceed? He is an interlocutor. What is an interlocutor? Literally, *interloquor* means "speaking between." Socrates inserts himself between companions and each other, between speakers and the subject being discussed, between teachers and their pupils, and, in general, between the elderly and the young, an intervention that cost him dearly.

A surprising etymology provides yet another defense for the valorization of intromitting. Our English term, "understand" was, for a long time, thought to be perfectly consistent with substance metaphysics. After all, "sub-stance" meant, as Locke emphasized, "stand-under." Invert the components, and, voilà, the metaphysical term meets its epistemological match, "under-stand." While it would make perfect sense for "understand" to result from simply combining "under" and "stand," such is not the historical case. Recent etymological research suggests a different story. The first component "under," derives from a transformation of the Latin prefix "inter," the Roman word for "between." "Understand," etymologically, means "stand between." It could just as well be spelled "interstand."[20] When we examine the most successful contemporary models of knowing, the sciences, we find practices that reinforce the indispensability of intermediaries. Scientists do not simply gaze out at their subject-matters, hoping for direct, unmediated access to truths. They construct experiments (mediating instrumentalities), work with colleagues (interlocutors), and present results at meetings of peers (interactions). Here as intromitters, the researchers presenting their results, serve mostly as messengers interpreting the work done by a research team.[21]

Disruptions and new equilibria

Given such considerations, opting for the para-site as a prototypical metaphysical figure, and for inter-position as a paradigmatic activity, will hopefully no longer seem like odd moves. Michel Serres actually takes this procedure one step further. Para-sites are not only understood as those beings with whom we must come into some equilibrium. Rather, their *positive* potential must be recognized. A *Scientific American* story reported how "parasites can foster greater diversity within an ecosystem" (Rennie, 132). Thinking along these lines, Lewis Thomas once speculated that a virus, might, in addition to its damaging possibilities, be a major engine of evolutionary change (Henig, 78–79). *E. coli*, for all the bad press it gets as a pathogen, is, by and large, a good friend to humans. Without it, we would be short on K and B-complex vitamins.[22] Animals born germ-free (read: free of interlopers) are, according to one microbiologist, "really wimpy. . . . [T]hey have thin intestinal walls, puny heart output, and require lots of vitamin supplements just to stay alive"[23] (Ibid.).

The parasite represents a conjunction of opposites. Promises of evil and good are woven into the very fabric of how things are. Abuse, decay, destruction are always possible. Our respose (responsibility), once it is oriented by the metaphysics of needy being, is not to seek elimination of the para-site. Rather our work, like that of artists, is to create conditions that allow the copresence of what were once considered incompatibles. One of nature's great eaters, *Bombyx mori*, can be quite destructive. It satisfies its voracious appetite with only one food, the leaves of a mulberry tree. But destructiveness is only one part of the story. In its larval stage *Bombyx mori* is better known as the silkworm. Now, if humans can figure out a way to live with the hungry larva, they can enjoy a fabric unlike any other. Similarly, if grapes are rotting on the vines, make sauterne. If bread is attacked by mold, make penicillin. If *Penicillium camemberti* has intervened, make cheese. "But when the arrow does not kill, when abuse is limited to within a certain threshold, it can happen that the relation evolves toward another equilibrium." When such a "rarity" occurs, says Serres, we can call it "justice." As with the cautionary tales presented at the beginning of this chapter, Serres suffers no illusions about the effort needed to reach this goal: "Difficult effort, exceptional, miraculous, human" (Serres 1980, 225).

Ortega y Gasset has drawn the implications for such a view within the context of liberal democracies. He praised liberal democracy as "the political doctrine which has represented the loftiest endeavour towards common life." Its greatness derives from how "in spite of being all-powerful," it "limits itself and attempts, even at its own expense, to leave room in the State over which it rules for those to live who neither think nor feel as it does, that is to say as do the stronger, the majority." Liberalism, the father of "needy being" metaphysics asserted, is "the noblest cry that has ever resounded in this planet. It announces the determination to share existence with the enemy; more than that, with an enemy which is weak." Such a noble expression of generosity, here Ortega agrees with Serres, is fragile. Humans, Ortega goes on, "appear anxious to get rid of it. It is a discipline too difficult and complex to take firm root on earth" (Gasset 1930, 76).

If we have an interest in not getting rid of them, then para-sites, whether invited to share the table or arriving unannounced, must be treated with care. They may threaten, but no system can improve without them. They provide the provocation, the dissonance that makes a move toward new harmony possible. A dinner table with no new guests is a safe place. It is also the place of redundancy and stagnation. The most vibrant system is hospitable to parasites. It can accommodate the most noise (Serres 1980, 321). No certainty accompanies these efforts. The intromitter is akin to the stranger or suppliant knocking at the door. Is the stranger Tartuffe who would unravel the carefully woven fabric of a family's life? Is it Shane,[24] the likewise single-named outsider whose presence helps break the cycle of constant battling and thus establishes a new, pacific order? Is it Babette,[25] hungry and alone, who will bring harmony and joy to an isolated community? There is no way of knowing ahead of time. We only know that taking up the creative challenge for moving to more inclusive levels of integration, when successful, provides rare moments of heightened harmony.

EATING PAUSE:
FONDUE FROMAGE

Since my wife and I met while we were both students in Switzerland, we have a special fondness for cheese fondue. With the fondue always served from a central container, and with each individual taking turns setting a bread-laden fork into the midst of others, the dish provides a good symbol for all-inclusive intromitting. Two little French terms are important to our ingredients and the cooking technique. Moitié-moitié *is how the Swiss refer to a fondue from two cheeses. This "half-half" version used Emmentaler and Gruyère, and we continue to find* moitié-moitié *to be our favorite. In blending the cheese and wine,* huit, *the number eight, provides the key movement: stirring in figure eights. Our recipe now is apportioned to serve two, but multiples of the wine and cheese can be adjusted for larger parties.* **Ingredients**: *Ceramic fondue pot, long fondue forks; 1 clove garlic, cut in half; 1/2 lb Emmentaler; 1/2 lb Gruyère; 3 tbsp flour; 2 cups dry white wine; 1 tbsp lemon juice; dash pepper; dash nutmeg; 2 tbsp Kirschwasser; baguette cut into cubes, wooden spoon for stirring.* **Directions**: *Rub ceramic pot with garlic; toss cheeses with flour; pour wine into fondue pot; set over medium* *flame. When small bubbles show on bottom and around edge of pot, stir in lemon juice and then handfuls of cheese, being sure to stir constantly (*huit, huit*) until each handful is completely melted. Keep this up until all the cheese has been added. Stir in spices and Kirsch (cognac would do as well). Serve immediately. If everything has turned into a lump (yes, this can happen if the stirring and cheese addition are not well coordinated or if one stirs in sixes or threes instead of* huits*), don't despair. It will work well the next time.*

NOTES

1. Epigraph by Herni Bergson from *The Two Sources of Religion and Morality* (1932). Translation by the author.

2. Macbeth, reflecting on what he is about to do, knows full well his responsibilities as host. "He's [the King] here in double trust. First, as I am his kinsman and his subject, Strong both against the deed. Then, as his host, Who should against his murderer shut the door, Not bear the knife myself" (Shakespeare, Macbeth, I, vii, 12–16).

3. The best example of this attitude can be found in Ayer (1946), chapter 6.

4. See Aristotle's *Metaphysics*, available in multiple translations, especially Book IV.

5. Metaphysics is important, for Ortega, as a map helping us with decisions about how to live. Existing and doing are correlative. Humans must inevitably make choices. "And the first thing he has to do is to decide what he is going to do. But in order to decide this, he must first frame a general interpretation of his surroundings, must formulate for himself a system of convictions about his environment; this he needs as a map so that he can move about among things and act on them" (Ortega 1958, 74). John Dewey also described metaphysics in similar terms, speaking of a "ground-map of the province of criticism" (Dewey 1925, 309).

6. Stephen Pepper, who helped extend the reach of Pragmatism, explored the significance of root metaphors in his *World Hypotheses* (1942). He spoke of "formism," built on the comparison with a blueprint and its materializations; "mechanism," rooted in the machine; "organicism," using the organism as the base analogue; and "contextualism," starting with something like the historical event and its multiple constituents unfolding over time. See the Pepper entry in the bibliography. See also Johnson (1980 and 1981) for a more contemporary take on the importance of metaphors.

7. In one of the most thorough studies of Aristotle's *Metaphysics* ever undertaken, Joseph Owens came to the conclusion that "entity" offered the most accurate English rendering of *ousia*. (See Owens, 149ff.)

8. In the third of his *Meditations* Descartes offers a more generous notion of substance, while preserving the notion of self-subsistence. "For example, I think that a stone is a substance, or is a thing capable of existing independently, and I also think that I am a substance" (Descartes 1984, 30).

9. Rousseau's state of nature appears in his *Discourse on the Origin of Inequality*. Locke's is described in his "An Essay concerning the True and Original, Extent and End of Civil Government" published as the second of *Two Treatises of Government*.

10. "The term is made up from *sitos*, which signifies primarily cereals (grain, but also food in general), and is also associated with *sitesis*, a form of state dining in Athens; and *para*, suggesting proximity and attendance" (Zaidman, 197).

11. "In its archaic ritual dimension, the office [parasite] is both a privilege and an obligation: a privilege shared with the priests, the old men and the women married for the first time, whereby they receive an honoured part of the meat (a third of the meat of two sacrificed animals during the festival of Athena Pallenis is shared among the parasites, another third goes to the priest, the rest to the 'contest' according to the inscription from the Anakeion (shrine of the Dioskouroi)" (Zaidman, 198–199).

12. "From the sixth century, Solon's imposition of *parasitein* on all citizens in turn perhaps indicates its antiquity and prestige at the same time as its obsolescence" (Zaidman, 200).

13. Readers should be made aware that some translations do not repeat the exact phrase that is in the original.

14. In nature, one of the best examples is the cuckoo. The most parasitic of them are among the wonders of adaptation, ruthless in deed and exquisite in deceit. Bothered by neither the protocols of hospitality nor the time-intensive work of feeding their young, or even, for that matter, hatching their own eggs, they sneak the eggs into the nests of other birds. While depositing their egg, they might help themselves to one of the other bird's eggs, carrying it off as food. The unsuspecting host keeps the cuckoo egg warm and, in a great feat of ingratitude, the new cuckoo hatchling pushes its fellow nestlings to their death. Having the nest to itself, it gets plenty of food, all at the expense of the hapless parent whose own chicks have been lost (Davies, 1–3).

15. The phenomenon of "cleaning symbiosis," in which tiny "cleaner fishes" feed themselves while providing important sanitizing functions for their larger hosts, is among the best known. Shrimp also exemplify interdependent benefits. "When the fish has approached near enough it remains motionless while the shrimp moves around over it removing debris and ectoparasites. The fish opens its gill covers to allow the shrimp to forage within them and also permits the shrimp to enter and leave its mouth. Very rarely does the symbiosis break down and the shrimp get eaten!" (Trager, 77). Another parasitologist credits even the malaria parasite with having a positive dimension. "On the credit side of the balance sheet, however, there is evidence that malaria prevents autoimmune diseases, such as lupos erythematosus, and inflammatory conditions, such as that scourge of the temperate zones, rheumatoid arthritis" (Desowitz, 131).

16. For an explicit use of the "parasite" metaphor by Hitler, see Zimmer, p. 18.

17. The main character in Smith's novel *Friends, Lovers, Chocolate*, introduces the word "intromitter." She has been accused of meddling. "I am not a meddler, Jamie, I am an *intromitter*. Yes, that's an old Scots law term which I rather like. It describes somebody who gets involved. A person who gets involved without good excuse is called a *vitious intromitter*. Isn't that a wonderful term? I, though, am *not* a *vitious intromitter*" (Smith, 239).

18. "Instinctively, that is what you were asking, what is always asked of a philosopher: what is your fundamental starting point? Existence, being, language, God, economics, the politician, and so on in ways that can include whatever is in the dictionary. . . . My answer: I begin, in a dispersed way, from relations, . . . Might I point out that each of my books describes a relation, often expressible by a singular preposition?" (Serres 1992, 150–151, my translation).

19. "The parasite's position is that of finding itself in between" (Serres, 1980, 309). Stressing the importance of "between" is not a move unique to Serres. The "between" is much discussed in continental philosophy. The twenty-sixth conference of the International Association for Philosophy and Literature, for example, had as its theme "intermedialities." Sessions abounded with titles like "In the Between," "The Third," "Hermes—the Intermediary," and "History, Negativity, Mediation." The theme has also been explored by Desmond.

20. In 1958, a dictionary of etymology could claim the standard view that "understand" was from the two terms "under" and "stand" (see Partridge). A 1988 dictionary offers the revised view that the etymology suggests "literally, stand in the midst of, stand between" (see Barnhart).

21. See the works by Ackermann and Latour in the bibliography.

22. "What the Heck is an *E. coli*?" at www.odh.ohio.gov/~/media/ODH/ASSETS/Files/eh/HAS/ecoli.ashx, retrieved 12/20/01.

23. Ibid.

24. Jack Schaefer's 1949 novel describes the classic interloper from nowhere. He does not have a last name and his first name may or may not be Shane. The outsider helps the farm family establish a stable life in the face of a threat posed by cattle ranchers, other interlopers who threaten the stability of settled farm life. In 1953 a famous movie version was released directed by George Stevens and starring Alan Ladd.

25. See the short story "Babette's Feast" by Isak Dinesen, and the Danish film version released in 1987.

Chapter Four

Knowledge

Carnal, Personal, Convivial

> If you hear that someone is talking behind your back, do not argue but rather say: "He obviously does not know me very well, there are plenty of other faults he could have mentioned."
>
> —Epictetus

FOOD AND KNOWLEDGE: I

Eating and drinking can be dangerous adventures. Poor Emperor Claudius was likely done in by his wife. She served up an appealing but death-dealing plate of mushrooms. We have seen how the unfortunate son in Camus's *The Misunderstanding* was murdered by what seemed a generously offered cup of tea. Anyone with food allergies realizes the importance of knowing the ingredients in any particular assortment of edibles. Medieval and Renaissance kings felt especially vulnerable. To get a good sense of whether any meal was dangerous, they inaugurated a practice known as "credence." Assistants would submit the food to various tests provided by the best science of the time. Someone would also actually taste (test) the meal. Should this faithful servant show signs of illness, the royal palate would be saved from ingesting poison (Visser, 139–140).

From this act of tasting-testing comes our word for a side table where food is set before serving it, *credenza*. We also get clues about the nature of knowing. To say "I know" in ordinary life is not a disinterested claim. It is one related to matters of concern. Detachment and disinterest are not the earmarks of cognition. Knowing is one mode of making our way in the world. It marks an act of confidence that opens the way for comportment of one sort or another. Since kings had to eat, they could not indefinitely withhold this confidence-that-leads-to-comportment. At some point, for example, after the chemical tests and after examining the servant-taster's reaction to a forthcoming meal, they "knew" whether it was safe or not. Or at least, they "believed," based on good enough evidence, that it was safe. Such situations of initial unease and subsequent confidence provide some initial lessons about food and knowledge. First, knowing in the ordinary sense has to do with matters of concern. Second, knowing is part of a feedback loop that involves acting. Third, there is no sharp line of demarcation between *knowing* and *believing*.

What we call "knowing" identifies a degree of credibilization, that, for all practical purposes, needs no longer be put into doubt. Kings made every effort to credibilize the claim "this food is safe." Still, imperfections in testing and delayed-action poisons could lay waste to the best tests. When there is longer time, a panoply of tests, and ample evidence from a variety of sources, the chances of error, though always present, approach a vanishing point. When doubt has been reduced to such a degree, the claim can be labeled "knowledge." There is, however, no difference in kind here, only a difference in the degree to which credibilization has led to confidence in guiding comportment.

FOOD AND KNOWLEDGE: II

An archetypal story from the Western tradition provides another way in which food and knowledge intersect. It's the tale of an overprotective father-figure. He wishes to shield his children from danger, harm, heartbreak, and disappointment. He seeks, in other words, to keep them from "knowing" these things. He sets forth a major interdiction; do not eat from the tree of the knowledge of good and evil. Not surprisingly, the children, although well fed and without a worry in the world, chafe at the limitations of their state. They live in a world with no struggle, but also without achievement. There is no pain, but no satisfaction. No relational strains, but no love. A third party (there's that "intromitter" theme again) enters the scene. It encourages violation of the interdiction. The woman's hand reaches out. She eats from the tree, sharing with her man. They enter a realm of new awareness. They will come to know pain *and* satisfaction, struggle *and* achievement, hurt *and* love. In general, this was after all the tree's name, they will come to *know* evil and, this also for the first time, good.

Their initial state cannot, strictly speaking, be described as "good." We depict it that way because we read our experience, that is to say our knowledge of both good and evil, back into the original setting. We do this by simply and artificially omitting the bad parts as if they and the good parts were not mutually implicated components of an inseparable package. Just as a world with no mountains has no valleys, so a realm without evil would also be void of "good." We tend not sufficiently to recognize this because we long for a world free from evil. In doing so, we tend to project a fanciful realm in which there is only what we know as good, ignoring the complementarity of opposites. Epictetus, as we saw in the previous chapter, knew better. We may not go along with his choice, but we can sympathize with his realization that to give up the evils in life, we also have to give up the goods.

Our couple, whose initial status was bland rather than good or evil, makes its choice to enter the world where the fusion of opposites holds sway. Having made their decision, the couple leaves the garden of overprotection. They enter the world of adult responsibility. Now, the burden is upon them to respond as contingencies and challenges arise. Risk, for the first time, becomes real. It must be faced without guarantee of success. The two have chosen to take their chances in a world of maturity, freedom, responsibility, and, what makes it all possible, knowledge.

To know is to eat from the tree of good and evil. Once again, knowledge intersects with matters of personal concern. In this case, knowledge is inseparable from living through certain situations. With our ancestral couple as an example we now can add the importance of experience over time as central to enhanced confidence and commitment, that is, knowledge. Biblical knowledge was primarily arrived at via "an intimate acquaintance with something" (Myers, 631). The man and woman, as they carved out their paths in life, as they lived through various experiences (the credence tables of life) came to "know" each other more fully. One particular "knowing," we call it "carnal," helped symbolize their commitment and keep it alive. It also moved them beyond themselves by resulting in the birth of their children. In this older sense, "knowing" had not yet come to be treated as a procedure disconnected from acting. It involved the doings and undergoings of the entire person. Hebraic "knowledge," as one interpretive source points out, "is an activity in which the whole individual is engaged." (*The Interpreter's Dictionary of the Bible*, 43). Knowledge, in this context, was primarily existential. Personal commitment was central in attaining it. Personal consequences flowed from it. Personal growth accompanied it.

KNOWLEDGE WITHOUT FOOD

Such a "knowledge-focused" reading of Genesis allows a special philosophical point to emerge: the kind of approach emphasized in this story has little to do with how philosophers deal with knowledge in the subfield called "epistemology." Many present and former students will be familiar with the stock examples from a typical philosophy class: the cat is on the mat, snow is white, grass is green. Such examples are well suited to an aseptic, cerebral, impersonal approach to cognition.[1] They isolate knowing, in what comes to be identified as the highest sense, from ordinary life. Instead, it comes to be grounded, not in its overall existential context, but rather in the depersonalized imparting of data.

How did we get from one paradigm, knowledge as "intimate acquaintance in a concern-centered environment," to another, "knowledge as disinterested observation of atomic facts"? At some point in history, just as Christianity was separating from its Jewish roots, a new player joined the field: neo-Platonic philosophy. It introduced the decidedly non-Hebraic understanding of human nature familiar to us today. Two separate components, body and soul, came to be posited as coexisting in the human being.[2] Carried by the Roman Empire and given a great boost by St. Augustine, neo-Platonism provided the new era with its lingua franca. So much was this so, that the developing religious movement, although rooted in non-Greek practices and attitudes, gradually allowed Greek, dualistic, conceptualizations to dominate. More and more, Christianity came to reflect the neo-Platonic rather than its own Hebraic inheritance. Traditional doctrines, like resurrection of the dead, evolved into the decidedly different "immortality of the soul" (Lazarus, we might recall, was really dead, not just temporarily separated from his soul). Two creedal formulations indicate the tension. The Nicene Creed, preserving the religion's ancestral inheritance, expresses hope "for the resurrection of the dead." Conversely, the Apostle's Creed, which, despite its name, was formulated centuries after the Apostles had died, reveals the impact of Greek body-soul dualism. It speaks of a "resurrection of the body."

This latter formulation came more and more to prevail, not only within Christianity but, because of that religion's dominance, throughout European culture. A particular philosophical trajectory then developed, one in which (a) the multidimensionality of human life came to be expressed in terms of sharp bifurcations, for example, mind/body, material/immaterial, body/soul, subject/object, matter/spirit, and (b) the two terms in the bifurcation came more and more to be understood as opposites. So sedimented has the neo-Platonic influence become, that dichotomous partitions that would have made little sense to the authors of Genesis, are second nature to us today.

EATING PAUSE:
FRUIT SALAD

Here is something that, given the abundant fruitfulness of their initial home, Adam and Eve could easily have concocted. It could also be called a "fruit cocktail," but that expression has now come to indicate a canned version from which most genuine fruit taste has disappeared. The options for mixture are variable. As is the case with most recipes, this one offers a basic pattern inviting modifications. **Directions**: *Take fresh fruit. Strawberries, apples, oranges, blueberries, peaches, pears offer one possible combination. Cut the fruit into bite-size bits, and place in a bowl. Pour orange juice over the combination. Add maple syrup to desired degree of sweetness. Enjoy. Variations around the theme are expected. Other juices may be used. A mix of cranberry and orange is popular in New England. Lots of different fruit combinations are tasty. Honey may substitute as the sweetener, but coagulation then has to be guarded against. If the fruits are fresh, local, and ripe, no sweetener need be added at all.*

DEPERSONALIZED EPISTEMOLOGY

When it comes to official, academic philosophical articulations about knowledge, a pivotal moment for crystallizing the issue can be specifically dated. The year was 1968. The author, Karl Popper. The title of his essay: "Epistemology Without a Knowing Subject."[3] If the embodied subject, mired in distractions, prejudices, and distortions, fascinated with the goings on at credence tables, could somehow be skipped over, there would result the highest triumph of total objectivity. Mind could confront reality directly without any distorting filters. Knowledge would be "independent of anybody's belief, or disposition to assent; or to assert, or to act. Knowledge in the objective sense is *knowledge without a knower*: it is *knowledge without a knowing subject*" (Popper, 109).[4] All "betweens," now defined uniformly as distortions and personal prejudices, are banished. Two poles only, object and mind, resonate in perfect identity. Embodiedness, personal involvement, and the "intimate acquaintance" that defined human knowing in the older paradigm, come to be dismissed. They now, in line with the mind/body split, get relegated to an area of mere feeling, a different category entirely than knowing.

Depersonalized epistemology was accompanied by its own myth, one quite different from that provided in the book of Genesis. Aiming at an absolute accuracy, unfettered by person-centered concerns, made good sense in a world now guided by the myth of "progress toward enlightenment."[5] In this newer story, the earliest epochs are not ones of innocence. Rather, the past is characterized as populated by "primitives" who lived in "dark ages." Escape from such darkness meant purposely leaving behind a world mired in blind obedience to tradition and superstition. Such a world was ignorant of the rational-empirical methods that alone would bring genuine knowledge. Only then, as in the story related by Immanuel Kant (1724–1804), could a new level of "maturity," one identified with Enlightenment, be achieved.[6] In this story, well-meaning, overprotective fathers do not figure prominently.

Quite the contrary. fathers, as representatives of the old order, have constantly to be overcome. They represent, after all, the primitive, dark age. Maturity, in the "tree of knowledge" story, had been linked to responsibility via knowledge. Now maturity comes to be associated with radical critiques that undermine and overcome in a wholesale way the inheritance from the past.

For our purposes, we can join this story in the early decades of the twentieth century. John B. Watson, pioneer in experimental psychology, father of behaviorism, proclaimed 1912 a pivotal year. His own field had turned a decisive corner. No longer would it follow a path marked by weak immaturity. It would instead strike out in a direction leading to a rigorous, robust adulthood. The choice had been stark: either "give up psychology or else to make it a natural science" (Watson, 6). Extolling how "brother-scientists" were "making progress in medicine, in chemistry, in physics," Watson urged adherence to the method that would bring parallel successes in his field (Watson, 6). Once the newly named "behaviorism" took hold, a practitioner could expect to satisfy important aims. "He wants to control man's reactions as physical scientists want to control and manipulate other natural phenomena. It is the business of behavioristic psychology to be able to predict and to control human activity" (Watson, 7). Watson here identified the watchwords of the new "maturity:" "science," "prediction," and, above all "control."

Watson's self-proclaimed pivotal year, 1912, also saw the publication by Bertrand Russell, of a well-received book, one that remains in print to this day. Most striking about this book is the mismatch between its title, *The Problems of Philosophy*, and its content. Russell's real concerns were problems of epistemology, the theory of knowledge. They were not those of philosophy in general. His book should have been called *The Problems of Epistemology*. Following a pattern we examined in the introduction, Russell spills plenty of early ink wondering whether the table on which he is writing is actually there. Outside of philosophy classrooms, no one, not even philosophers, really worries about this possibility. How then did such an issue become so dominant?

It all begins with the preliminary decision to bifurcate the person into body and soul, to separate mind from matter. These are the necessary prerequisite moves for detachment and depersonalization. What they do, in terms of this book's focus, is marginalize the stomach, not treat it as a major, integrated, component in the human person. This loss is serious, for the stomach serves as a constant reminder of interaction rather than isolation. Given the assumption of mind/body separation, however, a different trajectory comes to make sense. Mind came readily to be envisioned as a self-enclosed container. Ideas were its contents. With mind thought to be separate from body, it made sense to think of ourselves as having privileged cognitive access only to what was in mind. All other contact came via an untrustworthy "between," the body. This, in turn, created a special problem, how to accommodate what now had to be called the "external" world.

Once we assume that we can only know with certitude those impressions or representations contacted directly in our minds, that is, without intermediaries, a further question naturally arises: How can we be certain that these representations bear any relationship to what exists in the "external" world?[7] Having reached this stage we find ourselves in quite a muddle. It's a muddle that allows professors to produce plenty of tenure and promotion-securing essays. But it is a muddle from which, because it is based on a de-stomached, "make-believe," understanding of the human condition, there is no escape.[8] The only way out is to pose some questions that lead us to the neo-Platonic assumptions that have become second nature. "How the heck could we possibly have gotten in this mess?" "What are the assumptions that got us here?" "Might there be problems with those assumptions?"

Russell, though, did not think the muddle indicated a need for rethinking initial assumptions. He was not one for humble, self-critical formulations. When he came to wrap up his book, he envisioned an epistemological situation in which we were like little gods.

> The free intellect will see as God might see, without a *here* and *now*, without hopes and fears, without the trammels of customary beliefs and traditional prejudices, calmly, dispassionately, in the sole and exclusive desire of knowledge—knowledge as impersonal, as purely contemplative, as it is possible for man to attain. (Russell, 160)

Having achieved such an exalted, "purely contemplative" position, the personal dimension, pejoratively labeled "subjective," would have been successfully discounted. The channels of communication would operate in a perfect mediator-free fashion. Intromitters, causing noise, distortion, shifts in messages, would have been decisively banished. Who could doubt that this would be a good thing, especially with the examples of the physical and biological sciences as models?

TEXTUALISM

One year before Popper's essay, a book had appeared in France that offered a new metaphor, one that would challenge the depersonalized, God's-eye-view aspirations. The book's title: *On Grammatology*. Its author was the same Jacques Derrida we have already met in our discussions of hospitality. One phrase would come to resonate most powerfully within discussions about knowing: "There is nothing outside of the text" (Derrida 1976, 158). This phrase became a slogan of sorts. "Text" would now become the appropriate metaphor for describing subject-matters of inquiry. The earlier transformation of subject-matters into "objects" had encouraged the goal of pure disinterest: Russell's sheer seeing "as God might see." Such a model came more and more to be challenged as the twentieth century entered its final decades. The effaced subject now made its return everywhere, even, as the history and sociology of the sciences became more prominent, in the area that was its original inspiration, the physical sciences.[9]

The "everything-is-a-text" alternative offered itself as the exact antidote for the vices of depersonalized epistemology. To begin with, when it comes to texts, the inquiring subject who establishes, examines, and interprets them, cannot be overlooked. Second, the best of texts prohibit a God's-eye view. They bring with them a certain inexhaustibility. It makes little sense to say that we should now stop writing books about *Othello* or *King Lear* because *the* definitive interpretation has already been produced. Finally, the emphasis on texts leads to a particular kind of reverse marginalization. Facts, so crucial in the depersonalized paradigm, tend here to be treated as "constructions."[10] Words, paragraphs, events, exist as sounds and marks on a page or as operators in the world. They are perceptible. They *become* facts only when endowed with meaning. Because facts and meanings emerge together, it is not correct to claim that there exist "facts" prior to interpretation.[11]

The new paradigm for knowing, "pan-textualism" it can be called, got a huge boost in 1979 when Richard Rorty published his devastating critique of traditional epistemology, *Philosophy and the Mirror of Nature*. It would be hard, after Rorty, to privilege the single-method approach and depict mind, ideally, in terms of a mirror.[12] In essays that elaborate his thought, he provided explanations of how the central metaphor of texts allows for a more flexible, multifaceted approach to knowing. The older, "pan-objectivist," position suffered from one major flaw: it embraced the "myth of Nature's Own Vocabulary" (Rorty 1982, 198). If nature manifested, beneath appearances, a single, deepest vocabulary of its own, then the one method that got at that vocabulary would give *the* definitive picture of the world as it *really* was. The main danger here is the temptation toward a narrow reductionism. We start by assuming that one and only one vocabulary is suitable for attaining the truth about our world. Then a field is identified as the one that best articulates that vocabulary. Physics was often taken to be that field. The conclusion: physics alone gives us what is really real. Whatever is left out, typically the qualitative realm, comes to be treated as mere appearance.[13]

Because of concerns like these, researchers have tended to abandon the "one deepest vocabulary matched by the one field that speaks it" approach. Social scientists, to name one prominent group, now insist on developing methods of their own as the best ways for arriving at understandings suitable for their fields. Answering the question whether she, as an anthropologist, aspired to the model of physical science, Ruth Behar, answered categorically "I, at least, do not" (Behar, 6). Paul Stoller, in two important books with telling titles, *Sensuous Scholarship* and *The Taste of Ethnographic Things*, also rejected the old single-method approach.[14]

Thus far, especially with testimony from practitioners in the field, this insistence on interpretation and texts as a model for all investigation is not especially controversial. Even physical scientists, especially those involved with quantum physics, openly question the notion that they are simply mirrors reflecting a reality that emerges outside of our participatory activity. The Viennese physicist Anton Zeilinger states the case simply: "But I believe that quantum physics tells us something very profound about the world. And that is that the world is not the way it is independently of us. That the characteristics of the world are to a certain extent *dependent on us*."[15] While welcoming Zeilinger's overall claim, Rorty would reject the phrase "tells us something very profound about the world." Instead, Rorty willingly embraces the full consequences that follow from jettisoning entirely the idea of "Nature's Own Vocabulary." Within literary criticism, interpretations may serve various purposes. What they avoid is claiming "to have discovered the *real* nature of truth or language or literature." Indeed, "the very notion of discovering the *nature* of such things is part of the intellectual framework which we must abandon—part of what Heidegger calls 'the metaphysics of presence,' or the 'onto-theological tradition' " (Rorty 1982, 140). Here is where things get interesting. In a sort of wild pendulum swing, the "object" loses the absolute determinative control it once had. The inquiring "subject" with its multiplicity of interpretations now takes center stage. But, once again, as with the God's-eye view, what moves to the margins is the *credenza*, that intermediate set of tools and activities that gives us justifications for making claims about how the world is.

CONVIVIALIST EPISTEMOLOGY

Here is where a food-centered approach can offer a humble, earthier alternative to both the godlike mirroring of facts and the equally godlike construction of facts. Both of these positions derive from a one-sided overemphasis on either mind or its correlative creation, objects. Thinking of the stomach as a full participant in the human situation occasions important shifts in emphasis. The everyday eater is situated in a world that has to be dealt with and survived in. We are not thinkers first, eaters second. We are eater-thinkers. As such we are deeply implicated in situations within which we find ourselves. Our everyday practices as stomach-endowed creatures make us primarily engaged participants. Even the highly vaunted "theory" of philosophers, as Gilbert Ryle reminded us, is a particular kind of practice, a mode of making our way in the world.[16] We can, if, for specific purposes, we set our minds to it, suspend this primary engagement. Then we can assume one pose as creatures of laboratory detachment or another as inventive interpreters of texts. But these are derivative stances, taken up because of specific projects. They exist as appendages to our everyday more stomach-centered lives and their associated practices.

There is an outdated usage of a common word that captures both the centrality of practices and their continuity with intelligence. The word is "conversation." Its oldest meanings emphasize the various kinds of "converse," that is, dealings, with our surroundings.[17] To engage in "conversation," if we are to believe the Oxford English Dictionary, initially meant "consorting or having dealings with others." As the word's semantic range evolved from the fourteenth to the sixteenth centuries, the sense of engagement segued seamlessly and, I would say, appropriately, into "conversation" as we understand it today. Significantly, the *Oxford English Dictionary*, in defining "conversation" emphasizes a theme from the previous chapter: prepositions. "The action of living or having one's being *in* a place or *among* persons." "Occupation or engagement *with* things" (italics in original). We speak as a way of making our dealings with, by, for, and through our surroundings more thoughtful. "Conversation" as engagement and "conversation" as discourse are inextricably intertwined. Mind/body dualism skews this interpenetrating continuum, replacing it with an oppositional bifurcation.

When we emphasize the continuities implicated in "conversation" we have the opportunity for a rethinking of the semantic territory inhabited by "subjects," "objects," and "betweens." Depersonalized epistemologists privilege objects. Pan-textualists stress subjects. Both miss where the real action takes place, the prepositional realm of in-betweens. This is where a "convivial" epistemology can make a few humble suggestions. Each suggestion is built around a paradigm shift. When we think of knowing, the primarily analogue will no longer be either the detached observer in the laboratory or the interpreter who thinks of all subject-matters as texts. Rather the primary analogue shifts to personal acquaintance. This, in turn, emphasizes the multiple situations ("credence tables") that are lived through and the credibilized familiarity that results. There are three particular pivots around which a convivialist epistemology revolve. (1) "Converse" replaces mind-body dualism as the opening assumption. It does so by indicating the interpenetration of both actual interactions with surroundings and the conceptualizations in which those interactions are articulated. (2) Intermediaries, what happens on the *credenza*, will be highlighted rather than minimized. (3) The language of "subjects" and "objects" becomes obsolete. Instead we can now place the word "subject" where it belongs as that which seeks to be understood, the subject-matter in question. Subject-matter thus replaces the old "object." The curious humans become inquirers or seekers, not "subjects." They seek to make sense of various subject-matters in light of various purposes. The model tends to restore the "personal" dimension and is to be assimilated with rather than contrasted to the situation of "I" seeking to understand a "you."

REMEMBER ALL THE IN-BETWEENS

"Converse," indicating, at the same time, practices and the discourses about them, has already been discussed. The important result of those discussions: think of stomach, hand, heart, and brain as partners in our "conversations" with things. Those things, in addition to other humans, offer a sundry lot: subatomic particles, viruses, bacteria, other animals, insects, flora, tornadoes, and volcanoes, along with weather patterns of all sorts. If making our way in the world involves making our practices thoughtful, that is, fostering good, flourishing lives, then we need a growing familiarity with that world. By radically separating mind from objects, both the depersonalized and the pan-textualist approaches made the very kind of understanding we require into some sort of incomprehensible surd. The credence table approach, on the other hand, allows us a way of thinking about subject-matters that allow for multiple methods to permit the richness of what is to reveal itself.

As the sociologist of science Bruno Latour has pointed out, there is one effective way to demystify the process phrased in terms of how the mind can come to know objects. Do not begin by trying to answer that question. Rather rethink the assumptions and thus rephrase the question in a way that focuses on practices, on our dealings with things.[18] The puzzle, "Can mind know objects in a blanket sense?" is spurious. Such a question only makes sense within a specific conceptual landscape, one that assumes the spectator, detached attitude. When we think of a stomach-inspired approach and emphasize our dealings with things new questions come to the fore. The most appropriate question is, as Mary Midgley well put it, "What increases our understanding of the world?" (Midgley 1997, 86). What, in other words, helps us in our dealings with things? When we actually examine what researchers do, we find that they hardly ever think of themselves as minds sitting around waiting for a eureka moment, and still less as, say, therapists interpreting a dream. Instead they envision and undertake versions of the credence table experience, a series of experiments that, when successful, lead to new information that helps us make our way in the world.

If people who have climbed a rooftop and subsequently removed the ladder suddenly develop amnesia, they may wonder how they could possibly have gotten from the ground to their present heights. The same is true in epistemology. What needs to be done is to keep all the intermediary steps in mind, not forget them. In their informative book on ants, E. O. Wilson and Bert Hölldobler included a final chapter entitled "How to Study Ants." It was meant as a "primer of simple techniques for students and for the diverse population of field researchers who need to handle material quickly and efficiently" (Wilson and Hölldobler 1994b, 210). They list the sorts of procedures that lead from puzzlement about ants to enhanced understandings about them. Being thorough, they begin with tips for gathering ants, describe how to preserve specimens, what sorts of labeling techniques work best, how to keep colonies alive in the laboratory, what containers allow both vibrant ant colony life and optimal observational possibilities, even a formula for ant food.[19]

Before scientific papers are presented at conferences, published in journals, worked up into books, before, in other words, new understandings of our conversations with things become part of our conversations with each other, many procedures are undertaken. Some are pedestrian and ordinary. Others, especially construction of experiments, involve ingenuity and creativity. These are the "intromitters," the credence-table operations that convivial epistemology insists be kept in focus. They build the bridges between phenomena in their natural operations and knowledge as publicly adopted. Once again: prepositions. The members of a research team *with* their data, *with* their equipment, *with* their experiments, *with* their lab notes, *with* their critical peers, *with* the referees of professional journals, together they give us access to what the world is like.

I-YOU ACQUAINTANCE REHABILITATED

Unlike French and German, English has only a single verb "to know." The other two languages have double terms (*connaître/savoir*, *kennen/wissen*), which minimizes the chances of limiting the scope of "knowing." One term, *connaître/kennen* tends to emphasize the sort of knowing that arises from personal involvement, while the other stresses a more detached approach to understanding. The first is typified by acquaintance built up over a table with a history of shared meals. The other is typified by the dissection table. English-speaking epistemology, whether of the depersonalized or the textualist camp, tends to marginalize the first. Convivial epistemology, situated within a guest/host paradigm, reverses this valuation. The primary analogue is now acquaintance over time. When we think of knowing in its fundamental, that is, fullest, most fruitful and inclusive sense, it is this acquaintance over time that we should envision.

The term "trust" associated with the confidence gained via credence table procedures, takes center stage in this regard. "Trust" can have the sense of commitment, a confidence that certain factors (data, experimental results, lengthy association) have earned from us the response "yes, it is so." But trust can also involve the commitment of one's person. Two people clink glasses, look into each other's eyes, and promise to be faithful for life. The shared libation associated with a vow is an ancient practice. For the Greeks this use of drink was called a *sponde*, a solemn offering. Such offerings accompanied engagements of the self to some course of action. From the Greek root, we get a cluster of related terms whose link with drink has unfortunately been forgotten: *spouse, espouse, respond,* and *sponsor.* What they retain is the sense of a trusting act that binds oneself faithfully to others and to a way of living.

Within the social sciences, anthropologists are especially sensitive to this commitment-and-acquaintance dimension. Understanding another people requires a particular devotion, that of living with them, sharing their lives, eating their food. As a member of the community he was studying told Paul Stoller: "If you listen to us, you will learn much about our ways. But to have vision, you must grow old with us" (Stoller 1989, 83). Commenting on a particularly disconcerting ride in a bush taxi during his first visit to the Songhay, Stoller describes stages of growing awareness. What began as frustration, anger, and puzzlement gradually transformed itself into enjoyment and heightened understanding. But such a transformation could only result after *two decades* marked by uncounted bush taxi rides (Stoller 1989, 72).

When Jane Addams committed herself to open Hull House and offer hospitality to poor immigrants in Chicago, she did not primarily conceive the undertaking as charity offered by a superior to an inferior. She had been to college. She had taken the obligatory European tour. Now, as we saw in chapter 2, she sought yet another level of understanding. Living with the immigrants would not only yield a benefit to the poor and uneducated. It would also be a good thing for the children of privilege who "had developed too exclusively the power of acquiring knowledge and of merely receiving impressions" (Addams, 64). It was by living among the poor that young women "who had been given over too exclusively to study might restore a balance of activity along traditional lines and learn of life from life itself" (Addams, 72). It's a pity that the colloquial, double-directional use of "learn" (as in "he learned me good") has not gotten wide acceptance. Instead of the single-directional terms "teach" and "be taught," a verb is needed to indicate both teaching and learning. The verb, emphasizing interdependent relationship, much like the term *hôte*, would place the emphasis where it belongs: on the resonating reciprocities between partners in an endeavor.

The I-you trust most associated with personal knowledge is the one linked to the word "spouse." It identifies a commitment that leads to a lifetime of shared experiences, not to mention meals. Here, we go back to Genesis and a kind of knowing that can only come about if there is an antecedent confidence that the upcoming shared adventure will involve important transformations. It is an inclusive and growing knowledge, one that moves seamlessly between "knowing" as initial familiarity, as sexual intercourse, as growing commitment, as more sensitive discernment, as well as accumulation of information. Interestingly, the *Oxford English Dictionary* provides a similar trajectory as it traces the history of the word that is central to convivial epistemology, "conversation." There are other meanings of the term besides the ones we have already discussed. The word has meant the action "of being *in* a place *among* persons," "consorting or having dealings with others," "sexual intercourse or intimacy," "occupation or engagement with things," "circle of acquaintance," "manner of conducting oneself in the world," and "interchange of thoughts and words."

When awareness arises from lengthy acquaintance through shared experiences in various settings, we come not only to know in a fuller sense but also to an important realization: the "you" is inexhaustible. As chapter 2's discussion of the personalist philosopher Emmanuel Mounier pointed out, the other is "non-inventoriable," always has something more to offer, cannot be simply subsumed under a universal concept. Knowledge by increasing acquaintance, in whatever field, encourages the attitude of expecting "always something more," "always some surprise," "always some resistance to being easily categorized."[20] When the acquaintance paradigm is kept central, there is less temptation to think in terms of reaching a once and for all God's-eye achievement. After spending two years in Japan, Victoria Riccardi heartily endorsed the views of an American friend who is a longtime resident. After one week in the country he had proclaimed himself ready to write a book about the Japanese. After one year, he felt comfortable with maybe an article. After a long time, he thought he could only get out maybe one sentence.[21] In Levinasian terms, the other, as stranger, guest, or subject-matter of investigation, offers a manifestation of the infinite. Only a commitment to a shared life can begin to bring out the realization of that infinity.

Chinese translations of "subject" and "object" have the characters "host" and "guest" in them. This is a nice link, reminding us that all knowing can be considered an extension of "I-you" acquaintance. Given the guest-host metaphor, we might be tempted to think of ourselves, the researchers, as hosts. The alternative is actually more correct. It is the researchers who enter realms unknown to them. They are the strangers seeking to make their way in an unfamiliar realm. Following the guest/host metaphor, all knowing is thought of as resulting from a kind of long-term contact. This contact is accompanied by conversations, in the many senses of this term. The personal dimension had been obfuscated within spectator-based epistemologies. As we move away from these, there is an opportunity for rehabilitating the personal dimension and recognizing it as present, to some degree, in all forms of knowing. At that point, we will have recovered the sense that the safest general claim we can make about knowledge takes us back to Genesis where it "connotes an intimate acquaintance with something" (Myers, 63).

NOTES

1. Michael Polanyi, the scientist-turned-philosopher, warned about trivializing inquiry when the most prominent examples take the form "the book is on the table" (Polanyi 1959, 23). Although what I will develop goes beyond Polanyi, his work marks an important break with the tradition I will identify as "de-personalized epistemology." See especially *The Tacit Dimension*, and *Personal Knowledge*. Chapter 7 of the latter carries the title "Conviviality."

2. Plato's clearest statement is found in his dialogue the *Phaedo*, where the following is a typical claim "Now one part of ourselves is the body, another part is the soul? Quite so." (Plato 1977, 79b). Plotinus offers a more theatrical formulation: "The souls when they have peeped out of the intelligible world go first to heaven, and when they have put on a body there go on by its means to earthier bodies, to the limit to which they extend themselves in length. And some souls [only] come from heaven to lower bodies; others pass from one body into another, those whose power is not sufficient to lift them from this region because they are weighed down and forgetful, dragging with them much that weighs upon them" (Plotinus, IV.3. 15).

3. "Knowledge in this objective sense is totally independent of anybody's claim to know; it is also independent of anybody's belief, or disposition to assent; or to assert, or to act. Knowledge in the objective sense is *knowledge without a knower*: it is *knowledge without a knowing subject*" (Popper, 109).

4. Contrast this claim with that of William James from the days before philosophy had become over-professionalized: "It is almost incredible that men who are themselves working philosophers should pretend that any philosophy can be, or ever has been, constructed without the help of personal preference, belief, or divination" (James 1897, 93).

5. For a good outline of how progress came to be a guiding ideal, see the bibliographical entries under these names: Bury, Becker, Faulkner, and Randall. The last of these, surveying the history of ideas, indicated the novelty of progress as a general belief this way: "It is difficult for us to realize how recent a thing is this faith in human progress" (Randall 1926, 381).

6. Kant asserts that although it is not correct to claim that "we now live in an *enlightened age*," it is accurate to assert that "we do live in an *age of enlightenment*." This means living at time when "the obstacles to general enlightenment or the release from self-imposed tutelage are gradually being reduced" (Kant 1784, 8–9). Enlightenment is defined as "man's release from his self-incurred tutelage," where tutelage means the "inability to make use of his understanding without direction from another." With neither irony nor any recognition that what he is saying ought at least to occasion doubt about his diagnosis, Kant goes on to assert that his goal is deemed unworthy by at least half the human population. "That the step to competence is held to be very dangerous by the far greater portion of mankind (and by the entire fair sex)—quite apart from its being arduous—is seen by those guardians who have so kindly assumed superintendence over them" (Kant 1784, 3).

7. In 2000 the *Harvard University Gazette* published an interview with a philosophy professor who immediately problematized items in his office: "One of the basic questions in philosophy is the connection between mind and world. For example, here's a Coke bottle sitting on this chair, and there's a connection between the Coke bottle and my mental state. Ever since Kant, a big question has been, How do mental states succeed in being about things?" (www.news.harvard.edu/gazette/2000/02.03/heck.html, retrieved 4/19/2000).

8. One possible solution would involve identifying an outside spectator, "C," who could proclaim, "yes, indeed the representations in the mind, "A," do match up with objects in the world, "B." But even if such a third observer could be found, the problem would only be postponed. Now, we would need yet another outsider to validate how the representations in the mind of "C" matched with "D" (the correspondence of "A" and "B"). This infinite regress is known as the "third man problem" in philosophy.

9. See, Latour 1999, especially the chapters "Do You Believe in Reality?," "A Collective of Humans and Nonhumans," and "The Invention of the Science Wars."

10. In their reflections on historical methods, Martha Howell and Walter Prevenier point out that while the claim "there are no facts" only interpretations, is not embraced in its fullness by all historians, these latter have "long accepted a fairly mild version of this statement. Our entire craft is based precisely on the understanding that our knowledge of any event comes to us

70 Chapter 4

through sources which we know are *not* perfect reflections of 'reality,' which are constructions of reality, and which have to be decoded in order for us to understand what reality they construct" (Howell, 149).

11. Using rival readings of Blake's "Tyger, Tyger," which concentrate on the same term, while giving it widely divergent meanings, the literary critic Stanley Fish concludes that a "text" "is a *consequence* of the interpretation for which it is supposedly evidence" (Fish, 340).

12. Auguste Comte (1798–1857) had explicitly made mirror imagery central: the human brain, he asserted, must be "transformed into an exact mirror of the external order" (Brehier, 288).

13. Cp. the following from Marjorie Grene explaining Michael Polanyi: "*Personal Knowledge*, starting with the critique of the positivist claim for total objectivity in scientific knowledge, exhibited the culture of science as a subculture in our society, given existence and authority by our fundamental evaluations. Indeed, it is a subculture which claims for itself—and for which the layman claims—an overriding authority, over against all other evaluations or appraisals, which are conceived as merely 'emotional' or 'subjective' " (Polanyi 1969, xii–xiii). Alfred North Whitehead pointed out that if the division between a really real realm and one of appearance is upheld, then poets singing the beauties of nature would have to rethink their verses: "The poets are entirely mistaken. They should address their lyrics to themselves, and should turn them into odes of self-congratulation on the excellency of the human mind. Nature is a dull affair, soundless, scentless, colourless; merely the hurrying of material, endlessly, meaninglessly" (Whitehead, 80).

14. Christopher Tilley, in a book entitled *Interpretative Archaeology*, makes the case for treating the subject-matters of that field as "texts." Researchers are confronted by texts from other archaeologists and "the non-verbal text of the archaeological record that the archaeologist reads to construct his or her text" (Tilley, 12). Whereas the "object" can be isolated and controlled, the "text" is always accompanied by linkages that it cannot shed. In other words, *there can be no original text*. This means that the investigating subject, far from being a burden that should, ideally, be removed, is now given pride of place. Not just the subject presently "reading" the "text" but previous subjects as well. "Furthermore, the text is only available through a process of reading and what the reader understands or finds in the text is influenced by previous readings, other texts. Texts thus have a double dependence on others in their writing and their reading" (Tilley, 12).

15. Key scientists have always, Zeilinger claims, lifted "dividing lines in our minds." Newton lifted the line between action here and in the heavens, Darwin the animal/human line, Einstein the line separating space from time. "But in our heads we still draw a dividing line between 'reality' and 'knowledge about reality', in other words between reality and information. And *you cannot draw this line*" (Zeilinger). Niels Bohr had already explored this issue in the 1920s. Because the new discoveries in physics necessitated recognition of how measurement involved an interaction between "the object and the instrument of observation," physicists are led to reconsider "the problem of the objectivity of phenomena." (Bohr, 93). "The limit, which nature herself has thus imposed upon us, of the possibility of speaking about phenomena as existing objectively finds its expression, as far as we can judge, just in the formulation of quantum mechanics" (Bohr, 115). "Now, the quantum postulate implies that any observation of atomic phenomena will involve an interaction with the agency of observation not to be neglected. Accordingly, an independent reality in the ordinary physical sense can neither be ascribed to the phenomena nor to the agencies of observation" (Bohr, 54).

16. "Intelligent practice is not a step-child of theory. On the contrary, theorizing is one practice amongst others and is itself intelligently or stupidly conducted" (Ryle, 26).

17. Samuel Johnson, discussing how experience can be a good teacher, used the word "converse" in this way. Success in learning from experience depends, he pointed out, not so much on "solitary Diligence." It must, rather "arise from the general Converse and accurate Observation of the living World" (Fielding, 784).

18. See Latour, (1999), especially the chapter "Circulating Reference," and Latour (2004).

19. Food, after all, is important for ants as well as for humans. The nutritious mix of choice, named after its inventor, is called the "Bhatkar diet." "1 egg, 62 ml honey, 1 gm vitamins, 1 gm minerals and salts, 5 gm agar, 500 ml water. Dissolve the agar in 250 ml boiling water. Let

cool. With an egg beater mix 250 ml water, honey, vitamins, minerals, and the egg until smooth. Add to this mixture, stirring constantly, the agar solution. Pour the Petri dishes (0.5–1cm deep) to set. Store in the refrigerator. The recipe fills four 15-cm-diameter Petri dishes, and is jellylike in consistency" (Wilson and Hölldobler 1994b, 219).

20. Physicists apparently still have much to learn about the question: Why is ice slippery? "It's amazing," one physicist proclaimed. "We're in 2006 and we're still talking about this thing." The cluster of unresolved issues led one chemist to claim that ice "is a very mysterious solid" (Chang, F4, F1).

21. "Which is what is so bewitching about Japan: things seem so easy until you try to understand them. An American acquaintance now living in Tokyo said that after his first week, he felt he could write a book about the country; a year later, only a magazine article; after fifteen years, only one sentence. Remove the mask, draw the curtain aside, learn the language, and you face a web of complicated mazes" (Riccardi, 57).

Chapter Five

Art as Invitation

> As long as art is the beauty parlor of civilization, neither art nor civilization is secure.[1]
>
> —John Dewey

ARTISTS AND THE FOOD CYCLE

The novelist E. M. Forster was no fan of British food. Describing a particularly disappointing dining car meal, his prose resonated with the episode's glumness.

> At last the engine gave a jerk, the knives and forks slid sideways and sang against one another sadly, the cups said "cheap, cheap" to the sauces, as well they might, the door swung open and the attendants came in crying "Porridge or Prunes, Sir? Porridge or Prunes? Breakfast had begun. (Deval, 82)

Here was "gastronomic joylessness" at its worst. The service epitomized sheer functional eating: "Porridge fills the Englishman up, prunes clear him out" (Deval, 82). Forster's literary calling involved artistic transformation of words into stories that shone forth with beauty and meaning. The dining car episode, by contrast, offered nothing more than strict biological transformation. Edibles, energy, excrement—nothing more.

The mouth, as a novelist would well know, is not merely an opening for the intake of food. The human being is like a tube, said the philosopher F. J. E. Woodbridge. One end "praises God," the other "befouls the earth" (Randall 1940, 326). With Woodbridge's formulation we get a hint at the kind of complicated creature we are. Still, like many philosophers, he skipped over the mediating factor linking mouth to entrails. We are not just a tube. We are stomach-endowed creatures. The mouth does not simply praise God with spiritual words. Eating itself, as with the Sabbath meal or Holy Communion, can serve as central to worship. The production of waste and the worship of divinity do not mark two absolutely opposed activities. Somehow, when food is treated as sacred, they intermingle in ways that allow both to be revealed as good things.

Alfred Hitchcock, great master of the seventh art, once confided to François Truffault a plot for a film tracing the transformation of food. It would sort of be a societal version of Forster's porridge and prunes. Hitchcock would follow food from its "arrival in the city," through its final transformations into the "mess that's poured into the sewers" (Truffault, 320). Hitchcock never made that film, but in 2000, a Belgian artist gave yet another twist to the "porridge and prunes" theme. Wim Delvoye put together an art object, "Cloaca," which mimicked the transformational work of intestines. Its name referred to the Roman word for sewer, as well as a biological term for identifying certain avian and invertebrate excretory organs.

In 2002, a "new and improved" version went on exhibit at the Museum of Contemporary Art in Manhattan. "Cloaca" was a "vast contraption," a "room-sized intestine." Its combination of jars, tubes, computer-controlled pumps, acids and microorganisms functioned to one purpose: "generating feces." To succeed, the artwork needed to be "fed." Fortunately SoHo restaurants provided enough provisions for twice-a-day infusions. "Cloaca" as a stand-alone art object, treated the digestive process in isolation from any sacred aspirations. Here was something to be appreciated solely as an artistic creation. Although he had fashioned a piece that imitated one of biology's most useful processes, the artist rejected mixing art with utility. Reflecting on the types of works he favored, Delvoye insisted that "all art is useless" (Amy, 37).

By contrast, the nineteenth-century novelist and food lover William Makepeace Thackeray sought to bridge such sharp separations between art and life. In his "Memorials of Gourmandising" he upbraided those who eat and drink but "do not know the *art* of eating and drinking." He made a point of including cookery on his list of the "polite arts," a list that included music, painting, and architecture (Thackeray, 551). Concerning a rumor that "Master Shakespeare died of a surfeit, brought on by carousing with a literary friend who had come to visit him from London," Thackeray responded: "And wherefore not? Better to die of good wine and good company than of slow disease and doctors' doses" (Thackeray, 586).

Delvoye, the contemporary, and Thackeray, from the past, offer distinctively different takes on the nature of art. One creates a machine that mimics digestion but divorces art from actual eating. The other emphasizes continuities and, thinking in terms of refinement, welcomes, as arts, those refinements associated with all our appreciative faculties. As is often the case with sharp disagreements such as this, the very word in question is one whose meaning shifts, depending on the wider philosophical orientation within which it is set. In order to explore how the meanings of "art" correlate with general philosophical positions, and how a particular meaning would emerge within a stomach-and-mind approach to life, it will be necessary, first, to take a historical detour.

ART AS IMITATION: DECEPTIVE OR REVELATORY?

Imagine sitting at table salivating at the sight of a delicious rabbit about to be served. Then, imagine the surprise when the "rabbit" turns out to be a deception, a dissembling construction made of dough. Ancient banquets, as Herman Pleij points out, often focused not so much on the quantity of food as on the "artful arrangement of all those delicacies. Surprise courses and disguised dishes were among the high points of aristocratic dining pleasure" (Pleij, 137). Roman chefs, Pleij goes on to say, "earned their reputation by virtue of their mastery in falsifying foods" (Pleij, 140).

In her novel built around Chinese cuisine, Nicole Mones describes the heights of pleasure accompanying a particular surprise: ingesting what seemed to be one food only to get a quite different taste. A young chef envisions dishes he might prepare for an important competition. "For instance—what about tofu in the shape of a lute, stuffed with minced pork, flash-fried? And a chicken's skin removed whole, intact, then stuffed with minced ham and vegetables and slivered chicken meat and roasted at high heat until fragrant—?" (Mones, 64). Such dishes, with their deceit, touch mind as well as stomach. As they surprise, so they expand opportunities for the taster.[2] Speaking of another creation, the young chef asserts "this is a dish of artifice. See? It comes to the table looking like one thing. Like the plainest of food. Tofu. But you taste it and it's something different" (Mones, 228). The artistry at work here involves more than deception, since the meal must taste good as well. Still, transformation linked to deception suggests a theme around which Western discussions of art have revolved since its earliest reflections. One famous and telling anecdote involves, not humans, but birds seeking out food.

The painter Zeuxis, to hear Pliny the Elder tell it, was a cocky sort. His skill was such that he could re-create natural scenes better than nature herself. In an era of great artists, this was classical Athens, such arrogance could not go unchallenged. Parrhasius, giving no quarter when it came to self-confidence, threw down the gauntlet. There ensued a duel in paint, each competitor convinced of victory. Zeuxis went first. He drew back the curtain to reveal a tableau with grapes so realistic that birds swooped down to peck at them. Parrhasius, seemingly stunned, hesitated. Zeuxis, eager to claim victory, moved to lift the curtain himself, discovering too late that, he, like the birds, had fallen for a painted illusion (Pliny, 309–311).

Such a contest highlights several themes prominent in the philosophy of art. To begin with, out of all the arts, painting is made focal. Second, and fully in line with the focus on painting, a particular kind of artifice, imitation (*mimesis* in Greek), is considered to be the artist's highest calling.[3] It was just such imitation that bothered the first philosopher to engage in detailed esthetic reflection. Plato judged art as imitation to be a social danger. Free citizens had a particular calling. They needed to liberate themselves from falsehoods associated with mere appearance. Another realm beckoned, that of the "really real." Truth could only be attained if one gained access to this realm. Citizens of the ideal republic should not allow themselves to be taken in by deceit. So long as they remained in the world of distractions and amusements they would fall short of their civic calling. They would never grasp the difference between true justice and what passes for justice here and now. They would forever confuse images of beauty with true beauty. Imitative arts distract. They make people comfortable with the superficial, the self-satisfying, and the false.[4] For that reason, they need to be severely restricted, if not banished altogether.[5]

Plato's most famous pupil, Aristotle, thought his teacher had been inordinately harsh. By highlighting theater rather than painting, a more positive appraisal emerged. Drama, re-creating prototypical human situations, actually provides insight into truths about life. Unlike history, which deals with individual occurrences in their uniqueness, theater, exploring generic themes in their universality, is more "philosophical and more elevated" (Aristotle 1995, 59; 1451b 5–6). "Imitation," need not involve, Zeuxis/Parrhasius style, transformation aiming at deception. Tragedy, is a *mimesis* "of action and life" (Aristotle 1995, 51; 1450a, 16–17) that does not "relate actual events, but the *kinds* of things that might occur and are possible in terms of probability or necessity" (Aristotle 1995, 59; 1451a 36–38). "Imitation" re-creates and re-presents in ways that foster revelations about the human condition. Rather than encouraging distraction and falsehoods, it engages the audience with reality and truths.

Imitation, says Plato, is all about deception and distraction. A chicken skin should house, well, a chicken. Imitation, says Aristotle, brings us to new levels of awareness. Surprise tastes, we would say, open the palate in ways that had not heretofore been experienced. Imitation is bad says the teacher. No, imitation is good, says the pupil. The opposition could not be starker. Or at least so it may seem. For the historian of ideas, what sounds like a major disagreement turns out to be little more than a family squabble. On a deeper level there is absolute convergence. Art may be dangerous. Art may be revelatory. But art is first and foremost imitation.

ART AS EXPRESSION

If it were a Broadway play, "art as imitation" would have had a long and successful run. It was only by the end of the nineteenth century that it was finally closed down. By that point, imitation, as a generic characterization of art, had come to be viewed as doubly stifling. (1) It minimized the creative genius of artists. (2) It also limited the range of acceptable subject-matters for artistic production. Much better to go with a new, more liberating plot, "art as expression."

The novelist Tolstoy typified proponents of the newer theme. His essay "What Is Art?" reversed the traditional arrow of inspiration. Artistic creation does not begin with external objects. It originates with something internal: emotion. Suffused by a feeling, artists seek to "express" it creatively. The resulting product serves a particular purpose. It becomes a mode of conveyance, occasioning a similar emotion within the audience. "The activity of art is based on the fact that a man receiving through his sense of hearing or sight another man's expression of feeling, is capable of experiencing the emotion which moved the man who expressed it" (Tolstoy, 121).[6] Given such a power, the artist must take seriously the sorts of emotions being conveyed. Like Plato, Tolstoy thought misapplications of art could be corrected by appealing to a transcendental realm. For the novelist, after his religious conversion, the highest arts were those that fostered universal brotherhood.[7]

As was the case with those who offered variations within the "art as imitation" plot, so, too, there were family squabbles within the "art as expression" school. The British neo-Hegelian R. G. Collingwood highlighted a more active, more intellectual creativity on the part of artists. It was an error to assume an initial, fully articulated, emotion. Artists would then provide little more than external forms for conveying a meaning already clear and complete in itself. The actual process of artistic activity involves a more difficult challenge. What is initially felt is felt in a nebulous, if not incoherent manner. Artists, working with, not outside of intelligence, seek to make sense of the original inchoate feeling.

The emotion, as initially undergone, is more accurately labeled "oppressive."[8] It comes upon us ineluctably and confusedly. It grips us in its power. Artists, as reason-endowed creatures, tend to follow the admonition "I want to get this clear" (Collingwood, 114). Emotions move from oppressive to expressive when some understanding has been introduced. "The characteristic mark of expression proper is lucidity or intelligibility" (Collingwood, 122). Simple transmission is not "expression," but "arousal." Arousal and expression are differentiated by degree of intelligibility. Expression results when some effort at understanding has been accomplished. "A person expressing an emotion, . . . is making his emotions clear to his audience, and that is what he is doing to himself" (Collingwood, 110–111). Expression must arouse a true feeling, so Tolstoy thinks. Expression must explore the truth of an emotion, so Collingwood thinks. Plato and Aristotle all over again. The nature of expression might engender debates. Nonetheless, a shared assumption remains. Art is expression.

RETHINKING SPECTATOR AESTHETICS

For us, inheritors of both Greek antiquity and European modernity, the two paradigms become a source of contention. How, in the most general sense, is art best characterized? Imitation or expression? One ready answer: both. Why, after all, play the either-or game? There are many arts. Architecture, dance, music, sculpture, pottery, theater, opera, poetry, and calligraphy offer examples diverse and ample enough to accommodate both imitation and expression. Although tempting, there is one major philosophical problem with the both-and option. It fails to rethink more fundamentally the nature and role of the arts. For the fact is that imitation and expression, opposed as they are, represent two offspring of one and the same orientation. Underlying them both is our old friend the stomach-marginalizing "spectator."

So long as the spectator mind-set remains fundamental, so will its corollary, the "external" world as, not an environment of which we are an integral part, but something set over against us. When "objects" are emphasized, the external world becomes a sort of screen on which nature unfolds for our benefit. Artists can then attempt to imitate what they see. When "subjects" dominate, that same screen is transformed into a receptive surface. Artists become producers of objects expressed out of their subjectivity. The tension between the two positions seems unbridgeable. Indeed, it is unbridgeable, but only *if we remain within the spectator stance*. Moving to the stomach-mind blend known as the "convivial" approach changes things as significantly within the realm of art as it did within the field of knowledge.

When I provided a list of arts above, readers may have noted a glaring omission. In ordinary usage, one art, painting, has come almost to be synonymous with art itself. Painting's rise to supremacy as *the* art during the Modern period (1500–1900) is no accident. It owes much to the spectator attitude. The rise of museums as optimal settings for preserving and "appreciating" art also forms part of the fabric woven by "man" the spectator. Once paired together, the spectator stance and the museum setting gave birth to a special offspring, something called the "aesthetic attitude." Wim Delvoye's insistence on the nonutility of art indicates how he still seems to work within this context. Proper appreciation of art must not, according to this mandate, be contaminated by considerations such as those of interest or utility.

The self-reinforcing triad of (a) spectator stance, (b) museum-dominant setting, and (c) aesthetic attitude, provide a manifestation in art of a trend we have discussed in other chapters, the elevation of autonomy to the status of central good. "Art" becomes a special realm unto itself. It is one into which we can only enter as we leave aside everyday considerations of use and enjoyment.[9] Art appreciation, the spectator model asserted, requires a preliminary purification. Interests and concerns other than that of appreciating pure beauty must be purged. Only after such antecedent excisions, bracketing all prepositional dimensions, will spectators be able to assume the "aesthetic attitude."

Such a "view" (this is indeed the appropriate metaphor here) would have seemed odd to theatergoers in Shakespeare's time. The gap between audience and actors tended not to be pronounced at all. Productions took place in broad daylight, minimizing the gap between a darkened audience and lighted actors. With a stage that jutted out, it was hard for players and audience to think of themselves as viewers viewing the viewed. One commentator suggested that to recapture the sense of Shakespeare's Globe we would need to rid our minds "of prejudices and preconceptions born of familiarity with the magnified peep-show of today" (Lawrence, 3). Even in refined Paris, at a later time when the proscenium stage more sharply set actors apart, the attitude of audience-as-mere-spectator had not yet taken full hold. The *parterre*, the area immediately by the stage, continued to be populated by a gaggle of very active onlookers. As if indicating continuity, rather than a breach, between audience and actors, the *parterre* may even have helped Napoleon secure a sexual conquest. Arriving late, Bonaparte's appearance led, first, to an immediate demand: *Recommencez!* (start over). Later, when an actress uttered the line *Si j'ai séduit Cinna, j'en séduirai bien d'autres* (if I seduced Cinna I'll seduce plenty of others), "the *parterre* exploded in tumultuous applause, rising to its feet with all heads turning towards the First Consul's box." That same night Napoleon shared the actress's bed (Horne, 193).[10]

Audience activity in American theater actually involved food. The phrase "peanut gallery" referred to those in the least expensive seats. As is usual with this group, they were those least inhibited about taking on active roles of intervention. Their favorite snack, peanuts, gave them an opportunity for an activity of a particular sort: serving as projectiles. Such audience/actor interaction began to fade as the more medieval habits were replaced by genuinely Modern, that is, spectatorial, ones. Now there grew an unbridgeable gap between audience and players. The total triumph of the proscenium over the thrust stage sort of marks an important turning point. It symbolizes the end of lingering medieval practices, those that saw the arts flourish in squares, churches, and courtyards.

Reintegrating a more interactive grasp of the arts requires an approach that puts the whole spectator framework into question. Western philosophy, as we have already seen, did just that in the early decades of the twentieth century. John Dewey, linking this wider shift to aesthetics, took some major steps away from what he called the "museum conception of art" (Dewey 1934, 12).[11] The first example cited in Dewey's *Art as Experience* is not a painting, but a building, the Parthenon. Here is a work that, in its original setting, stood as an integral component of a living community. By starting there, Dewey was sending a signal. He wanted to reverse the marginal/focal arrangement that had dominated Modern aesthetics. No longer should we treat as focal those arts most amenable to the "aesthetic attitude." Those would move toward the margins. The center would now be occupied by arts in which the interactive dimension is less detachable. The fullest aesthetic experience would come to be associated with an inclusive setting dominated by integration not autonomization.[12]

We can also get some help in rethinking fundamental orientations by looking at commentators outside the Western tradition. Dewey came to the relational-contextual grasp of things via Hegel and Darwin, but the most prominent worldview emphasizing interactions and relations preceded them by several millennia. Buddhism, accepting as central, *pratitya-samutpada*, "conditioned co-origination," rejects the primacy of autonomous, detached existence. "Everything is conditioned, relative, and interdependent. This is the Buddhist theory of relativity" (Rahula, 53). This "theory of relativity," really a "theory of relationality," emphasizes interlocking attachments. It presents a sort of convivialism writ large, one that finds *with* to be an accompaniment to anything anywhere. Such a perspective discourages both the spectator stance and its accompanying aesthetic attitude.

THE WAY OF TEA

Yanagi Soetsu was born the same year, 1889, as Martin Heidegger, Gabriel Marcel, and Ludwig Wittgenstein. Like his Western contemporaries, he developed into a man with a mission. Worried that the Japanese were forgetting their traditional handicrafts, Yanagi, a pupil of the Zen master D. T. Suzuki, coined a word and invented a movement. The word: *mingei*, "arts of the people." The movement: also *mingei*, aimed at recalling the wonder and attractiveness of the practical arts.

Yanagi's discussion immerses his readers in a ritual that affirms Buddhism's commitment to interconnections and interdependencies, *Cha-no-yu*, the Way of Tea. Right away, several contrasts with spectator aesthetics emerge. First, the aesthetic setting is a convivial, interactive one. Others are present as participants. Second, the situation is continuous with ordinary life. Food and drink, the most basic biological necessities, form the ceremony's core. Third, integration and fullness, rather than separation and isolation, become prized qualities. The ritualized aspects of the ceremony, the landscaping, decorations in the room, the clothing, the cooking utensils, sounds associated with preparation, the tea itself, when taken in combination, make up the situation. Fourth, the relation of artist to audience can be compared to that of guests and host.[13]

In such a setting, "Art," focused on the entire situation and its conjunctions, that is, charm *and* utility of a cup or a pot, has little to do with either imitation or expression. Some of the Korean potters most admired by Soetsu worked, according to him, almost un-selfconsciously. Years of experience made the movement of hands, clay, wheel, and kiln a single, interlocking loop. "Sure," a Western aesthetician might proclaim, "what you say is fine for people who make pots and cups, they are artisans not artists." But this criticism begs the question. The aesthetic detachment so prominent in the West already assumes the segregation of the fine arts (amenable to the aesthetic-attitude) from crafts (uncongenial to such an attitude). Such question-begging takes us to the heart of the matter. Here we are confronted with a situation in which philosophers engage in what they do best: ask basic questions about core, automatically accepted, assumptions. Are we to remain within the built-in dichotomies of the Modern cognitive landscape, or are we willing to take a chance on listening to people working within a different one, be that landscape Western and non-Modern or non-Western?

Two immediate changes result from switching to intellectual landscapes cultivated by people like Dewey and Yanagi. (1) Instead of Art, it is better to speak of arts, plural and with a lower case *a*. (2) From among the arts, painting no longer holds the privileged status accorded to it within the world of spectator aesthetics. Instead, other arts, ones emphasizing participation, take their turns in the center. The tea ceremony, from Yanagi's discussions serves as one new exemplar. Dewey's opening emphasis on architecture offers another.

Combining architecture and Buddhism, the great Javanese monument of Borobudur indicates how different exemplars can take us in different directions when thinking about art. One book describes Borobudur as "neither a temple, a place of worship, nor a sanctuary. One does not go there to pray but to bask in a spiritual universe. It is a magical place, a gigantic antenna that gathers forces and thoughts, condensing them into a lesson that pilgrims only learn by degrees" (Frederic and Nou, 16). Borobudur, a "gigantic antenna" whose realization is incomplete without pilgrims streaming through it, offers itself as one good model for rethinking the nature of the arts within a convivial context. Rather than mirroring or expressing, a primordial fact about this architectural, sculptural, didactic, and religious wonder is simply its power of attraction. It is a kind of "host," which, although static, nonetheless draws, actually requires, guests.

ART AS INVITATION

Such a simple move, toward invitation and away from imitation/expression, may seem pedestrian and obvious, but it substantially alters inherited predispositions about art. Unfolding the full impact of what it means to treat the arts as modes of invitation will allow us not only to move beyond the imitation/expression debate. It will also allow us to think of the arts apart from museums, apart from the fine art/useful art split, apart, in the end, from the apartness that has sequestered art for over four centuries. The new approach, associated with the tea ceremony's emphasis on guest and host, centers on two related terms: *invitation* and *truth*. Together, they lead to the ultimate invitation provided by art, that which asks us to imitate it, a kind of *reverse mimesis*.

Chaucer's "Prologue" to his *Canterbury Tales* specifically introduces the theme of reaching out, that is to say, invitation. His pilgrims are headed for Canterbury, site of a shrine serving as an antenna, drawing believers from far and near. The prologue's location itself serves as a subsidiary antenna, another locus for gathering, the Tabard Inn. Chaucer's world was pre-Modern, but his attitude resonates with that of both the post-Modern Dewey, and the non-Western, Yanagi. Instead of spotlighting either imitation or expression, Chaucer opens with an inn, its host, and a reaching out.[14] The inn depicted by Chaucer, along with the tea ceremony highlighted by Yanagi, situates us in contexts emphasizing the more stomach-friendly continuities with ordinary life. So much is this so, that our ordinary connotation of "aesthetic," indicating that which is detached from ordinary experience, can barely survive in these settings. Yanagi recognizes this explicitly. There is, he says, "no such thing as Buddhist aesthetics conceived of as an independent branch of learning" (Yanagi, 129).

The word, "aesthetic," can be preserved, but only if it alters its connotations in line with the new, non-Modern semantic landscape. No longer would it signify what *remains* after a process of eliminative abstraction. It would now connote what *emerges* when an experience has been successfully integrative. Ultimately, the "aesthetic" applies most prominently to the fullness of lived experience. "Not only did the Tea masters enjoy beauty with the eye and contemplate it with the mind, but they also experienced it with the whole being. We might say they comprehended beauty in action. Tea is not mere passive appreciation of beauty. To live beauty in our daily lives is the genuine Way of Tea" (Yanagi, 179).

Inviting beauty to cooperate with use

Yanagi, true to this integrative and participatory ideal, finds that a typical antagonism, that between beauty and use, makes little sense. Far from being opposed to use, beauty is actually enhanced as a result of it.[15] "Without using there is no complete seeing, for nothing so emphasizes the beauty of things as their right application. Through use, therefore, the Tea masters approached still closer to the secrets of beauty" (Yanagi, 178). We are brought back here to the contrast between mind-focused and stomach-friendly perspectives. Minds as spectators require only visual recognition for identifying beauty. For stomach-endowed humans, necessarily engaged in practices, such a perception is partial and distorting. The kind of awareness consistent with lived experience depends on how we respond to invitations for engagement with things. The "beautiful" becomes a way of identifying certain satisfying, culminatory, complex engagements. It is not, in its most comprehensive sense, a matter of mere ocular perception.

Such an orientation is actually not absent from the Western tradition. We only consider it so if we myopically identify "Western" tradition with "Modern Western Tradition." Umberto Eco has made a point of noting how integrative emphases were dominant in pre-Modern, medieval culture. *The* Western tradition is an abstraction. There are many dimensions, often conflicting, that make up the strands forming the Western heritage. The medievals, certainly an important constituent, simply did not recognize sharp ruptures between beauty, utility, and goodness. The idealization of such divisions as categorical goods was a later accretion (Eco, 15). Reflecting on this situation from the vantage point of the late twentieth century, Eco looked for a corrective to the excessive emphasis on bifurcations. He hoped for some recovery of "the positive aspects" of the medieval attitude, "especially as the need for integration in human life is a central preoccupation in contemporary philosophy" (Eco, 16).

The Middle Ages were dominated by particular artworks: cathedrals. By their very nature these buildings served as invitations. Yanagi's Zen-influenced aesthetics, highlighting the tea ceremony, likewise invites participation, one that is of the most direct, tactile sort. Such an emphasis may seem to indicate a turning away from "cognitive" interpretations of the arts. Plato and Aristotle spoke in terms that associated arts with truths. Tolstoy and Collingwood were more circumspect. Still, Tolstoy's emphasis on universal brotherhood indicated his commitment to a certain truth. Collingwood's emphasis on "understanding" indicated his cognitive preoccupations. The art as invitation approach, emphasizing integration and participation, certainly rejects the notion of arts as nothing more than disguised, more easily digestible forms of philosophical or scientific propositions. It blocks the notion, as old as Plotinus, and famously defended by Hegel, that the "content of art is the Idea" (Hegel, 70).[16] Thinking of art as invitation does much to combat attempts at treating art as little more than a prettified package for conveying some conceptualization arrived at separately in philosophy or science.

EATING PAUSE: ANCESTOR'S SALAD

Having spent time living in Lyon, a city with an inviting and excellent food culture, we are naturally inclined toward Lyonnais-style recipes. In one cookbook devoted to the region, we even found a recipe that shares the name with a long-ago ancestor. He was Etienne de Nevers, a seventeenth-century adventurer who left for New France. The dish: salade de Nevers. It's a strange inclusion for a Lyonnais-area cookbook since the town of Nevers is nowhere in the neighborhood. Still, we took to the salad. We love the basic ingredients, olive oil, Dijon mustard, Roquefort cheese, and bacon. **Directions**: *Mesclun mix for 4 people; 6 slices bacon; 3 tbsp wine vinegar; 1/2 tbsp Dijon mustard; 2 to 3 tbsp Roquefort cheese at room temperature; 3 tbsp olive oil; 4 hard-boiled eggs (I prefer them just short of hard boiled so the yolk is a bit runny); 2 slices good bakery bread; 2 large garlic cloves; olive oil; salt; pepper. Place the lettuce mix in a bowl. Cook the bacon until crisp and set aside. Boil the eggs and set aside. Make the dressing: mix together vinegar, oil, mustard, and cheese. Prepare the croutons: heat olive oil in a pan with the garlic. When the oil is hot and saturated with garlic flavor, cook the bread slices until brown on both sides. The oil must be hot so that the bread gets crisp quickly. Mix together the mesclun, bacon, and dressing. Season with pepper and salt. Cut the bread into croutons. Add them and the sliced eggs to salad. Serve.*

"TRUTH" AS DOUBLE-BARRELED

At this point, it is important not to overreact. Art as invitation does discourage thinking of arts as nothing but imaginative ways of packaging ideas. Still, we should not commit the same error in reverse, denying all connection between arts and truths. The kind of rigid segregation that isolated truth as a product of science and limited beauty to the realm of art typifies a particular intellectual outlook. It represented the outlook challenged in the opening decades of the twentieth century. Dewey published *Experience and Nature* in 1925. *Art as Experience* followed in 1934. In Europe, a seismic shift occurred in 1927 with the publication of *Being and Time*. A decade later, its author, Martin Heidegger, published his reflection on aesthetics. *On the Origin of the Work of Art* is startlingly direct: "*Art then is the becoming and happening of truth*" (Heidegger 1971, 71). The claim might be direct but Heidegger's prose is often arcane and obscure. Nonetheless, a key insight from him can be borrowed and given a life of its own if it is resituated within a convivialist context.

To help weave Heidegger's claim within the orientation being defended here, two detours are needed. The first takes us to the Middle Ages. The other to Pragmatism. Before medieval distinctions got turned into Cartesian bifurcations, a thinker like Thomas Aquinas could embrace several meanings for "truth." In his essay *On Truth* he identified three. It is only the second that is familiar from epistemology-centered philosophy: "truth is the conformity of thing and intellect." The first meaning cited by Aquinas actually had more to do with being than knowing.[17] The "truth" of something is the fullness of what that thing is. It is hard for us, brought up in a spectator world, to be comfortable with this understanding. Still, ordinary usage provides some assistance. It preserves relics consistent with the more expansive, that is, not strictly epistemological, usage of "true." When we speak of a "true friend," or of "true love," we know perfectly well what we are saying. What we are saying indicates patterns of comportment more than representations in the mind. Hanging on to such usages helps prepare the ground for retrieving the long-forgotten ontological dimension of truth.

The lesson from Pragmatism can provide further assistance. Pragmatists savored words that blurred the boundary between subjective and objective. James and Dewey referred to these as "double-barreled" (Dewey 1925, 18). "History" provides a prime example. The word indicates occurring events. It also indicates the human attempts at retelling those events. "History" moves back and forth freely between the realm of occurrence, or "converse" in the language of the previous chapter, and the realm of telling, "conversations" about the occurrences. In official philosophical terminology, the difference is that between the "ontological" and the "epistemological" realms. "History" is double-barreled because it has a kind of oscillatory existence, unable to exist neatly in either categorization. Mere occurrences are just that, simply ongoing events. They become history only when recounted. The recounting in itself is, on the other hand, just storytelling unless it is grounded in some complex of evidence about the initial occurrences. As a result, it is correct to say both "history does not change" and "history does change." The occurrences and their narration form an indivisible cluster.

Food terms offer the same blurring of boundaries. "Nutritious" indicates properties associated with particular foods. It also signals the way in which the comestibles are transformed by the organism. With such terms, it makes little sense to speak strictly of "objective" properties or of "subjective" construals. Prepositions, once again, rule. Whatever is nutritious is so *for* some organism *on account of* properties present both in the food and the eater. The "nutritious" undulates. It is rooted in the foodstuff, but meaningless apart from the incorporating entity. Its status is prepositional. Like "history" it eludes simple single-barreled classification.

What can this possibly have to do with arts and truths? During its lengthy stay in the world of epistemology-dominated Modern philosophy, the term "truth" was radically subjectivized. It became simply a property of mind. That is to say, it was forced to become single-barreled. Now, after Heidegger and Dewey, conditions are ripe for reviving truth's double-barreled dimension. It, like "history," can be understood as oscillating between existential and cognitive significance. Each being-in-the-world as a specific composition of possibilities, as just this particular manifestation, presents us with a new "truth." An event becomes "history" as it unfolds. It is this very unfolding that allows it to become "history" in the other sense, that written in books. So, too, any art work, as a particular fabrication, is a "truth." Its truth resides in its manifestation of just this particular cluster of possibilities. The complexity of what this new fact involves then calls forth human understanding as it attempts to formulate truths in language.

ART AS TRUTHFUL/UNTRUTHFUL

The arts, by adding to the furniture of the world, provide works that are, in this sense, truth-ful. But this "truth-fulness," in both nature and art, reveals something special and often overlooked. It is a revelation that takes us back to a theme from chapter 3. Any making involves com-posing, that is to say, selecting, mixing, blending, and putting together. Before it comes to realization, an artifact may take many possible directions. We can think here of what James Davidson pointed out with regard to a master stylist: "Plato was a famously careful writer. After his death a tablet was found among his possessions with the first eight words of the *Republic* written out in different arrangements" (Davidson, 25).

The limiting side of such a move must now be highlighted. Just as hosting means welcoming some while rejecting others, so art as truth-ful contains within itself a difficult recognition. Any "composition" will have both permitted entry to certain elements and rejected others. Jambalaya is not shepherd's pie, *Aida* is not *La Bohème*, Borobudur is not Chartres, the order of Plato's first eight words is not the ones he rejected. The pool of possibilities from which such selections are made contains much that continues to go unrealized.[18] The pool stands for a combination of energies and ingredients whose status remains that of possibility. It identifies the realm of the "not-now-in-play." When the Greeks dealt with that which was not manifest, they told the story of Lethe, the river of forgetfulness. Cross the river, and memory is erased. In this sense, "not-now-in-play" means "set aside or forgotten, for now at least." The "lethic" was the forgotten. By contrast the "a-lethic" was the "true" as manifest and no longer forgotten.

When they engage in "factivity," the processes of making,[19] artists serve an important function: they rescue the not-now-in-play from oblivion. They allow the flowing forth of the forgotten from the hurly-burly of simple potentiality. Any particular "composition" can be thought of as the "no longer covert." The ancient Greeks, as William Barrett has pointed out, did not have a term that matches our "true." The word we translate as "true" meant "evident, manifest, open, present" (Barrett 1978, 145). Their word was *aletheia*, "un-forgotten."[20] Each making, as a rescuing from the "not-now-in-play" becomes a new *alethes*, that which has now become overt. In our vocabulary, thinking in double-barreled terms, we can now translate this as a new "truth." It actualizes a particular cluster of possibilities. But the actualization of possibilities, the opus, inevitably excludes as well. Every act of making entails a sort of permission. Every permission, in turn, necessitates some omission.

"Truth," when considered in ontological and in artistic terms, takes on significance quite contrary to what had been a dominating epistemological dream of modernity: total transparence. Such a transparence had frightened the Czech philosopher Jan Patočka who associated it with totalitarianism. After all, the drive to absolute clarity can easily become allied to the drive for absolute control. The longing for total transparency provides a setting where prediction and control, power and order dominate. Isolate these, ignore ambiguity, interdependence, neediness, surprise, and the dangers are not merely theoretical.[21]

By contrast, the position defended in the convivialist context suggests not only that total transparency is a dangerous political ideal. Strange as it may seem, truth itself is inherently incompatible with perfect transparent clarity. "Truth is untruth," says Heidegger, "insofar as there belongs to it the reservoir of the not-yet-uncovered, the un-covered, in the sense of concealment" (Heidegger 1971, 60). When Frenhofer, the master painter in Balzac's "The Hidden Masterpiece," refuses to limit his brushstrokes, continuing to add more and more lines and colors, the result is a mess. His desire to leave nothing out has the effect of allowing nothing in. The canvas resembles more the representation of pure possibility than anything else. As such, it stands as unbalanced concealing. By refusing to omit, it cannot permit.

The modern dream of a final, perfectly clear achievement of Truth now appears to have been not only erroneous but a dangerous delusion. Artists, in their quest for pushing back the limits of necessity, act as a healthy antidote. Recognizing the limitations associated with truths, admitting omission as a part of construction, should keep us all sensitive to the need for constant efforts at reform. In that way, omissions are, at best, provisional. This helps explain why artists regularly chafe within totalitarian societies. They recoil from the regime's inherent need for single-minded cleansing and eliminating. They reject its guiding assumption that the favored inclusion/exclusion arrangement is final and ideal. Their calling takes them in an opposite direction. They create or make things out of the forgotten and the eliminated. They make new truths happen.

Possibility, necessity, creativity = truths

Here is where the social significance of the arts comes in to play. Art as distraction or escape, the kind of concern that so bothered Plato, remains a genuine problem. Plato left a positive legacy, encouraging citizens always to ask questions about the gap between "real" virtues and the manifestations found in the world. Good Platonists continue probing the gap between "true piety" and what they see around them, "true courage" and what passes for courage here and now, "true justice," "true beauty," and so on. To emphasize this constant need, Plato depicted a bilevel world. Platonic reformers seeking a truer version of the virtues had to leave the here and now in order to gain access to the "higher" realm. Only then, having been exposed to "true" justice, "true" beauty, and other ideals, could they formulate genuine plans for reforming the here and now.

Such a scheme had one great strength: it kept people focused on how any particular social manifestation fell short of certain ideals. When taken literally, though, the image of another realm could lead to stifling intransigence. Power-hungry rulers could find in Plato a ready excuse for dictatorship. They could claim to be the ones armed with "truths" from the transcendent realm. In turn, this claim could be used to justify imposition, by force, of a particular scheme on the rest of society.

Can the "art as truthful-untruthful" recognition preserve the benefits of Plato's scheme while minimizing its disadvantages? It can certainly try. A new image takes center stage: that of a community at whose gates resides an unending stream of supplicants. We can translate this image into more strictly conceptual terms by learning from a contemporary Pragmatist, Thomas Alexander. Of the conditions that allow any entry or ex-istence, literally, any "standing forth," to take place, three are especially prominent. Being a philosophy professor, Alexander employs Greek terms for these conditions.[22] There is *apeiron*, literally, "un-bounded," indicating the "continuum of pure possibility." (This is the crowd clamoring for admission.) Then there is *ananke*, "necessity," the inherent limitations and restraints of the situation. (Some elements within the *apeiron* are simply incompatible with each other. Some are incompatible with pre-existing structures within the city.) Finally, there is *agon*, the "struggle" between possibility and necessity (debates and efforts to accommodate supplicants) (Alexander, 158 note 74).

Staying with the English equivalents and thinking in artistic terms I would make one emendation, substituting "creativity" for "struggle." "Creativity" indicates the drive and ability to com-pose, harmoniously, ingredients that had previously been separate or even incompatible. Successful artists, whether in the fine, the utilitarian, or the political arts exemplify a creativity that bends and stretches "necessity." A big long poem, loaded with theological and philosophical insights and all written in *terza rima*? Impossible, say the skeptics. Then along comes Dante. Working within constraints, yet pushing beyond the limits of what those necessities seem to entail, here is the mark of artistic creativity.[23]

Art as invitation, understood within the context of *possibility*, *necessity*, and *creativity*, offers a model that supplants the bilevel structure of Plato. The greatness of arts increases in proportion as they bring varied and conflicting elements to a creative realization, holding them together in some sort of harmony. Exclusion, as we have amply seen, will always be with us. Each composition as it includes, also excludes. Far from encouraging quiescence, this should be taken as prompting us to take seriously the need for breaking through seemingly intractable limits. Dewey, sensitive to the demands of a multiethnic, pluralistic democracy, phrased the ideal this way:

> Since aesthetic objects depend upon a progressively enacted experience, the final measure of balance or symmetry is the capacity of the whole to hold together within itself the greatest variety and scope of opposed elements. (Dewey 1934, 184)

Note how Dewey formulated his optimal situation. It is not a fixed program for a final scheme that once and for all achieves an ideal state. No matter how well organized is the city, many goods remain unrealized. Many evils, in other words, remain in need of redress. We face an ongoing task, reforming and reconstructing, so that the "greatest variety and scope of opposed elements" can coexist. Because every attempt will continue to leave good combinations outside the city's walls, no ultimate resting place is possible. The work of the arts, and of philosophy, in other words, is ongoing and ever unfinished.

Reverse mimesis

This unending need for creativity that allows co-possibles to emerge within the limits of necessity, helps us grasp more fully the many levels of "invitation" associated with the arts. Any making, first of all, results from the artist's invitation, even insistence, that varied constituents cohabit in ways that can be judged as beautiful and good. Such compositions then serve as invitations in another regard. Like the "antenna" that is Borobudur, like the innkeeper from the *Canterbury Tales*, artworks draw people to them. They serve as invitations for attention, participation, and commentary.

A painting bought at auction and kept in a collector's vault has become, to use a Deweyan distinction, an "object" not a "work." Its invitational dimension, its "work," has been blocked. The ultimate invitation of an artwork takes us back to the topic of imitation. Imitation is restored as central, but now in a novel sense, one that sort of reverses the Greek notion of *mimesis*. No longer is the work an imitation. It is we who are invited to be the imitations of the work. Absent Plato's transcendent, ideal realm, we must find another way of formulating the gap between ideal and real. Artists who succeed in making real what had heretofore been considered impossible provide just this sort of inspiration. The rest of us can then consider artistic effort as exemplary. "To live beauty in our daily lives," says Yanagi, "is the genuine Way of Tea" (Yanagi, 179). The work of art, says Dewey, offers a challenge to perform a "like act of evocation and organization" (Dewey 1934, 278). The making of artworks, as embodiments of new clusters of possibilities brought together in the face of necessity, provide a dynamic model for us to imitate.

"Makers," in the oldest sense of the term, were those who kneaded, who engaged in the work necessary for transforming basic ingredients into bread. Prior to either imitating or expressing, artists are most fundamentally kneaders of material, makers. The results are compositions, and, as such, epiphanies, revelations of what had hitherto been hidden. They bring new truths into the world. When well done, the works invite participation, contemplation and conversation. Invitees thus become co-makers of sorts, ensuring the works' resilience by returning to them century after century. Ultimately, co-makers take up an important personal task. They become makers of their own lives, mimicking artists, and inventing some manner of reworking the present so that hitherto unknown possibilities see the light of day.

NOTES

1. Epigraph by John Dewey from *Art As Experience* (Carbondale: Southern Illinois University Press, 1939).

2. Mones creates a theoretical text in her novel, one that explores Chinese cuisine's subtleties and compositions: "Chinese cooking accumulates greatness in the pursuit of artifice. Although we say our goal is *xian*, the untouched natural flavor of a thing, in fact we often concoct that flavor by adding many things which then must become invisible. Thus the flavor is part quality of ingredients and part sleight of hand. The latter can go to extremes. The gourmet loves nothing more than to see a glazed duck come to the table, heady and strong with what must be the aromatic *nong* of meat juices, only to find the "duck" composed entirely of vegetables. The superior cook strives to please the mind as well as the appetite" (Mones, 161).

3. "Epic poetry and Tragedy, as also Comedy, Dithyrambic poetry and most flute-playing and lyre-playing, are all, viewed as a whole, modes of imitation" (Aristotle 1995, 1147a, 14–16). "Can we also call the painter a craftsman and maker of such a thing?—Not at all. Then what will you say he is in relation to the bed? This, he said, seems to me the most reasonable name to give him, namely he is an imitator of that which the others made" (Plato 1974, X, 597d, e).

4. "Imitative art, then, is far removed from the truth, and that is why, it seems, it can make everything, because it touches only a small part of each thing, and that an image. . . . So too with sex, anger, and all the desires, pleasures, and pains which we say follow us in every activity. Poetic imitation fosters these in us. It nurtures and waters them when they ought to wither; it places them in command in our souls when they ought to obey in order that we might become better and happier men instead of worse and more miserable" (Plato 1974, 598b and 606d).

5. In the last book of his *Republic* Plato says that "it was reasonable for us to banish poetry from the city earlier." (Plato 1974, 607b). He goes on to praise the charm of poetry and welcome efforts by its champions to make the case that "it not only gives pleasure but is useful to cities and to human life." He concludes, however, that such a case has yet to be made (Plato 1974, 607d).

6. This kind of expression is not to be confused with direct stimulus-response causation, such as one person's yawning leading others to yawn. "Art begins when one person with the object of joining another or others to himself in one and the same feeling, expresses that feeling by certain external indications. To take the simplest example: a boy having experienced, let us say, fear on encountering a wolf, relates that encounter, and in order to evoke in others the feeling he has experienced, describes himself, his condition before the encounter, the surroundings, the wood, his own lightheartedness, and then the wolf's appearance, its movements, the distance between himself and the wolf, and so forth" (Tolstoy, 121–122).

7. "And as the evolution of knowledge proceeds by truer and more necessary knowledge dislodging and replacing what was mistaken and unnecessary, so the evolution of feeling proceeds by means of art—feelings less kind and less necessary for the well-being of mankind being replaced by others kinder and more needful for that end. That is the purpose of art" (Tolstoy, 231). The "kinder and more needful" feelings are later identified with Christian ideals. "The religious perception of our time in its widest and most practical application is the consciousness that our well-being, both material and spiritual, individual and collective, temporal and eternal, lies in the growth of brotherhood among men—in their loving harmony with one another" (Tolstoy, 234–235).

8. "When a man is said to express an emotion, what is being said about him comes to this. At first, he is conscious of having an emotion, but not conscious of what this emotion is. . . . From this helpless and oppressed condition he extricates himself by doing something which we call expressing himself" (Collingwood, 110).

9. "Taste is the faculty for judging an object or a kind of representation through a satisfaction or dissatisfaction without any interest. The object of such a satisfaction is called beautiful" (Kant 1970, 96).

10. The actress, known as Mlle. George, described the seduction this way: "He undressed me little by little, and acted as my *femme de chambre* with so much gaiety, grace and decency that there was no resisting him." The next morning "the future Emperor thoughtfully helped her make the bed, 'witness of so much tenderness'" (Horne, 193).

11. "Many a person who protests against the museum conception of art, still shares the fallacy from which that conception springs. For the popular notion comes from a separation of art from the objects and scenes or ordinary experience that many theorists and critics pride themselves upon holding and even elaborating" (Dewey 1934, 12). For Dewey, this is linked to the more general problem of detaching humans from the lived environment of which they form a part. The analogous problem in epistemology, he calls the "spectator theory" of knowledge (see Dewey 1929, 19).

12. The unusual overlap here between Dewey and medieval thought did not go unnoticed. Hence, Umberto Eco: "Medieval aesthetics, together with the Greek tradition, can suggest the ideal of a new *kalokagathiia* [integration of the beautiful and the good], and create a sense of the harmony of reason. This has already happened in such naturalistic philosophers as Dewey" (Eco, 118–119).

13. Cp. "Rikyu Koji regarded such a relation between guest and host as the ultimate and ideal state to be achieved in Chanoyu. When all the ornaments, both material and immaterial, are left out of Chanoyu, it is only the relationship between guest and host that remains. The union of guest and host is the basis of Chanoyu, and the ideal of Chanoyu lies in this union" (Sen, 1–2). Describing the Way of Tea, another commentator translates the relationship into Western terms: "A common goal and a common effort toward that goal replaces the individual and independent aims of the actors (we can call them that because they have lost their exclusive passivity). In place of the relationship of host and guest, a new reciprocity appears which we may call fellowship" (Jordan-Smith, 30).

14. Chaucer's most worthy successor in this regard is Henry Fielding. He prefaced his *Tom Jones* with an explanation that specifically compares the author to "one who keeps a public

Ordinary." Any such "honest and well-meaning Host" will provide a "Bill of Fare, which all Persons may peruse at their first Entrance into the House: . . . As we do not disdain to borrow Wit or Wisdom from any Man who is capable of lending us either, we have condescended to take a Hint from those honest Victuallers, and shall prefix not only a general Bill of Fare to our whole Entertainment, but shall likewise give the Reader particular Bills to every Course which is to be served up in this and the ensuing Volumes" (Fielding, 25).

15. Schopenhauer, very much within the spectator, detached attitude of Modern European aesthetics, urged what he considered to be a crucial distinction with regard to still-life paintings. As we saw in the first chapter, so long as what was depicted on canvas did not suggest utility (hunger and its satisfaction in this case), then it could be contemplated aesthetically, that is to say, bracketed from the interests of the will (Schopenhauer, 207–208).

16. Cp. "But since we have spoken of art as itself proceeding from the absolute Idea, and have even pronounced its end to be the sensuous presentation of the Absolute itself, we must proceed, even in this conspectus, by showing, at least in general, how the particular parts of the subject emerge from the conception of artistic beauty as the presentation of the Absolute" (Hegel, 70).

17. This sense is best exemplified in a citation from Avicenna: "The truth of each thing is a property of the act of being which has been established for it" (Aquinas, 6–7). For Aquinas, the ontological sense of "truth" is related to his theology of creation. "A natural thing, therefore, being placed between two intellects is called *true* in so far as it conforms to either. It is said to be true with respect to its conformity with the divine intellect in so far as it fulfills the end to which it was ordained by the divine intellect. . . . Even if there were no human intellects, things could be said to be true because of their relation to the divine intellect" (Aquinas, 11).

18. Suzuki associates the idea of some initial font of possibilities with the important Buddhist concept of "emptiness" (*sunyata*). "As Rikyū says, the water that fills the kettle is drawn from the well of mind whose bottom knows no depths, and the Emptiness which is conceptually liable to be mistaken for sheer nothingness is in fact the reservoir (*ālaya*) of infinite possibilities" (Suzuki, 298).

19. Etienne Gilson, the historian of philosophy, utilizes this term in his discussion of art. See Gilson 1965, 9, 18.

20. Heidegger defines *aletheia* as "unconcealedness." "Truth means the nature of the true. We think this nature in recollecting the Greek word, *aletheia*, the unconcealedness of beings." He then goes on to complain that even the Greeks did not draw out the full implications of what this way of thinking truth involved. "The nature of truth as *aletheia* was not thought out in the thinking of the Greeks nor since then, and least of all in the philosophy that followed after. Unconcealedness is, for thought, the most concealed thing in Greek existence, although from early times it determines the presence of everything present" (Heidegger 1971, 51).

21. Anne Dufourmantelle explains the connection "Patočka interpreted the crisis of the modern world and the decline of Europe in terms of a totalitarianism of everyday knowledge. To reason on the basis of the values of the day is to be prompted by the wish to define and subjugate the real solely in order to attain a quantifiable knowledge pledged to technological values" (Dufourmantelle, 38–40). "Man is meant to let grow in him what provokes anxiety, what is unreconciled, what is enigmatic, what ordinary life turns away from so as to get to the present agenda" (Dufourmantelle, 38).

22. The pattern identified by Alexander also deserves to be expressed in Greek terms because it owes much to the fragments of Anaximander and the *Timaeus* of Plato.

23. This is not the same; it must be noted, as simply breaking taboos, simply producing works that have some shock value. The heart of the matter involves com-possibility, not just doing something that violates what had been disallowed simply for the sake of doing so. One can break taboos easily by violating *one* previous restraint. Coming up with a work that provides new *com*-possibilities is a much more challenging task. Breaking the barrier of rhymed verse, for example, does not identify a more creative production than offering new ways of showing what can be done within the limits of cadence and rhyme. Douglas Hofstadter has examined closely the intersection of constraints and creativity in his *Le Ton Beau de Marot*.

Chapter Six

Clock Time/Stomach Time

To everything there is a season, and a time to every purpose under heaven.
—Ecclesiastes

WHEN DOES THE NEW TEA YEAR BEGIN?

In *Untangling my Chopsticks*, her book about *kaiseki*, food accompanying the Japanese tea ceremony, Victoria Riccardi describes a traditional way of reckoning time. "The special opening of the sealed tea jar, for example, which marked the beginning of the new tea year, used to be determined by the yellowing of yuzu citrus fruit in late October, not by a set date, which is currently November." Such temporal measuring, following nature's flexible lead, was abandoned when Japan switched to the Gregorian calendar in 1873. The new schema severed old connective tissues linking ritualistic response to specific natural occurrences. "Suddenly," as Riccardi puts it, all the food, flowers, weather, colors, and numerous other seasonal aesthetics involved in the tea ceremony and tea kaiseki fell slightly off track" (Riccardi, 234).

Such associations may have been lost, but a great gain was surely made in efficiency. After all, under the original schema, what kind of advanced notice would one give a caterer? What date could be printed on invitations? When would one prepare the hors d'oeuvres? The older way of reckoning time was characterized by contingency rather than control, dependence rather than autonomy. We who are children of the Enlightenment tend to dismiss the "yuzu fruit" approach to time as perhaps quaint but, given our need for prediction and control, certainly inefficient and frustrating.

The linguist Benjamin Whorf, having lived among the Hopi, offered a less wistful judgment than that pronounced by Riccardi. Instead of lamenting a loss, Whorf doubted whether the Hopi had a proper sense of time. They certainly did not grasp time "as a smooth flowing continuum in which everything in the universe proceeds at an equal rate" (Pinker, 63). Time, for Whorf, meant *one* thing. That one thing, a succession of instants quite independent of natural occurrences, provided a self-sufficient, separate means for measuring temporal flow. In this way, Whorf situated himself in the tradition crystallized by Isaac Newton's pronouncement: "Time exists in and of itself and flows equably without reference to anything external" (Greene, 46).

This last phrase "reference to anything external" identifies the key demarcation point between an Enlightenment conception of time and that whose loss is mourned by Riccardi. Interestingly, in one significant way at least, it also parallels a demarcation between Newtonian and Einsteinian physics. As Brian Greene explains it in *The Fabric of the Cosmos*, for post-Einsteinian physics, reference to something external, such as gravitational fields, is now known to affect time. Counterintuitive or not, "the closer you are to the sun, the slower your clocks will run" (Greene, 531, note 3).

Einstein's challenge to eighteenth- and nineteenth-century paradigms in physics was matched in philosophy by thinkers like John Dewey and Martin Heidegger who began to question assumptions that had guided "Modern," that is, post-medieval, thought. We might call them incipient "post-modern" thinkers except that (1) this label has become a lightning rod for various specific doctrines, and (2) the sorting out of epochs in terms of linear progression, for example, ancient, medieval, modern, post-modern, represents a prototypically "Modern" mode of reckoning, one that thinks of time as unfolding along a line of ever-progressing stages.

Jose Ortega y Gasset summed up the situation in the early twentieth century by saying that "we are now living in an era of intense crisis in which man, whether he likes it or not, must execute another great about-face." Why was such a change needed? The old, "Modern" ideas had begun to manifest their limitations. "Is it not obvious to suspect that the present crisis proceeds from the fact that the new posture adopted in 1600—the modern posture—has exhausted all its possibilities, has reached its farthest limits, and thereby has discovered its own limitations, its contradictions, its insufficiency?" (Ortega 1958, 69). Whatever name the new epoch comes to possess, the philosophical shift at the turn of the last century was real, as were parallel ones not only in the sciences but in literature, painting, music, and architecture.[1] Such a shift sent ripple effects throughout the Modern worldview, including its notion of time.

Had Whorf done his linguistic research in China, original home of tea ceremonies, he would have found no term directly corresponding to our "time." This point becomes the centerpiece for a careful and helpful analysis by the philosopher and sinologist François Jullien. The word *riyue*, Jullien points out, means, literally, "days and months" (Jullien, 118). Additionally, as a language without verb conjugation, Chinese does not encourage neat separations of past, present, and future. Using such linguistic clues, Jullien takes a different approach from that of Whorf. Selecting a particular take on time as *the* correct one unduly limits the complexity of human experience. As a way of fostering a richer grasp of that experience, he welcomes the difference between post-Enlightenment European and traditional Chinese understandings. The two modes of thinking, the latter more concretely experiential, the former a product of abstractive compartmentalization, sort of need each other, or at least that is what I, following Jullien, hope to indicate in these reflections.

HOW CAN PHILOSOPHY HELP?

Reconstructing and rehabilitating the "yuzu fruit" conception of time requires an ear for unfamiliar voices. Some of these will come from alternative philosophical traditions. Some will come from our own. One surprising voice will be found in the ordinary rumblings of the organ I am making central to my analysis. Borborygmi, marking intervals signaling hunger, offer one way to mark out temporal passage. Stomach-temporality, more directly related to ordinary experience than even "yuzu fruit" chronology, is neither, *pace* Newton, disconnected from "reference to anything external" nor, *pace* Whorf, a "smooth flowing continuum in which everything in the universe proceeds at an equal rate."

Stomach time could not be taken seriously, cannot today be taken seriously, so long as the default starting-point for eighteenth- and nineteenth-century philosophy, humans as detached minds standing over against the world, remains dominant. Fortunately, the twentieth century witnessed several philosophical revisions of that central assumption. We have already discussed how American Pragmatism, for example, moved from modernity's emphasis on autonomy/separation toward an orientation consistent with our post-Darwinian status as bio-social beings. John Dewey, as in the previous chapter, stands as an especially good guide. He may be the philosophical tradition's most stomach-friendly thinker. We saw, in the introductory chapter, that there were a few others, the *u* and *h* thinkers, but except for Hume we know little about their actual relationship to food. From what we do know of Hume (as described in chapter 1), he may have been stomach-friendly in an "I love to gorge myself on good food" sort of way, an attitude signaled by his wide girth.

Dewey, announcing a shift away from received assumptions, actually made theoretical hay out of our food-dependent condition. It was he, after all, who established an experimental school in which the stomach took a central place. "One of Dewey's curricular obsessions," Louis Menand has pointed out, "was cooking" (Menand, 323). The justification for such an emphasis goes to the heart of whether we think of humans as essentially minds or as fully embodied beings. In the latter case, the practices associated with the stomach, far from being problematic, become emblematic of the human condition.

What has any of this to do with time? The rehabilitation of interdependence allows for a renewed appreciation of the "yuzu fruit" interconnection of things. Such a shift brings with it two important corollaries: (1) *Instead of moments escaping, time comes to be understood as opportunities surging forward.* Temporality no longer need be thought of one-dimensionally as an ever-escaping sequence of standard units. It comes to be considered, on the "yuzu fruit" model, as a cluster of possibilities tending toward us. (2) *Time relaxation rather than time anxiety.* A particularly prominent contemporary anxiety, "chronomania," the frantic concern with not wasting "time," is directly linked to the time-as-disconnected-from-anything-external attitude. Rethinking temporality allows for a more relaxed, welcoming posture toward emerging eventualities.

Can the "yuzu fruit" Humpty Dumpty be reconstructed? Yes, if we are willing to piece together components from diverse sources. Just as the previous chapter drew on helpful hints from Japan, so this one draws on China. Both Jullien's explanations of Chinese time sensibility and American Pragmatism's emphasis on human practices help overcome the sedimented prejudices toward separation, autonomy, and disconnectedness. Iconographically, help will come from two well-known paintings. Together, these considerations will culminate in a new root metaphor for understanding temporality: the seasons.

This metaphorical move comes from François Jullien. He points out that in traditional China, seasons, not clocks, provided the primary analogue for thinking time. The central Modern Western assumption of humans (subjects) and the world (objects) set in opposition to one another would have struck Chinese thinkers as odd. It does not seem odd to us. But that is because we have inherited a particularly post-Cartesian construal of ourselves and the world. This is the construal summarized by Dewey as the "spectator theory." It assumed that the basic relationship of humans to the world was that of a mind, that is, an outside spectator, accumulating neutral observations about matter.

MODERNITY'S FASCINATION WITH DIVORCE

The spectatorial self had not always been prominent. Greek mythology, in its wisdom, had understood the importance of mind not isolating itself as an outside observer. Mind (*Psyche*) needed to be blended with a force linking it to things, and what better force than love (*Eros*).[2] *Eros*, urging *Psyche* toward connections and relations, would discourage detachment. Rationality worked best, not as disembodied/disinterested, but when it had a real affection for things. Even "philosophy" after all, means *love* of wisdom, or, maybe even better, considering the epistemological reflections of chapter 4, the wisdom of *love*. (Serres, 2002b, 8).

Psyche, however, suffering from a sort of seven year itch, longed to be free. It sought liberation both from *Eros*, the drive that implicated it in things other than itself, and from *Soma*, the body, its longtime partner. In the early seventeenth century, *Psyche* sued for divorce. Modern philosophy really gets its start in the divorce court presided over by Rene Descartes. The famous dualisms and binary oppositions, against which twentieth-century philosophy railed, got their start with what could be compared to a judicial decree. Descartes pronounced *Psyche*, Mind, and S*oma*, Body, as riven by differences irreconcilable. Not only that, but the settlement he imposed favored Mind entirely. It got its main demand: freedom as autonomy. Having jettisoned *Eros* and *Soma*, it assumed the status of self-reliance, dismissing neediness, dependence, and attachment as impediments associated with its former life.

Left aside in all of this was our formidable friend, *Gaster* (stomach). Here was a partner that would prove more difficult to divorce. Philosophers did not immediately recognize the difficulty because, mind-intoxicated, they dismissed the stomach as insignificant. How strange this seemed to a Chinese thinker. Humans may, in great numbers, have circumvented a bodily activity like sex, said Lin Yutang, but "no saint has yet circumvented food and drink." The stomach along with its needs, its dependencies, its attachments, should not be considered as burdens. It was Lin who formulated the felicitous label "stomach-gifted." The practices associated with eating open us to possibilities for connection and celebration. This is so true that "the best arrangement we can think of when we gather to render public homage to a grandfather is to give him a birthday feast" (Lin, 44).

Birthdays, we all recognize, present typical markers of time. Time can be represented by any marker of change or alteration. In this sense the stomach stands as one of biology's most familiar timepieces. This link is preserved etymologically in the word "meal," whose oldest significations include "measure" and "time." Anchored in the Indo-European root *mē*, to measure, the word "meal" indicated, initially, a measure in general and, more specifically, a measure of time. Our term "piecemeal" still echoes this older sense. Thus when we, as Lin suggests, think of a feast to celebrate an elder's birthday, we are un-selfconsciously relinking temporality with the stomach.

Psyche, Mind, in its haughty imperiousness, had tried to rise above such feasts, linked as they were to *Eros*, Interconnection, and *Soma*, Body. Doing so meant attempting also to transcend *Gaster*. Here, Mind met its match. Several hours of hunger would reorient Mind from theoretical contemplation to a practical search for food. Heedless of such biological commonplaces, the Cartesian tribunal, declaring *Psyche* to be self-sufficient, imposed at the same time a particular value hierarchy. Autonomy was no longer to be decried as unreal fantasy. Self-sufficiency now catapulted to exemplary status. No wonder this tradition ignored *Gaster*. The stomach cannot consider self-reliance as any sort of ideal. It is immediately, irrevocably connected to and dependent on its surroundings.

MILLET'S TIME VERSUS HOPPER'S

This tension between connection (*Gaster*) and separation (*Psyche*) provides the source out of which our two conceptions of time emerge. Their differences can be highlighted by using iconographic representations in which the stomach plays a prominent role. Millet's *Angelus*, for example, assumes a stomach-centered world. As such, it situates the participants in a nexus of intersections. The scene depicts a couple observing a particular ritual. The place is clearly defined, a field just outside of town, still within sight of the local church's steeple. One temporal span, afternoon, is transitioning into another, evening. Time flows via intervals that may be stretched and shrunk in various ways, depending on the activities with which they are associated. Some are relatively short as in the bowing of a head. Others lengthen as accompanied either by the sun's diurnal trajectory, or by the periods of planting, cultivation, growth, and harvesting.

Such an expanding series of spans, multiple and variously measured, emerges in a matter-of-fact way when time is inseparable from external events. What about reversing the order and looking for the shortest fundamental constituents? What are the ultimate simples out of which these spans are constructed? Here is the first surprising answer of stomach time: there are none. Time is not here thought of as a kind of line made up of distinct points. Spans, defined by the flux and flow of ongoing activities, cannot be separated from those activities. The paradoxes formulated by Zeno (ca. 495–430) long ago problematized the notion of a series emerging out of an infinite number of discrete units. How, he asked, could we ever get from here to there if we have to cross an infinite number of spatial units in a finite number of time units? Reaching a fixed goal, on such a scheme, should be impossible. Yet, every day, we manage to get from here to there. In the same way stomach temporality problematizes the notion of time as composed of ultimate simple units. This "ultimate simple units" construal, admittedly, is particularly well suited to certain purposes, those of efficiency and control. But it is neither the only possible conceptualization, nor the one closest to the actual flow of experience.

Zeno had highlighted a real problem. While the mind can divide things in various ways, the results of such mental abstractions should not uncritically be read back into reality as if they were its primordial and thus ultimately real constituents. Dewey identified this procedure as the "commonest of all philosophical fallacies" (Dewey 1925, 352). We are primarily creatures of practices. The things of ordinary experience, are "objects to be treated, used, acted upon and with, enjoyed and endured, even more than things to be known" (Dewey 1925, 352). Applied to temporality, this means that our experiences, dependent as they are, on use, enjoyment, and interaction, can best be considered in light of such practices. Within this sort of "fluid" rather than "atomic" world, the ultimate instant, that abstract construct so crucial for efficiency, power, and control, no longer retains its primacy. It can be grasped for what it is: a specific mode of interpreting time for particular purposes. Temporal durations, when considered in relation to practices, are spans composed of spans. Codependence goes all the way down. Borrowing the Chinese metaphor, time is a season composed of seasons.

Although this manner of speaking seems alien to us, the philosophical riches of our own language remind us how this has not always been so. In *Tom Jones*, Henry Fielding, describing behavior immediately following the death of a character's mother, refers to the action as "very indecent at this season" (Fielding, 200). The Oxford English Dictionary tells us that "season" comes from a term eminently related to the stomach, *serere*, the Latin verb "to sow." In common contemporary usage, "season" identifies, paradigmatically, one of the four recurring periods of the year. Examined historically, "season" turns out to be fundamentally heteronomous. It is dependent on some activity (linked to what is external). We speak of the planting, the harvesting, the hunting, or the fishing seasons. The dictionary's four pages devoted to the term include meanings indicating a university term, a court session, movement toward ripeness or maturity, and the fit or proper time. One phrase, harsh to our ears, goes to the heart of the term's extension. Autumn, the expression goes, is drifting away "through all its seasons."

Comparative etymology is also helpful, The Mind-centered and the Stomach-centered conceptions of time reveal complementary developmental trajectories. Our English word "time," consistent with its divorce-friendly connotation, derives from the Indo-European root **di*, to cut or divide. Romance languages, growing from a different root, tend to emphasize, not surprisingly, *romance*: linkage, connection, reaching out. Their words for time go back to the Latin *tempus* signaling the action of stretching, as with the cognates "extend," "portend," "attend."[3] English emphasizes ultimate divisions, the constant disappearance of homogeneous instants. Latin suggests time stretching toward us.

These differences take on special significance when we examine their ramifications. First, time, divided into a series of instants, suggests linearity, an ongoing, unending succession of moments, a timeline. *Tempus*, seasonality, suggests periods, repeating patterns, a set of cycles. Second, the way "season" invites a modifier, for example, "rainy" season, "tourist" season, "hunting" season, links temporality to ongoing events while pluralizing it. Third, time, as the autonomous ticking away of instants, privileges not only ultimate simples but an ultimate neutrality. Time considered apart from external conditions is nothing but a value-drained datum. "Valuing" becomes a subjective imposition onto an initially neutral backdrop. Seasonal time knows no such neutrality. Linked as it is to practices, it remains irredeemably immersed in a world of preference and avoidance. Finally, the *Psyche/Soma* split in Modern thought got a bit contagious. Everyone, it seems, was heading for divorce court. One prominent pair, time and space, had been inseparable from Aristotle to Leibniz. Their divorce was announced most famously by Isaac Newton. Thinking of *tempus* as composed of seasons discourages the isolation of time from space. The growing season, the rutting season, the dry season, the planting season, these all involve the intersection of localities and temporalities.[4]

Millet's painting takes on relevance in light of these reflections. It represents the lived experience of *tempus*. Though painted in the mid-nineteenth century, the characters inhabit a pre-Modern world, a world in which breaking up is hard to do. Millet's depiction is suffused with significance resulting from jumbling together, in a hard-to-separate mixture, solar movement, harvest, memory, religious heritage, community, fatigue, hunger, and hope. Time is not a fixed measure of disappearing, uniformly constituted units, ticking away autonomously. In Millet's world *the* present is constituted by what is *present*.

In spite of its overtly religious theme, Millet's scene is driven by something more fundamental than the church bell's call for a reverential pause. It is the couple's location, rather than the religious commemoration, that takes on special significance. They have toiled in the field because of the stomach's incessant demands. Various temporal spans intersect in that place: the Sun's trajectory, Autumn coming to a close, memories of spring and summer. The couple notes the day's end by pausing reverentially for the spirit and then by heading home to pause nutritionally for the body. Mechanical clocks are not a dominant presence, nor need they be. Time is real. But this is stomach time, a heteronomous parceling out of spans according to conditions presented by the couple's setting.

EATING PAUSE: SWEET POTATO SOUFFLÉ

The fall harvest season marks an opportunity for celebration in many ways with Thanksgiving in the United States as exemplary in this regard. My first teaching position was at a historically black school affiliated with the United Methodist Church, Clark College in Atlanta. Just before one Thanksgiving the departmental secretary shared her sweet potato soufflé recipe with me. It's been a family favorite ever since. Because this is holiday fare, the recipe is for eight people. **Ingredients**: *3 cups mashed, cooked sweet potatoes; 3/4 to 1 cup sugar; 1/4 cup milk; 2 eggs; 1 tsp vanilla; 1/4 cup melted butter; 1/3 cup flour; 1 tbsp grated orange peel; 2 tbsp fresh orange juice.* **For the topping**: *1 cup chopped pecans; 1 cup brown sugar; 1/4 cup melted butter; 1/3 cup flour.* **Assembly**: *Combine sweet potatoes, sugar, milk, eggs, vanilla, melted butter, flour, orange peel, and orange juice. Mix well. Pour into a 2-qt baking dish. Combine topping ingredients and scatter over the mixture.* **Cooking**: *Place in 350-degree oven for 40 minutes or until bubbly. Garnish with pecan halves.*

HOPPER'S DIVORCE WORLD

Millet's world is by no means our own. A more familiar scene, one centered on Time rather than *tempus*, was painted eighty years later. With Edward Hopper's *Nighthawks* we find a community whose main points of reference have little to do with Millet's world. Instead of fields surrounding a village, there is the omnipresent city. We are immersed in a concrete, steel, and glass environment. Gone are the signs of planting, cultivation, harvesting. Gone are the traces of the Sun's natural trajectory. Gone, too, are the supple hues of dusk that distend boundaries and blur the separations between humans, earth, and sky. Light is now artificial and contrived. Harsh verticality and disconnection rule. In the distance (across the street, actually) the modern world's replacement for a steeple stands out in sheer isolation: a cash register. Not only has the agricultural world completely disappeared but, along with it, the theme of rooted interrelatedness. Division and self-enclosure now dominate.

The lonely figures even seem to be imprisoned, there being no obvious mode of egress. We may well be looking at a diner, but where, we might ask, is *Gaster*? Strangely, the stomach is present by its absence. Hunger-induced activities, dominant in Millet, hardly appear. No longer does seasonal time, the bouquet of possibilities surging toward us, dominate. Artificial light, abetted by a cash register society, reflects and reinforces the dominance of autonomous Time. No surprise here, since Time is itself part and parcel of a world dominated by isolation, division, and forlornness. "Killing time" could serve as an alternative title for the painting. The victim might be an evening, but as M. F. K. Fisher noted, "an evening killed is murder of a kind, criminal like any disease, and like disease a thorough-going crime" (Fisher, 41).

Hopper's characters exhibit a condition fully in line with the Indo-European root *di: isolated individuals, severed from the earth, from their communities, from transcendence, and from each other. Division and divorce dominate. Such characters, insular in their solitariness, favor sullenness (the pejorative cousin of sole-ness) over solemnity. The world of Hopper is a desolate one in which Time hovers as an invisible presence. Just as Millet's painting gave us an anachronism, a post-Enlightenment painter providing a pre-Enlightenment depiction, so Hopper's painting also involves an interesting reversal. We are now situated in the mid-twentieth century, but the scene depicted immerses us rather in Time as envisioned by earlier thinkers: the grand neutral backdrop of ever-disappearing instants.

CHRONOMANIA

While such absolute Time flowing "uniformly on" may be "without regard to anything external," the same cannot be said for those whose lived experience is shaped by it. When clock time completely displaces stomach time, a special anxiety ensues. No longer do we live in *tempus*, the cluster of opportunities and impediments immersing us in a call-and-response sort of world. Autonomous Time, privileging freedom as disconnection, considers all external demands to be inherently burdensome. Time is experienced as a disappearing deposit of instants (1440 minutes or 86,400 seconds per day). Each string of instants, optimally, would be set aside for self-originating and self-directed activities. Pesky externally generated demands, however, keep interfering. Strings of ever-perishing instants then become a battleground. They can be set free by autonomy, or they can be "lost" in servitude to heteronomy and obligation.

Certain externally imposed obligations we cannot avoid. Employment, for most of us, falls into this category. Conceding such a loss, the battle moves elsewhere. To liberate the remaining temporal units, other instant-usurping activities must be eliminated. Actions thought of as natural and inherently worthwhile in a call-and-response kind of setting, now come to be viewed as impositions. Take bedtime stories. Who has time? One solution: a 1983 volume entitled *One-Minute Bedtime Stories*. But why stop there? That volume's success led to *One-Minute Birthday Stories*, *One-Minute Teddy Bear Stories*, and even *One-Minute Christmas Stories* (Gleick, 142).

Not surprisingly, stomach-related activities become special targets for elimination. Nutrition remains an iron-clad necessity. Time-obsessed individuals wish to dispense as much as possible with necessity, replacing it with autonomy, that is, as many self-sufficient instants as possible. Eating presents a special challenge. Heteronomy wins this battle. Regrouping, however, autonomy strikes, guerilla-like, in skirmishes it can win: those involving the preparation and ingestion of meals. Fast-food establishments have naturally mastered the techniques for avoiding "wasted" time. A *New York Times* article pointed out how the Boston Market chain more than halved time of service (11 minutes to 5) "by requiring customers to select their meals from a menu board and pay at the front of the line instead of ordering cafeteria-style and paying at the end." The article goes on to tout how "value meals" ordered by a single number rather than by an enumeration of various items, cuts time of service as well (see Feder). James Gleick, in his book *Faster, the Acceleration of Just About Anything*, recounts what is an extreme case. A Japanese restaurant owner devised a pay-by-the-time-you-spend-eating scheme. His restaurant featured a punch-clock. For patrons, it's all you can eat, pay by the minute. Customers rush in, load up on food, speed eat, and rush back to punch out. So popular is the concept that, "when the restaurant prepares to open at lunchtime," Gleick points out with delicious irony, "Tokyo residents *wait in line*" (Gleick, 244).

Autonomous Time brings with it what I would call "chronomania," constant fretfulness about wasted moments. Chronomania as a way of life requires palliatives. Though Plato, as we saw in the previous chapter, would disapprove, it is distraction and amusement that tend to dominate in this regard. Barring either, Time can be occupied by simply sitting, mostly isolated, in a late-night eatery. Hopper may have situated his characters in a diner, but no stomach-induced rhythms of temporality emerge. There is neither plate nor piece of food in sight; just mugs and two large, forlorn coffee urns, isolated in vertical rigidity. Evening brings social solitariness to prominence. Humans are forced to confront (as did existentialists like Jean-Paul Sartre) the repercussions of being a spectator self: isolated individuals confronting a neutral, meaningless world.

MIND AND STOMACH REUNITED

"Boredom," it is worth recalling, emerged in English only in the mid-nineteenth century. How, we might ask, did humans ever manage without this now ubiquitous term? Well, seasonal time, in its call-and-response dimension, kept us plenty occupied. Autonomous Time, on the other hand, by disengaging temporal flow from ongoing events, encourages an attitude of ironic detachment. Hopper has depicted disconnected characters getting through yet another lengthy series of lonely instants. Time is autonomous and oppressive, space is meaningless, and amusement and distraction have their limits. Boredom rules.

Autonomous Time will not and need not go away. Our world of airline schedules, conference calls, and global positioning systems is too dependent on it. It has proven a marvelous boon for organizing and coordinating lives. In its move to prominence, however, it has overly marginalized another sense of time, that which Jullien discovered in traditional Chinese society, Millet depicted in a pre-urbanized Europe, and Riccardi celebrated in pre-Meiji Japan. Our world has seen the triumph of the spectator subject and the trumping of Millet's *Angelus* by Hopper's *Nighthawks*. This is where we have been led by the divorce court model of philosophizing. Our new young couple, *Psyche* and *Gaster*, offers us matrimonial hope. With their union, we can go a long way toward a more balanced perspective.

NOTES

1. Some key dates: Monet's paintings of Rouen Cathedral, 1892–1895; Einstein's paper on special relativity, 1905; Ford Motor Company founded, 1903; Marcel Proust publishes first volume of *A la recherche du temps perdu*, 1913; Stravinsky's "rite of spring" debuts, 1913; Carson, Pirie, Scott Building in Chicago, designed by Louis Sullivan, 1899; first television transmission, 1925; James Joyce publishes *Ulysses*, 1922; see Boisvert, 2000.

2. The full story, not just the symbolic elements of blending love and mind, can be found in *The Golden Ass* by Apuleius.

3. See Klein, s.v. "temporal" and "time." The actual etymological situation, as reported in various sources, is more complicated. The Oxford English Dictionary, for example, takes "time" back only to its Teutonic root, which means, not divide, but "stretch." On the other hand, Partridge, s.v. "temper" and "tide," traces *tempus* back to a root indicating, not stretching, but cutting and dividing. Philosophically, the importance remains the same: time lives at the intersection of two tendencies, dividing and stretching, both of which have to be preserved in some sort of tension.

4. We have here the concrete, ordinary experience version of Hermann Minkowski's powerful 1908 claim announcing the triumph of Einsteinian relativity: "Henceforth space by itself and time by itself, are doomed to fade away into mere shadows." Cited in Galison, 164.

Chapter Seven

Fraternity as a Political Ideal

And crown thy good with brotherhood
From sea to shining sea!

—Katherine Lee Bates

THE SPORTS BANQUET AS A MODEL?

"Sports Banquet Ends in Trophy Fight" went the headline. Accompanying it was a photo featuring a food- and blood-strewn table. Such a story seems not only distressing but incongruous. For that reason it also seems a little unbelievable. Indeed, it is fictitious, a product of writers at *The Onion*. Knowing that we are reading a satirical piece transforms the distress into humor, especially since we know banquets to be havens of harmony and good behavior. Maybe that is why they make good targets for lampooning. Lucian, the second-century satirist, populated one banquet, not with athletes, but with philosophers. Mocking Plato's *Symposium*, Lucian depicted an ever-degrading situation, culminating in an all-out melee. Yes, his philosophers were throwing not only food but punches and actually drawing blood. The melee got its start when representatives from the rival Epicurean and Stoic schools turned to fisticuffs over who deserved the plumpest chicken (Lucian, 455–457).

Outside of satire, banquet decorum typically prevails. Open bloodletting associated with fights over a particular fowl or over a trophy are the exceptions. Wedding banquets, the setting envisioned by Lucian, rarely erupt in all-out altercations. They are helped in that regard by having gathered together a grouping of people, who, in most cases, are fairly homogeneous. For ancient symposia, the "in most cases" qualification was unnecessary. Homogeneity of participants characterized a Greek symposium, whether Plato's, the most famous, or those of Xenophanes and Plutarch. In such settings "fraternity" poses few problems. It is readily attained because it is allied to social exclusivity.

Sports banquets offer a different setting. Athletes from a city high school present a more varied mix. Indeed, celebrations that culminate a sports year offer one of the few situations in which people from different races and differing economic strata regularly share the same table. True, this is not universal. It is more common with football and basketball players than it is for the golf or tennis teams. Still, the banquet marks one time when the question used as the title of a book on race relations, *Why are all the black kids sitting together in the cafeteria?* need not apply.

As they sit around enjoying their entrées, lasagne maybe, or a choice between chicken and a vegetarian dish, team members, having spent a season in a shared endeavor, manifest a sort of interethnic, interracial camaraderie often lacking outside the realm of sports. This lack is evident even in large, multiethnic democratic republics devoted to universalist ideals. Such republics may have long since granted citizenship and full voting rights to a mixed group of individuals. Still, they can remain, in other ways, close to the Greek model of symposium-style exclusivity. It might thus seem to be a no-brainer to suggest that the contemporary republics would move closer to approximating their ideals if sports banquet fraternization were extended into the wider community. But just at this point does the discomforting role of philosophy come into play. Despite its place in the triumphal "liberty, equality, fraternity" slogan of the French Revolution, tough questions can still be raised about the third member of this triad. Among philosophy's embarrassing provocations is the following straightforward question: Should "fraternity" be an essential component of democratic republics?

Here is a philosophical topic that forces us to examine a sphere where the table and political philosophy intersect. Republics built around the pillars of freedom and equality, it could be argued, arrive at their optimal conditions when two qualifications are met: (1) equality of opportunity is widespread and (2) plenty of leeway is allowed for freedom in charting one's life trajectory. Generalized camaraderie, as glimpsed at the sports banquet, may offer a nice addition to the mix. Why, however, make of it an essential ingredient for a healthy republic? Freedom should mean freedom to choose one's tablemates without prodding or coercion. Equality of opportunity can exist without mandated forced camaraderie among individuals who have little in common. The table, in general, and its guests, in particular, can be considered as existing within the private, not the public realm.

CRITICISMS OF FRATERNITY

Making co-citizen friendship a private option rather than a public goal would seem consistent with what commentators have discovered about human nature. History and empirical evidence might well indicate how fraternity was a misguided, not to say dangerous, ideal from the beginning. After all, democratic republics must maintain a healthy wariness with regard to *substantive* goods. These are specific behaviors determined by one group to be beneficent for the entire population. Theocracies typically embrace and enforce a wide range of substantive goods: which religion to practice, what foods are suitable and which taboo, whether divorce is acceptable, what can be read and what is forbidden, how to dress, what music is allowed, what counts as "pure" and what "impure."

Democracies tend to be restrained when it comes to prescribing substantive goods. The scales of their policy judgments tilt in the direction of allowing wide leeway for individuals to define their own conceptions of a good life. Democracies fear how, metastasized beyond a certain limit, a commitment to substantive goods limits freedom to flourish. After all, there is a wide assortment of dispositions and talents manifested in human lives. The envisioning of substantive goods in terms of a generous, flexible range, rather than a restrictive, compulsory list, comes to be central in a democratic republic. Enforced friendship would then seem to be one of those substantive projects that are better left to individual initiative than to governmental mandate.

There are other, more specific concerns about fraternity. Freud warned that universal brotherly love might be a high-sounding ideal, but a typical mode of achieving it is fraught with difficulties. Too often social bonding is galvanized by a technique as devastating as it is effective: identification of a scapegoat. Nothing more assuredly brings people together than a shared enemy.[1] While critical, Freud at least admits that brotherly love is a high-sounding ideal. An earlier, more strictly political criticism had dismissed fraternity as not even worthy of theoretical praise. Only dewy-eyed utopians, guided by some saccharine, illusory fellow-feeling could possibly think of universal brotherhood as a good. This, at least, was the position of James Fitzjames Stephen writing at the height of the Victorian era. Let's get real, he says. How should I respond to someone who is false, calculatingly cruel, and ungrateful? Easy: stigmatize and punish. "In the first place, I for one do not love such people, but hate them" (Stephen, 230). Stephen asserts that "General philanthropy" cannot be justified by empirical evidence. "Many men are bad, the vast majority indifferent" (Stephen, 226). Those who praise fraternity do not live in the world of concrete experience. Instead, they worship and serve "humanity in the abstract" (Stephen, 222). "Are we all brothers?" asks Stephen. No. "Are we even fiftieth cousins?" No again (Stephen, 240).

These criticisms need to be taken seriously. Adding fraternity to the liberty and equality mix can lead, in practice, to restrictions on freedom and promotion of inequalities. The kind of fraternity in evidence at a Greek symposium countenanced a rigid class society, male/female segregation, and slavery. Fraternity, for those who extolled it while making the French Revolution, had moved beyond slavery but had still embodied, in practice, the continued subordination of women. Ethnic fraternity can lead to ethnic cleansing and genocide. Let's face the human situation as it is, say the critics. This may involve harsh truths, but social policies based on truths reap greater benefits than those based on syrupy self-delusions. When we return to our opening question, "Should fraternity be an essential component of democratic republics?, it seems that the three concerns just identified conspire to answer "no." Democratic republics have no business mandating substantive goods. The scapegoat temptation is all too prevalent. Let's not pretend we are all cousins, let alone brothers.

MEALS AND FRIENDSHIP AS CENTRAL TO POLITICAL PHILOSOPHY

Such objections were not always dominant. Aristotle, in an early systematic reflection on politics, could not envision doing so without mentioning either meals or friendship. Indeed, he linked the two by prescribing communal meals as ways of fostering co-citizen affiliations, something he considered crucial to a good society.[2] For the ancients, producing a political philosophy always involved both *structural considerations* (i.e., discussions of different types of political organization, monarchy, oligarchy, tyranny, democracy, etc.) and the *social practices* considered essential for nourishing particular political systems (Schmitt-Pantel, 234). Here is where communal meals came in. They offered one outstanding example of such practices.

Aristotle understood that formulating a constitution as an abstract framework for politics was necessary but not a sufficient condition for a flourishing community. A vibrant civic life required observances, practices, rituals, which not only reminded participants of their shared commitments but also wove threads of mutual linkage between them. Our own time has seen a renewed interest in how shared ritualized practices, say bowling leagues, provide the kinds of cohesive mini-communities within which civic virtues are nurtured and practiced.[3] The specific Aristotelian suggestion, mandatory public meals, seems, however, quite unworkable. Ours, after all, is the era of fast food and the drive-through. We make do, not with public, but private celebrations, like the sports banquet. For us, food and politics exist in different compartments.

If ancient Greek were our language, the conjunction of food and politics would not sound so strange. Recovering the meaning of their correlation requires us to take an indirect tack. John Dewey, speaking American English, repeatedly emphasized how, beyond formal political structures, a flourishing democracy required a set of virtues associated with its ideals. Only when those ideals were translated into virtues, habitual dispositions for citizens to act in certain ways, would the ideals become living realities. Democracy, Dewey was fond of saying, is a way of life embodied in the daily practices of citizens. It is "primarily a mode of associated living," not merely a system of political organization (Dewey 1916a, 93). That, at least, is how he addressed his point to an early-twentieth-century American audience.

Had he been a contemporary of Aristotle, he could have said "democracy is a *diet*." *Diaita*, the original Greek term, means "way of life," or "manner of living." Its associated verb, *diaitan*, indicates the act of arbitrating, or governing one's life. The latter sense continues to be echoed in the use of "Diet" to identify legislative bodies, as in Denmark and Japan, or obscure historical references as with the pun-inviting "Diet of Worms." More surprising is the way in which our ordinary, culinary, sense of the term was also significant for classical thinkers. Pauline Schmitt-Pantel's study of Greek banqueting practices makes this quite clear. Plato and Aristotle, she writes, take us back to a time when "describing the meals of a city was an integral part of coming to understand the *politeia* [sociopolitical structure] of that city" (Schmitt-Pantel, 242). For Plato and Aristotle, a city's character emerged not simply from its constitution, but also from its ritualized observances. Indeed the two had to be interwoven. Observances without constitutions are aimless. Constitutions without observances are empty.

CIVIC FRIENDSHIP REQUIRES LIGATING PRACTICES

The need for institutionalizing ritualized practices becomes important if we accept, as Aristotle did, how community depends on more than shared geographical boundaries and a common set of laws. There must also be *philia*, a kind of "friendship" that affiliates the state's members. For readers who prefer German words to Greek ones (philosophers, never meeting an unusual word they do not like, draw heavily on both), a ready substitute is available. The key distinction is usually phrased as that between *Gemeinschaft*, a "community" in which there is a high degree of shared customs, beliefs, and practices, and a *Gesellschaft*, a "society" whose members are held together by external, instrumental, and impersonal aims.

Aristotle, a *Gemeinschaft* type, considered the best indications of communal ties to be those associated with the hearth. This was the province of the goddess whose very name means hearth, "Hestia." Hestia's earthly abode was the *Prytaneum*, a sort of multipurpose room/dining hall, in which a perpetual fire was carefully tended. The Roman version was the goddess Vesta. Her hearth fire was tended by six virgins. So important was the flame, that not only were these young women forbidden from consorting with men, but they faced the threat of being buried alive should the flame go out. Such a central flame served as what can be called either a "bonding object" or a "rallier," a medium of shared activity whose lines of centripetal force draw together those touched by it. Hestia's presence both in individual homes and at the city's center was significant in this way. The political community was not to be considered a mere *Gesellschaft*, just an agglomeration of distinct individuals. The state was a *Gemeinschaft*, a "community of families." As such it was only natural that it would have its own central "hearth with an ever-burning fire as the symbolic center of its life" (Lenardon, 630). Ligating objects or activities are found wherever a touchstone or action takes on the linking activity once associated with Hestia.

We have long since given up on a central hearth. We have even forgotten how the emphasis on fostering family-like affiliations lingered on in politics well after Aristotle. Historically, friendship (religious and political versions, admittedly sexist: "brotherhood," "fraternity") maintained a level of prominence at least through the nineteenth century. The most famous international exhortation came with the French Revolution's slogan, which, in 1789, complemented the ideals of "liberty" and "equality" with that of "fraternity." Well before that revolution, however, colonists headed for Massachusetts heard what would become a famous sermon from their first governor, John Winthrop. He reminded his compatriots how the great divergence of human character, far from being a flaw, was divinely ordained so that "every man might have need of others, and from hence they might be all knit more nearly together in the Bonds of brotherly affection" (Winthrop, 79–80). In the late seventeenth century, the most prominent American city celebrated *philia* by calling itself "brotherly love," Philadelphia. The concern with brotherhood was even prevalent enough to find its way into documents dealing with commerce. The Champlain Canal, site of great commercial activity, would seem an unlikely place for such a concern. Yet an 1812 report explained how canal commerce would "strengthen the bands of union and preserve brotherly affection in the great American family."[4]

Such exhortations have gone the way of the central hearth. Large contemporary states make no special effort to erect some version of communal dining areas. Even when individual homes have one, a household's hearth, for which the Latin term is *focus*, no longer really serves as the home's "focus." The food-centered hearth has been replaced by the spectator-centered television. Here is the new "focus" around which people gather. It may not glow 24/7, but it comes fairly close to replacing the eternal flame guarded by the Vestals. As a result, bonding objects in our world tend no longer to be associated with central activity relating to food. They tend instead to be spectatorial. The Super Bowl is probably the most significant. Televised presidential inaugurations and New Year's Eve programs offer other, lesser, examples.[5] These onlooker activities do foster some sense of bonding among those who make up the nationwide audience. Because they are spectatorial and to a great degree impersonal, what they foster is better called solidarity, common interest in a particular undertaking, than fraternity, the co-citizen friendship promoted by Aristotle.

EATING PAUSE: GRANDCHILDREN "THUMBS UP" BROWNIES

Families offer the first model of friendship. On a visit to our grandchildren, Charlotte, entering grade 2, mentioned a love of brownies. This was as good a prompt as any for Grandpa to make some. When brother Léo, age 3, tasted the finished product, he gave a spontaneous thumbs up. What pleased them is a simple, typical brownie recipe suitable for making with children. As chocolate purists, we prefer a nut-free version. **Ingredients**: *1 stick of butter, melted; 3/4 cup cocoa powder; 1 1/4 cups sugar; 1/3 cup flour; 2 eggs (the larger the better); 1 tsp vanilla (optional); and 1/4 tsp of salt.* **Directions**: *(a) Blend sugar, cocoa, and salt in bowl; (b) mix in melted butter; (c) stir in vanilla (if using); (d) add 1 egg and blend; (e) add other egg; (f) stir in flour until well mixed.* **Cooking**: *Have oven preheated to 325 degrees; line standard pan (8x8x2) with foil, leaving some overlap; grease the foil with either butter or spray oil; add batter. Bake for 20 to 30 minutes. Top should be crusty and inner layer soft and moist. Inserted toothpick should come out with a few bits of chocolate on it. Use foil to remove brownies from pan. Cool, then cut into pieces (size of pieces is up to the family).*

FROM FRATERNITY TO *COMMUNITAS*

In today's large, heterogeneous states, it is not surprising that fraternity receives much less emphasis than the two other prongs of the French Revolutionary slogan. Besides the kinds of objections raised by Stephen and Freud, its gender specificity and historical affiliations render it suspect. Its inherently sexist name and original male-only application, for example, limit its contemporary attractiveness.[6] In American discussions, fraternity tends to be eclipsed by Jefferson's "pursuit of happiness," a pursuit that can easily be carried on by remaining within already established socially exclusive webs of affiliation, or even completely outside webs of affiliation.

The first issue that has to be dealt with, then, is the word itself. The term "fraternity" is ill-suited to democratic societies. It brings with it inexpugnable associations: (a) the automatic exclusion of all females, and (b) class and race oppression. To sidestep the unavoidable historical connotations, I will borrow a word coined by the anthropologist Victor Turner. He reached back to Latin and spoke of *communitas*. Here, admittedly, is a clumsy term, especially compared to the common "fraternity." It brings, however, two advantages: (1) It is not hampered by antecedent, antidemocratic associations. (2) No really suitable English synonym is available.[7] What the term suggested to Turner was "an essential and generic human bond without which there can be no society" (Turner, 97). The key term for large, multiethnic republics is "generic." The political bond in question can no longer be based on ethnic, class, gendered, or genealogical qualifications.

Here is where the American high school sports banquet, especially if male and female sports teams are celebrated together, is superior to the banquets of the ancient Greeks. In the older setting, "fraternity" meant camaraderie among men of a certain social class, and only among them. When fraternity is metamorphosed into *communitas*, the sports banquet takes on a place of special prominence. It now comes to serve as an exemplar for preserving what was best in the Greek model, while moving beyond its antidemocratic elements. Such a banquet serves as a rallier or a ligating milieu. It embodies important centralizing activities or points of contact that occasion the bonding together of individuals who would otherwise remain disembedded.

COMMUNAL MEAL:
BOTHERSOME DISTRACTION OR INDISPENSABLE MEDIUM?

For Aristotle, friendship, happiness, community, politics, and the common good all found a happy intersection at the table. Even in the ancient world, however, such a celebration of food-centered activities was not universally championed. The great moralist Plutarch (46–127), whose writings provided ethical edification from the Renaissance through the nineteenth century, placed an anti-food diatribe in the mouth of no less a source than the great legal reformer Solon. Plutarch's Solon has dismissive ideas about eating. The text in which the discussion occurs is another symposium from the classical era. This one is usually translated as the *Dinner of the Seven Wise Men*. Solon's utterances make one thing crystal clear: he considered the stomach a source of nothing but trouble. The digestive tract, incessant task master that it is, distracts and draws us away from our more important callings. "The English," Voltaire once dismissively exclaimed, "have one hundred religions but only one sauce" (Deval, 81). If we are to believe Plutarch, that single sauce would still have been too many for Solon. It would be a great good, Plutarch has the latter assert, to need very little food. An even greater good, actually "the greatest good," he says, "is to require no food at all" (Plutarch, Sec. 15, 415).

The very banquet of the seven wise men provided him with a telling example. Echoing a theme prominent in Plato, Solon asserts that eating is nothing but a distraction from higher callings. Only after completing the meal could the participants undertake intelligent discourse. Solon would never, as did Lucian's Epicurean and Stoic, stoop so low as to get into a fight over who had the plumpest chicken. The digestive organs lead us astray because they "afford us no perception or craving for anything noble" (Plutarch, Sec. 16, 159, 421). Our lives would be so much better, Solon suggests, if the demands of the stomach could be permanently quelled (Plutarch, Sec. 16, 423). Solon even had a friend, Epimenides, who came up with an early version of Professor Wogglebug's meal-in-a-pill. The product fashioned by Epimenides when ingested, would allow individuals to "go all day without lunch or dinner" (Plutarch, Sec. 14, 411).

Another guest at the *Dinner of the Seven Wise Men* took exception to Solon's denigration of our eating practices. Cleodorus, a physician, spoke out in their defense. His argument went right to the heart of the matter. Step one: say "yes" to the human condition in its fullness. Immediate result: embodiedness need not mark us as flawed. The twentieth-century British philosopher Peter Strawson once attempted a rigorous description of life in a disembodied state. When no cheating is allowed, that is, no allowing properties and abilities only possible in an embodied state, the results are rather grim. Homer, literary license in full use, had cheated when he sent Odysseus to the underworld. Everyone spoke and acted just the way they would in the world of the living, except they were now just shades or souls. Philosophical accuracy, as Strawson indicated, takes us in a different direction. As disembodied individuals there would be no perception of anything around us, no sounds, no smells, no sunsets to marvel over, no hugs for children, no movement. All in all, a sorry, self-enclosed existence with some cognitive activity but only thinking about the act of thinking itself.[8] Thinking along similar lines, Cleodorus worries about denigrating the experience of table. Take away episodes of shared eating, he says, and a self-enclosed existence is what you are moving toward.

Meals offer especially fruitful affiliation-creating opportunities. They provide occasions for multiple connections, associations that go well beyond the range of any exclusive social circle. Depending on how we approach meals, they can help us overcome many a self-centered forgetfulness. They stand as reminders of how we are linked to and dependent on the fertile earth, on those who work the land, those who transport, market, and sell the food. They also link us to those with whom we are in a face-to-face relation at table. In ritualistic meals, the vectors extend to others who, in various locations, are engaging in the same observances, as well as to ancestors whose practices we are continuing. For Cleodorus, a world freed, Solon-style, from the demands of the stomach, would also, of necessity, be a world marked by "dissolution." First "dissolution of the household," subsequently the disengagement from all other linkages: to friends, to gods, to the earth (Plutarch, Sec. 15, 417).

COMMUNITAS: CULTIVATED, NOT FOUND

Here is where the double suggestion made by Aristotle (co-citizen friendship and communal meals) returns to prominence. He recognized how social concerns, like Cleodorus's worry about dissolution, had to be addressed in terms of societal rituals. For him, this meant that a society seeking something like friendship, not just neutral co-citizenship, would have difficulty encouraging such *communitas* outside of tangible rituals. His suggestion of meals in the *Prytaneum* was rooted in a most basic biological necessity. Admittedly such a proposal is not attractive today. Our world is one in which a Solon-like utilitarian attitude toward food has become overwhelmingly prominent. Warren Belasco reports that when ordinary people are asked to project what human food intake will be like in a hundred years, many reply "Oh, probably pills" (Belasco, 253). Trying, in such a context, to extract something of value from Aristotle, we are faced with the issue of whether anything can be rescued from communal dinners.

One way to address this issue is to make an admission that is more realistic than pessimistic: *communitas* cannot be understood as some preexistent fact that we have simply failed to recognize. Here is where a touch of Deweyan Pragmatism is helpful. "Ideals" are identified as such precisely because they *do not* preexist. They serve as what Dewey calls "ends-in-view," prescriptions that allow "reconstruction" of existing conditions. Adopting ends-in-view to guide transformations requires the same kind of imaginative inventiveness that artists, as we saw in chapter 5, bring to their work.[9] Political artists delve into the realm of possibility and seek to realize new combinations in the social realm. With regard to *communitas*, this means making an effort toward new realities, allowing them to emerge within concrete interactions.

Since *communitas* does not preexist, its status can only be that of a desideratum, something to be striven for. That only raises the further question, the one asked at the beginning of this chapter, whether it should be adopted as a goal at all. When we examine contemporary conditions, I think it is possible to answer in the affirmative. Multiculturalism, a reality for large, industrial democracies, offers some important opportunities and challenges. As we have seen in earlier chapters, the blur of possibilities from which all peoples and cultures arise can never be fully instantiated in any single manifestation. The "infinite," to paraphrase Levinas, is always beyond any particular instance arising out of it. Each individual and each grouping of individuals can thus benefit from the infusion of talents and perspectives that others bring with them. Within such a context, bland homogenization cannot be considered as a kind of ultimate good. Such a homogenization, necessarily finite and single, would encourage self-idolatry. Such self-idolatry, in turn, merges easily with allophobia, fear and rejection of what is different.

A humble recognition, by contrast, of how the infinite is manifested in many ways among many peoples, encourages a dynamic pluralism of identities. The aim would be to multiply contacts that allow for fruitful interactions, transformations, mixings, and blendings. We are faced here with another kind of tension, and another lesson in the importance of moderation. Absolute ethnic purity and absolute mingling and blending would provide bland homogenization. Vibrant societies maintain a combination of communities-in-interaction, which is to say, communities-in-formation. Bo Diddley, the early Rock musician, exemplifies this emphasis. In doing so, he utilizes a food metaphor and points to a city whose culinary, musical, and racial mixtures exemplify what can emerge from fruitful cross-fertilization.

> I'm classed as a Negro but I'm not: I'm what you call a black Frenchman, a Creole. All my people are from New Orleans, the bayou country. French, African, Indian, all mixed up. I like gumbo, dig? Hot sauces, too. That's where my music comes from, all the mixtures. (Rammel, 128)

Unfortunately, what goes by the label "multiculturalism," need not be considered in terms of interaction, transformation, cross-fertilization, and hybridization. It can be interpreted as fostering cultural isolation (by emphasizing inflexible, unchanging components making up the "multi").

Moving beyond the "isolated communities" view of multiculturalism, though, brings with it an important challenge: the loss of social cohesiveness. Robert Putnam's studies have shown that, in the formal language of social science, "diversity and solidarity are negatively correlated" (Putnam 2007, 142). Elaborated in a straightforward way, Putnam points out that where there is great social diversity, there is

> lower confidence in local leaders . . . lower political efficacy, lower frequency of registering to vote . . . less expectation that others will cooperate to solve dilemmas of collective action . . . lower likelihood of giving to charity or volunteering . . . fewer close friends and confidants . . . more time spent watching television and more agreement that 'television is my most important form of entertainment. (Putnam 2007, 150)

Admitting the difficulties of making a multicultural society work is actually the prerequisite for arguing that fraternity be made central to the inspirational ideals of democratic republics. As *communitas*, it can serve an important counterbalancing role. The democratic ideal of "tolerance," important and successful as it is, suffers from an important drawback. It does not adequately encourage active engagement with others, a fact amply attested to by Putnam's research. What Dewey labeled a "fraternally associated public" (Dewey 1927, 303) fails to be promoted via mere toleration. The point of resurrecting fraternity as *communitas* is to complement tolerance with a more activist ideal.

COMMUNITAS AS FRATERNIZATION

When Dewey discussed fraternity, he characterized it as "association and interaction without limit" (Dewey 1919, 53). In an earlier work, he had made clear the criteria that were to serve as "a measure for the worth of any given mode of social life." These took the form of two questions: "How numerous and varied are the interests which are consciously shared? How full and free is the interplay with other forms of association?" (Dewey 1916a, 88, 89). With these questions we have a mode of judging whether a republic is satisfied with tolerance or moves to embrace *communitas*. Specifically republican virtues, habitual dispositions to act in certain ways, need not be limited to the procedural ones of mutual deliberation, respect for law, and tolerance. They can also include the activist dimension of *communitas*: fraternization (Dewey's "association and interaction without limit"). A vibrant democratic republic will commend and encourage active intermingling between members of the various subcommunities that make up the wider state. Such interactions, will, typically, add to the various groups that make up the nation via transformations and creolizations The aim of *communitas* as fraternization can be well expressed in the terms given us by Putnam. It seeks to promote interactions that will help reverse the negative correlation between diversity and solidarity.

For our initial question, we can now propose an answer, one that even involves meals. Fraternity, metaphormosed into *communitas* as fraternization, does take on a special importance in multicultural democratic republics. Thinking in terms that blend Aristotle and Dewey, we also have some criteria for determining whether *communitas* is a living presence or not. If democratic republics seek a measure for determining the degree to which fraternization has become a *diet* or "way of life," they can ask certain questions. Are interactions between the many groupings that make up the wider nation-state narrow and one-dimensional, or are they diverse and ample? How free, flexible, and common are the movements among, between, and within the subcommunities? How prevalent are blendings and mixings of individuals from diverse subgroupings? These sorts of diagnostic questions take us back to high school sports banquets. The size of today's nation-states, large beyond what an Aristotle could even envision, make his project of enforced communal meals unfeasible. There is a way, though, to reintroduce meals into discussions of political philosophy. True, they can no longer be mandated. That approach has gone the way of forced church attendance. But their presence or absence can be diagnostic. They can provide a sense of how the Dewey-inspired questions are being answered in practice.

Here then, is a ready test for determining if *communitas* retains an aspirational status matching that of liberty and equality. We can say that societies in a substantive, not just a procedural sense, live out the democratic ideal when their tables reflect the mixed ones of the sports banquet. To what degree is fraternization, the transformational model of blending and mixing, an important living presence? For an answer, look at who is seated around the table. A democratic republic that defines hopes and practices in line with its ideals will be one in which there is free and easy commerce between all of its citizens. It will be one that encourages those citizens to make an extra effort of inviting to their tables individuals not typically present. In that way we can preserve the Aristotelian connection between shared meals and co-citizen friendship. We can then combine diet, as foods ingested, with *diaita*, a way of life embodying republican virtues.

NOTES

1. "It is always possible to bind together a considerable number of people in love, so long as there are other people left over to receive the manifestations of their aggressiveness" (Freud, 61).

2. For example: "As to common meals, there is a general agreement that a well-ordered city should have them" *Politics* VII, 10, 1330a 4–6; "For friendship we believe to be the greatest good of states and the preservative of them against revolutions" *Politics*, II, 3, 1262b 8–9.

3. See Elshtain and Putnam (2000).

4. The report is cited on a historical marker by the canal in Waterford, New York.

5. For an insightful and easy to read examination of how television has become a center for contemporary rituals, see Goethals.

6. The French Republic, although inspired by the tripartite slogan, nonetheless was constructed, as Joan Landes puts it, "against women" (Landes, 171). Carole Pateman's study of social contract theories from a feminist perspective emphasizes what is too often overlooked "Almost no one—except many feminists—is willing to admit that fraternity means what it says: the brotherhood of *men*" (Pateman, 78). A helpful discussion with my colleague, the political theorist Laurie Naranch, led me to these sources.

7. "Solidarity" indicates shared dedication to a project, rather than general friendship. "Sodality," although more in line with general friendship, is too outdated for even someone as retrieval-friendly as myself. *Comitatus*, the social cohesiveness celebrated in *Beowulf* is overly associated with societies in which loyalty to the chief is paramount. The medieval Islamic philosopher of history Ibn-Khaldun coined the term *asabiyya* to indicate the communal comradeship that helps hold societies together. Like *comitatus*, *asabiyya* is rooted primarily in tribal loyalties, although Ibn-Khaldun sought to make of it a sense of general comradeship. See Mahdi, 196–197.

8. Macquarrie, 51, describes this position. Strawson had imagined what life would be like for a soul having survived death and existing separately from its body. "There would be no perception of a body related to one's experience, one could not be perceived by other people, and there would be no way of initiating changes in the physical world. Two consequences seem to follow. Such an existence would be utterly solitary, and the individual so existing would have to think of himself as a *former* person and would have to live on the memories of his past, for there would be no new perceptions or social contacts."

9. For a good analysis of how important is imagination in Deweyan ethical thought, see Fesmire.

Chapter Eight

Religion, Recipes, Negligence

"Come in, come in (to the kitchen), the gods are here too."[1]

—Heraclitus

I BRING A CASSEROLE, THEREFORE I AM RELIGIOUS

Imagine a grade school project for a multireligious society. The children have been asked to bring in an item symbolizing their religion. The first child says, "I am Jewish, and this is a Star of David." The second, "I am Catholic, and this is a crucifix." The third says, "I am Protestant, and this is a casserole" (Sack, 7). This anecdote, originally from the Internet, is repeated in Daniel Sack's study *Whitebread Protestants: Food and Religion in American Culture*. The book explores the importance of potluck dinners, picnics, and other church-centered meals in providing a sense of "popular piety." This, the author declares, is especially important to a reform tradition that had consciously moved away from older practices of popular religion, focusing instead on the Word (Sack, 96). In the absence of public rituals, it is food, Sack says, that "provides Protestantism with a popular religion" (Sack, 96).

Linking casseroles and Protestantism not only makes sense in terms of social practices, it also hearkens back to the original religious ceremony within Christianity, the fellowship meal, known by the Greek term for altruistic love, *agape*. Dennis Smith wrote a detailed book seeking to answer the question "Why did early Christians meet at a meal?" His answer was simple and straightforward: because they were continuing "a pattern found throughout their world," a pattern rooted in the Greek *symposium* (Smith 2003, 285–286). What the *agape* meal made central was how it served as a bonding activity, what I have called, somewhat clumsily, a ligating activity. The sharing of food created, among the participants, a bonding event that made them into a fictive family, in which they could call one another brothers and sisters and think of themselves as part of the family of God. In this sense, the meal became the means for community formation, or, to put it differently, the theology of community came to be intertwined with and brought to experience by the ritual (Smith 2003, 283).

Smith's qualifier, "fictive," although important, can be misleading. A better label, following a suggestion of Michel Serres, would be "adoptive." Christianity is, Serres suggests, a religion of adoption (Serres 2001, 176). The virgin birth story breaks, on the paternal side, with blood lineage, while lack of offspring by the religion's founder eliminates consanguinity on the descendant side. As emerging "adoptive" families, the participants needed a ceremony in which their newly forming affiliations could be celebrated and strengthened. What better than sharing meals "in a great banqueting hall"? There, at tables "overflowing with food and wine," bonds of relationship could be fostered (Smith 2003, 284). The older symposium, as we saw, tended to be restrictive. There were strictures about who could sit around the table. Within the adoption model, the "controversy over the boundaries of the table," that is, what are the antecedent marks by which invitees are chosen, now had a novel answer. There is no antecedent mark. The new host in the Gospels "has opened the doors to everyone" (Smith 2003, 285). A ministry now highlighting the "poor, the captives, the blind, the oppressed" finds no better means of conveying this emphasis than the "imagery of the meal" (Smith 2003, 269). Here is a setting in which disparate individuals can come together and work at constructing a new community.

RELIGION IS NOT FAITH

The connection between religion and food goes beyond the *agape* meal and its successors: potluck dinners, church picnics, and formalized communion. It indicates something more general about the nature of religion. The intersection reveals the importance within religious communities of something other than the typical focus on creeds. Rituals and observances, "practices" in the terminology of this book, play every bit as much a central role in the religious way of life as do the shared core commitments. Commitments *and* observances provide the ingredients for bringing forth a religious community. Thoughtful reflection ("theology" is its formal name) adds a third prong. This last is important if religious life is not to transform itself into one of two ever-present usurpers: magic and superstition.

The tripartite blend (commitment, observances, thoughtful reflection) is not always recognized in popular consciousness. Religion's importance, evidenced by its pervasiveness and tenacity, often comes mixed together with confused intellectual articulations. These tend to simplify religion, providing neat shortcuts that translate it into what is essentially a set of cognitive claims. These claims are special, however. They reject typical scientific and logical justification. Rather, they are based on "faith." The situation is like what William James said about the schoolboy's definition: "Faith is when you believe something that you know ain't true" (James 1897, 29). So prominent is this way of dealing with religion that popular language tends to use the terms "religion" and "faith" interchangeably. Sam Harris's book attacking religion, for example, is entitled *The End of Faith*. In the same vein, popular language also tends to use the label "believer" as synonymous with "religious individual." Such ways of speaking limit discussions of religion by directing them into a particular channel. They highlight one aspect: belief. Here is a one-sided cognitive emphasis that makes good sense within the mind-only approach to philosophy. When the stomach and its associated activities are added to the mix, alternative suggestions move toward the center. The most important of these would be to avoid the epistemologically influenced synonyms, "faith" and "believer." Instead of highlighting repetitive practices like communal meals, a better choice would be to speak of committed religious individuals as making up "communities of the observant." Such a phrase draws attention, more holistically, to the communal, ritualized activities that help foster and strengthen the basic commitments. It also shifts the context for understanding what "faith" means.

"Faith," removed from the mind-only orbit, comes to be understood as something like "being faithful," an act associated with the entire person. Faithfulness would emphasize not a checklist of cognitive claims, but an engagement with and subsequent fidelity to a central figure or tradition or set of texts. Unfortunately, some religious individuals revel in the "believe what is not believable" attitude. They halt discussion with some version of the claim attributed to the Christian church father Tertullian, "I believe because it is absurd" (*credo quia absurdum est*).

Not surprisingly the identification of religion with (a) faith, and (b) of faith as embracing belief in the unbelievable, has occasioned criticism. The twenty-first century opened with especially harsh broadsides; broadsides that got traction as violence, such as the attack on the World Trade Center, were justified in the name of religion.[2] In an earlier critique, composed late in the twentieth century, before 9/11 had focused attention on militancy and murder in the name of religion, John Searle had offered a more moderated, but equally devastating critique. His calm voice makes the criticism all the more powerful. While teaching in Venice, he heard the story of a church with the unusual name "Madonna of the Orchard." Initially, the church was to have honored St. Christopher, patron of travelers. The helpful saint was moved aside by a miraculous event. Wanderers found a statue of the Madonna in a nearby orchard. Such a find would lead today's parishioners to ask a simple question: Who put it there? To long-ago believers, the event gave evidence of supernatural intervention. The statue, they believed, could only have fallen out of heaven. This "miracle" was an occurrence best commemorated by renaming the church.

Searle relates this story as an indication of how removed we are from our ancestors. Today, skepticism would be exhibited generally, even by church officials. The statue-falling-out-of-the-sky story "is not a possible thought for us because, in a sense, we know too much" (Searle, 34). Knowing so much leads us to take for granted a natural, non-miraculous view of things. We no longer need fall back on faith or religious mysteries to explain what seems inexplicable. The puzzling has been transformed into the someday-it-will-be-explained. "Odd occurrences," according to Searle, "are just occurrences that we do not understand" (Searle, 35). So far have we come, that thinking people no longer "even raise the question of God's existence" (Searle, 34). Religion is little more than a cultural remnant from a less enlightened time.

RELIGION: COMMITMENTS REINFORCED BY PRACTICES

A dismissal like this is based on (1) a reaction to real nonsense pronounced by "people of faith," and (2) an epistemological focus that is typical of philosophers who emphasize mind while neglecting the stomach. From the "stomach-is-also-part-of-the-human-condition" perspective, I would like to revisit the notion of religion as relegated to the status of a museum piece. It is possible, I will argue, to reconceptualize the issues of religion and nonreligion in ways that make them both respectable topics of discussion.[3] The manner of reaching this destination may offer some surprises. Clues for reconceptualization will come from the area central to this book, reflection on food. A neologism created by switching one vowel will provide the terminological key. This neologism, "symbal," in turn, will be linked to the construction of the "ligature line," a new criterion for sorting out the secular from the religious.

Readers who have worked through the previous chapters will not be surprised to read that a loosely Pragmatist orientation rooted in our dealings with things is well suited as a source for guidance in this alternative approach. Not only is it food-friendly, but it is so because it is built around a web of principles that discourage totalizing pronouncements. This cluster of traits, *rootedness in the life-world*, *centrality of practices*, *experience as revelatory*, and *the irreducibility of pluralism*, identifies important general background assumptions. Of these, the centrality of practices takes on the most significance. What does it mean to claim that the life-world is conditioned by *praxis*? It means that, unlike academic philosophers who tend to overgeneralize from their self-appointed roles as specialized thinkers, most humans most of the time (and even professional philosophers much of the time) are engaged participants in varied patterned processes. These processes have emerged as significant and meaningful ways of dealing with our surroundings. A farmer milking a cow or tapping a maple tree, a father and grandfather building a swing set in the backyard, a mother balancing a checkbook, city planners holding public meetings, rural residents digging a well, neighbors gathered for a Fourth of July cookout, these are prototypical examples of the practices that need to be remembered in an adequate philosophical grasp of things. Many problems occupying professional philosophers, as we saw in chapter 1, take on an entirely new complexion when we keep in mind, as representative human actions, those marked by our *dealings* with things.

If religion, at its center, is a cognitive enterprise dependent primarily on the prominence of miraculous intrusions, then Searle and the other critics make a good case. There is not much room for it in our demystified world. Religion, in this context, depends on the existence of a divinity who resembles a powerful, yet bribable human being. In other words, an idol, not a god. This micromanager not only intervenes but does so in ways that, by definition, are beyond human powers of comprehension. Credulous religious followers make this characterization easy. Many "believers" actually want magic rather than religion. They are not satisfied with the other-directed exhortation of Mother Theresa:

> The fruit of silence is prayer.
> The fruit of prayer is faith.
> The fruit of faith is love.
> The fruit of love is service.
> The fruit of service is peace.

Instead of her focus on personal transformation, they are really interested in calling on special (bribe-friendly) powers in the service of their own ends. As a result, they often confuse praying with asking for special self-centered intervention ("Let my will be done" instead of "Let Thy will be done"). In the end, though, divinity as bribable-superbeing must always retreat in the face of experimentation and refined techniques of explanation.

Taking account of humans as stomach-endowed participants in practices, we can rethink such formulations. Here is where substituting "communities of observance" for "communities of faith" pays dividends. What was once figure becomes ground and vice versa. On the widest perspective, taking into account religions of all sorts, what emerges as integral is *praxis*. There are sets of practices reinforcing what a community accepts as an inspirational focus for developing a form of life. In some cases, so interwoven are observances, histories, and commitments that certain traditional languages have no separate word identifying the detachable entity called "religion" (Mbiti, 2).[4]

Matthieu Ricard is a Buddhist monk. He holds a Ph.D. in molecular biology and is the son of Jean-François Revel, the French philosopher noted for his book *Neither Marx nor Jesus*. Revel's work has contributed eloquently to a post-Enlightenment tradition that cast suspicion on both religion and totalitarian politics. His son, unhappy with what he perceived to be the emptiness of a secular attitude, decided, as a mature man, to leave the laboratory for life as a Buddhist monk. An engaging dialogue between father and son has been translated as *The Monk and the Philosopher: A Father and Son Discuss the Meaning of Life.*

What Ricard says early in the book reinforces the importance of observances. "There are a lot of very interesting things in Buddhism, but it's important not to lose yourself in purely theoretical book study. It might distract you from practice, which is the very heart of Buddhism and all inner transformation" (Revel, 9). Here, once again, is the observance/faith figure-ground reversal. Instead of first insisting on creedal assertions and then discussing practices, there is an initial emphasis on practices as leading to enlightenment. In Ricard's case, there can be no appeal to an interventionist divinity, since within the Tibetan Buddhism he practices, there is not only no such divinity but no divinity at all (Revel, 89).

RECIPES AND CEREMONIES OF SITUATED-NESS

We are now in a position to take up eating as a way of helping us rethink the issue of religion in general, and, in particular, to formulate new identifying marks for sorting out religion from nonreligion. An ordinary, food-centered, practice celebrated yearly will serve as point of departure. What is unique in this particular example is how the practice occurs in a situation where individuals are denied the opportunity for ordinary observances. We are in what Karl Jaspers called *Grenzsituationen*, those ultimate or boundary situations that force serious reflection about the human condition. The scene is as follows: a child holds in her hand a lump of mashed potatoes to which some sugar has been added. Circumstances, though, occasion the participants to violate the principle of noncontradiction. It is the early 1940s. The place is Terezin, a Czechoslovakian transit camp established by the Nazis. The date is that on which the child was born. The food in her hand is no longer a serving of potato. It has become a birthday cake (DaSilva, xxxvii). The inmates are observing what might be called a "ceremony of situatedness." Not only is a birthday being commemorated, but the child's place within social geography is reinforced. Ceremonies of situated-ness are inversely proportional to processes of dehumanization. Lacking physical weapons, the prisoners fought dehumanization by attempting to preserve practices associated with ordinary life.

One commentator, discussing inmate life at Terezin, uses the language of spirit. A simple event, in this case the observance of a birthday, becomes a "revolt of the spirit" (DaSilva, xxiv). "Spirit" and "spiritual" are words with a lengthy history. Originally, "spirit" translated the Greek *pneuma*, which means breath. Eventually, it came to be associated with the soul and with an aspect of life opposed to matter. But the original meaning of breath is still relevant when speaking of the "spiritual revolt" at Terezin (DaSilva, xv). The prisoners realized that the ultimate purpose of incarceration was to extinguish their communal breath. That wider "spirit" did not reside in any single individual, but in a people with overlapping inspirations and aspirations, clusters of criss-crossing personal histories celebrated in communal rituals. How did the inmates combat communal asphyxiation? Under impossible conditions, some camp women developed an imaginative way to keep the community breathing: they remembered recipes. Yes, recipes! Not only remembered them, but had heated discussions about the "right" way to prepare favorite foods such as Viennese dumplings and chocolate strudel. They also wrote down the recipes, hoping that the spirit embodied in the written word would survive the ordeal (DaSilva, xxxi).

The book that relates the story of these women is called *In Memory's Kitchen*. Neither philosophically rigorous nor sophisticated, it is built around recipes written in the camp. Prominent academic philosophers would almost certainly dismiss it as marginal to their professional interests. This would be a mistake. Precisely because these women situate us in a different life-world from that of a professor's study, they help open new paths for reflection. Caught in an extreme and deadly environment, their response can guide our reconfiguration of the conceptual network commonly associated with discussions of religion.

"SYMBALS" VERSUS NEGLIGENCE

Two images from Terezin will guide my reflections: the little girl's handful of potatoes, and the women copying down recipes on hard to find paper. Conceptually, the terms "symbol" will play a key role. One neologism, the transformation of "symbol" into symbal," will minimize ambiguity. It will help provide novel, yet definitive criteria for characterizing what it means to be religious. It will also indicate how food practices provide a key to the new understanding.

For articulating such an alternative, we must return to *In Memory's Kitchen*. "Food" says the introduction, "is who we are in the deepest sense.... Our personal gastronomic traditions, what we eat, the foods and foodways we associate with the rituals of childhood, marriage, and parenthood, moments around the table, celebrations—are critical components of our identities" (DaSilva, xxvi). Such a claim, although accurate, is narrow. It is restricted to the human plane. Food practices can actually help us understand how our identities have taken root in a context that extends beyond the human sphere. If we take our stomach-gifted situation seriously, it attests not only to alliances and connections in the human realm but also to the natural realm. The entire web within which we find ourselves is marked by ligatures, threads of conjunction, between ourselves and the life-world at large.[5]

Let's go back to the birthday celebration. The handful of mashed potatoes is a nexus for intertwining linkages. In the strictly etymological sense of the word, it is a "symbol" (*sumballein*, the Greek original, indicates the movement of throwing things together). Because the word "symbol" has multiple uses, a minor vowel emendation creating the neologism "symbal" will indicate the single, etymologically inspired sense of "that which links together." "Symbal" and "symbalic" will identify occasions in which multiple strands are not only present but brought to consciousness and celebrated. The Native American smoking tobacco and exhaling first in each of the four cardinal directions, then above, below, and finally on the body of the smoker, is engaged in a "symbalic" action. The ritual acknowledges the joining of "self to the cosmos" (Tedlock, xii). Eating a handful of potatoes to celebrate a child's birthday is an activity that can be described as "symbalic" It conjoins various dimensions: the physiological, moral, cultural, personal, social, and agricultural. These are all connections the child's captors hoped to sever. The captors' work, quite literally, was "diabolical," the effort to divide or throw things apart. What they sought was a progressive de-ligaturing aimed ultimately at breaking the link with life itself.

The prisoners' response of celebrating birthdays and copying down recipes involved the contrary move of re-ligaturing, or, in our technical term, symbalizing. The child is not an isolated individual. Likewise, women remembering recipes think of themselves as allied to a wider whole. Both the child and the women belong to a community, the community is linked to others in the outside world, to ancestors, and to those not yet born. The links embodied in recipes, if recognized, go further still. They blur the culture/nature boundary. Recipes and birthday cakes not only weave together memory, tradition, and community but also the soil, sun, rainfall, as well as those who plant, cultivate, and harvest. A birthday observance, especially under conditions of impossible hardship, signals something of importance beyond an individual's move into another year. Its role as a rallier now makes more manifest what is usually only tacit. It "symbalizes," that is to say, summons up the interlinkages via the observance.

When a powerful enemy seeks to sever linkages, there is a natural and worthy antidote: reemphasizing ordinary life practices. Those of us not faced with such terror may take the linkages for granted. Our time, says Michel Serres, is one characterized by negligence (Serres 1990, 81). "Negligence" here carries the specific sense of ignoring linkages. For Serres, negligence, more than anything, is the opposite of religion. ("Negligion," a convoluted invention, would offer the appropriate antonym to "religion.") Enlightenment-style philosophies centered on mind, along with post-Enlightenment practices associated with industrialization and urbanization, cooperate, not surprisingly, in accelerating degrees and levels of neglect. Together, they tend more and more to isolate us from the interconnections on which we depend. They, in other words, facilitate the retreat from religion.

Especially neglected is the activity needed for growing and cultivating food, an activity that best typifies religious sensibilities. "Agriculture," says Serres, "is a religious practice." Farmers cannot overlook the interconnections and multiple dependencies on which success at raising crops and livestock depends. "Every religious crisis is a crisis of agriculture; all religious residue is a way of resisting, at the same time, the metastases of the city and those of industry" (Serres 1974, 246). Life, even in a port city like New York, can be lived in total neglect of the tides, and can surely be lived in neglect of the optimal planting season. Dependence on meteorological and soil conditions, on farmers who grow food, laborers who harvest it, and truckers who deliver it, these can readily receive but scant attention.

The women of Terezin attempted to restore, via food practices, the dimensions their captors wished to force into permanent neglect. Through these practices, even if only imagined, they could celebrate who they were in their ordinary, pre-internment lives. Biological necessity, although inseparable from food, here took on a secondary importance. There were no supplies for apple strudel, chocolate cake, stews, and roasts. Writing out recipes was rather an occasion for acknowledging the connections that affiliated the residents of a household with a particular community, and ultimately with the world itself. Neglecting the practices meant losing one's identity. Recalling recipes and keeping the practices alive offered a mode for interlacing the various strands out of which identities were composed.

THE LIGATURE LINE

This concrete struggle to maintain ceremonies of situatedness provides clues for articulating a schema that will help reformulate the issue of religion. It will do so by situating the issue in a context different from the epistemological one, the one in which it is typically set by most commentators, friend and foe alike. In Searle's formulation, for example, the separation is clear-cut. On one side we find belief in miraculous occurrences requiring *super*natural explanations. On the other, good sense coupled with scientific research. Phrased in this way, the issue is already settled. The good-sense-coupled-with-science camp is the only defensible one. Set out schematically, the either-or would look like this:

128   *Chapter 8*

Non-religion ———————————————————————————— Religion

Figure 8.1.

Content for determining membership at one pole or the other can be registered on a sister line:

Reject supernatural explanation ——————————————— A God which explains
for the as-yet unknown   the inexplicable

Figure 8.2.

Framed in straightforward terms, this comes down to "either an atheistic attack on or a typical theistic defense of traditional religion" (Searle, 34). There are really only two camps, and inclusion/exclusion depends on the issue of God's existence.

A more suitable schematization, one taking into account the more muddled range of human experiences, can be drawn. It recognizes the importance of practices and incorporates the stomach-inspired emphasis on interdependencies. For lack of artistic creativity, I call it simply, the "ligature line." For purposes of classification it offers a spectrum rather than a simple dichotomy. Occupying a particular place on this continuum does not automatically identify one as more or less good, more or less immersed in the sensual, more or less ascetic. It has nothing to do with embracing or escaping the here and now. There is no necessary connection between one's place on the continuum and belief in or denial of occurrences or phenomena in daily life that can only be explained by recurring to a transcendent force. Having had a religious experience, despite its personal significance, is not essential to a place on the "religion" end of the spectrum.

Instead of such usual markers, and in opposition to a sharp either-or approach, the new schematization encourages thinking in terms of a continuum. The newer lines, one for categories, the other for content, would look like this:

Non-religion —— secular —— minimally secular —— minimally religious —— religious —— Religion

World as alien—— social solidarity——solidarity with natural forces —— path not of our making ——"three jewels"

Figure 8.3.

Now we have a continuum based on the various *kinds of ligatures* that are embraced.

Any trajectory toward the end "religion" is marked by acceptance of linkages beyond merely anthropocentric affiliations ("social solidarity"). The category "religious" is marked by adding cosmocentric connections to the anthropocentric ones. Our activities are taken to be working *in conjunction with* what is best in the very nature of things. Moving fully into the "religion" end of the ligature line requires acceptance of further linkages. Re-ligion (often said to be rooted in *ligare*, to bind), is embraced when the bundle of ligatures includes some version of what Buddhists identify as the "three jewels," the Buddha, the Dharma, and the Sangha. Generalized, these identify (1) an inspirational center, either a religious founder or a guiding narrative; (2) a cluster of teachings about the place humans occupy in the scheme of things; and (3) conscious commitment to membership in a community of shared practices.

The end-terms on the category line remain the same as in the Searle-inspired schematization. In between, though, comes a range of options. Increasing levels and kinds of ligatures mark the distinctions as one moves from nonreligion to religion. There are some important implications related to the suggested spectrum. It is possible to occupy the religion end of the spectrum whether one is a monotheist, polytheist, or even, as with Buddhism, a nontheist. What is needed are (1) a conscious embrace of a particular narrative or figure, (2) commitment to the significance of a cluster of life-guiding texts, and (3) membership in a community of observances.

The more controversial middle area is occupied by what, following John Dewey's example, I have identified as "religious." Situating people at this range involves distinguishing, as ordinary language now tends to do more and more, between "religious" and "religion." Membership here depends on embracing a cluster of ligatures that link us to other persons *and* to the natural world, while resisting the "three jewels" stretch of the continuum. We are now at the fuzzy border where secular and religious meet. This is the maddening (to commentators who like clean classifications) position articulated by Dewey in his *A Common Faith.* The religious (separable from "religion") attitude, he says, "needs the sense of a connection of man, in the way of both dependence and support, with the enveloping world that the imagination feels is a universe" (Dewey 1986, 36). Translated into the language of this essay, Dewey is suggesting minimal criteria for belonging to the range identified by "religious" but not "religion." Humans must not think of themselves as imposing structures and meaning onto the world. There has to be a humble recognition of "dependence and support." The "religious" individual thus works in conjunction with what is best in the social and natural spheres. The individual does so, however, outside of any creedal commitment to supernatural forces.

The middle part of the line shades into the secular end at a point where Deweyan style "dependence and support" on anything extra-human no longer is thought to have any validity. The position expressed by the French existentialist philosopher Albert Camus in his novel *The Plague* offers a good example of this threshold. The main character, Dr. Rieux, is devoted to the service of his fellow human beings. He works tirelessly to ease the suffering and save those who have been afflicted by the plague. He is also not in any sense religious. When asked about why he is so committed to serving his fellow human beings, he replied that he saw himself as "fighting against creation as he found it" (Camus 1948, 127). Here is the exemplary case of someone at the nonreligion end of the ligature line. Creation, with its diseases that inflict indiscriminate suffering, does not deserve any gratitude or celebration. Unlike individuals on the religious end of the spectrum, he denies and rejects linkages with the extra-human world and the possibilities of working with them.

Camus here depicts a kind of honest embrace of truth coupled with a determination to do good. Giving up on good would be to give in to unnecessary suffering. Accepting religious comfort would be to give up on truth. The modern ethic, as Alan Ryan well put it, is an ethic of authenticity. Such an ethic demands "that we face the grim truth about the world—particularly the grim truth that it cares nothing for us and our purposes" (Ryan, 360). Nature and cosmic forces are not considered to be either particularly good or supportive in the struggle for good. Indeed they often offer obstructions that must be overcome. We have here arrived at the paradigmatic de-ligatured state that characterizes the nonreligion end of the continuum. Allegiance beyond the human realm is out of the question. Good can be created, but, Camus-style, it involves rebellion and is wholly a human product.

Attitudes characterized as religious, on the other hand, accept not only some dependence on, but need for support from, forces that are neither made by nor for us. The point is emphasized by one of Dewey's students, John Herman Randall. Central to the religious vision, says Randall, is what allows us to live in a way that we recognize ourselves as "cooperating with what is most real in the universe. It is this ideal perspective born of religious vision, and this sense of partnership with the best the world contains, that gives to life that central and unifying meaning which men find in their religion" (Randall 1968, 74).

Given this context, that of "cooperating with what is most real in the universe," we can take a few small steps for altering the terms of the opposition as set forth by Searle. Earlier formulations, situated within an epistemology-dominant context, were framed in terms of "faith" as a cognitive alternative to evidence and reason. The most pressing question seemed to be: Must we resort to a supernatural agency for explaining what we cannot now understand? That question can now be relegated to the periphery and replaced by a Randall-inspired alternative: "Is the sacred an integral component of existence?" Some religious traditions, it must be admitted, neglect the "partnership with the best the world contains." They relegate the sacred to a special *super*natural realm. This may be good for power politics (power going to those who control access to the other realm), but it distorts religious experience. Because it accepts a Dr. Rieux–style rejection of creation, it must locate the holy and the sacred in a wholly different realm.

The ligature line approach, by contrast, focuses on the degree to which the pervasive presence of the sacred is affirmed (on the religious half of the line) or denied. When it is affirmed, it brings several ramifications in its wake: (1) It relativizes the "everydayness" aspect of our lives, that is to say, the prosaic, literal-minded, utilitarian workaday world. This is accomplished by justifying a wider significance. (2) It provides a different set of lenses for examining the realm of biological and cosmic processes. For the Hobbesian lenses that highlight strife and competition, it substitutes more ecological ones that examine how, in addition to strife and competition there is also cooperation and symbiosis. (3) It serves as a guard against dissolution and as a lure toward wholeness, or full, inviolate health, the etymological source for "holiness." (4) It minimizes the Promethean situating of humans in a separate and superior realm. In doing so it blocks an ever-present temptation to think primarily in terms of power and control.

AN EXEMPLARY MEAL

The best religious observance in this regard is food related, the Shabbat meal within the Jewish community. Here, to my mind at least, is one of the truly great human inventions. Soup, gefilte fish, chicken, two breads, salt, wine, vegetables, potatoes, and dessert—the makings of the meal are ordinary enough. But the ordinary here exudes the extraordinary. The sacred, neglected, or ignored in so much of our everyday lives, comes to be explicitly recognized and celebrated. This celebration does not take place by turning away from the ordinary, by dismissing the importance of food and wine as "mere" material things. Rather their sacred character is welcomed along with the day of rest. These are seen as gifts for which we should be grateful. The home is already pervaded by the sacred, if only we will take the time to acknowledge it. The Sabbath prayers and songs accompanying the meal make such acknowledgment explicit.

Here is an important observance that embodies the awareness of the holy in the very dynamic of family life. Without the ritualized observance, such awareness would remain an abstract, detached one. The awareness comes to be more fully pervasive as one engages regularly in the weekly practice. With the ritual, a cluster of activities and ingredients, patterned, ritualized behaviors, signal the importance in a way that cannot be felt apart from the observances. Everything conspires to make the awareness fully human, and holy (i.e., whole) not merely cognitive: a special tablecloth and maybe utensils, two breads, a cup full of wine, blessings, specially prepared dishes, invocations of dependence and gratitude, all culminating in good eating.

If all of this makes sense, we can understand why cherishing practices by preserving recipes was not only a proper but a religious way of resisting diabolical forces fomenting a people's extinction. Ordinary kitchen practices have much to teach us about links and liaisons. To grasp these lessons we must set aside "negligion," our willful neglect. Taking the table seriously, ligatures of all sorts present themselves as candidates for acknowledgement. How far will this symbolic dimension go? For the secularist, it extends to humans and their strivings for companionship and constructing goods. For those on the secular/religious border, it includes, in addition, awe, appreciation, and some cooperation with the nonhuman, natural world. Those who have moved into the religious stretch of the line admit as well some link to a dimension that defines propriety, a dimension to which they must adjust themselves. For those who can consistently be classified as embracing religion in the fullest sense, the ligatures extend to some central narrative or figure, some teaching, and a community that defines itself by patterned observances. Many of those observances will make a central place for that obvious carrier of symbolic force, food. It's not at all a bad idea, then, when symbolizing a religion, to bring in a casserole.

EATING PAUSE:
POTATO-CAULIFLOWER CASSEROLE.

We borrowed this recipe from the kitchen of our son Alex, daughter-in-law Lorène, and their children Charlotte and Léo. "Gratin de Chou-fleur" is delicious and easy to make. **Ingredients**: *2 lbs of potatoes; 6 oz Gruyère cheese, grated; 1 cauliflower head; 1 clove garlic; salt and pepper; 2 tbsp butter; 3 tbsp flour; 1 cup of cream (heavy cream is best, regular cream is okay, half-and-half comes close, milk will do).* **Assembly**: *Peel and cut potatoes into thin slices. (Cubes work also so long as they are parboiled for about 1 minute.) Cut apart the cauliflower and steam for 20 minutes. Make a white sauce by melting the butter, whisking in flour, and gradually stirring in the cream. Rub the casserole dish with the garlic. Arrange the potatoes and the cauliflower in the pan. Sprinkle half of the cheese on the mixture. Add the sauce, which should come just short of completely submerging the casserole's contents. Sprinkle in salt and pepper to taste. Spread the remaining grated cheese over the ingredients.* **Cooking**: *Cover with foil and bake in preheated 400-degree oven. Remove the foil and brown for another 15 minutes.*

NOTES

1. Translation by the author.
2. The uncontested leader in this regard is Richard Dawkins. He has been joined by Sam Harris, Christopher Hitchens, and Daniel Dennett. See the bibliographical entries.

3. The most thorough recontextualization in this sense comes from Charles Taylor's Gifford lectures published as *A Secular Age*.

4. The pattern for thinking of religions in this way is not radically novel. It has been made prominent by anthropologists like Clifford Geertz. "Whatever role divine intervention may or may not play in the creation of faith—and it is not the business of the scientist to pronounce upon such matters one way or the other—it is, primarily at least, out of the context of concrete acts of religious observance that religious conviction emerges on the human plane" (Geertz, 112–113).

5. For religious articulations that recognize interdependence as central, none is more direct than the Buddhist notion mentioned in the art chapter, that of *pratitya samutpada*, the "conditional or causal interdependence of all things" (Kasulis 1981, 43). Matthieu Ricard describes phenomena as arising "through a process of interdependent causes and conditions. Nothing, he says, "exists in itself or by itself" (Revel, 122).

Conclusion

The enjoyment of the table belongs to every era, every culture, all levels of society, in all countries every day; it mingles with other delights, and is always there to comfort us in times of their loss.[1]

—Jean Anthelme Brillat-Savarin

MEAL OF THE FUTURE?

Meals often begin with an aperitif, and this Parisian banquet was no exception. Its creators were self-proclaimed "artists." For them "artist" was a calling sharply differentiated from, and superior to, mere "artisan" (Marinetti, 70). The defining mark of their "art" was total dedication to "creative originality" (Marinetti, 21). This perhaps explains the aperitifs in question. The base, a red wine, seemed promising. But plain wine, let's face it, is nothing if not "artisanal." If "creative originality" were to be the rule, "artists" could not let it stand alone. So, in this case, glasses contained not only wine but bits of cheese and chocolate, citron syrup, and bitters. Reporting the reaction, even a supporter had to admit seeing some "grimaces." Still, the same reporter noted that a few patrons (very few would be my guess) asked for seconds (Marinetti, 88).

When it came to appetizers and entrées, the "creative originality" impetus went into full flourish. A diner might be served the "tummy tickler" whose ingredients included a disk of pineapple, combined with "sardine, tuna and nuts" (Marinetti, 88). A favorite of this group, "totalrice," a medley of "rice, beer, wine, eggs and Parmesan cheese" also made its way to the appetizer selection (Marinetti, 89). Soon a special multisensory treat was the order of the day. Because these artists loved the speed and efficiency of airplanes, the innovation was called "aerofood." Various vegetables and fruits were eaten with the right hand. Simultaneously, the left moved over a surface of different textures: velvet, silk, sandpaper. "Wild jazz" was played by an orchestra and waiters sprayed "the napes of the diners' necks with a strong perfume of carnations." On it went, fourteen courses in all, including "salami immersed in a sauce of coffee and eau-de-Cologne" (Marinetti, 89).

This banquet, along with others of a similar vein can be found in *The Futurist Cookbook*, first published in 1932. Its author Filippo Marinetti had already been responsible for several *Futurist Manifestos* at the turn of the twentieth century. Now he focused his polemical energies on Futurism's relation to food, an area so mired in tradition and hopeless passéism (a very bad word for Futurists) that it had to be completely revolutionized. The meal described above, let's face it, would have hardly been edible, let alone enjoyable. But this turns out to be quite beside the point. Futurists were prophets of the new. They dismissed old-style cooking as having paid scant attention to "aesthetics." That was now changing (Marinetti, 67).

The vulgar artisans of cooking suffered from a particular failing. They were too solicitous of the stomach. This organ, a "crude materialist," served as nothing but an obstacle in culture's struggle for progress (Marinetti, 91). Needless to say, the predilections of those who continued to think in stomach-centered terms must be rejected. Who were these hopeless passéists? Why, housewives of course. In a dramatic flourish, the Italy-based Futurists had declared pasta a forbidden food (Marinetti, 47).[2] "Hold on there," "wait a minute," "this is ridiculous," went up a chorus from those actually preparing meals in the homes. Recalcitrant to new trends, old-fashioned, and stuck in passéism, some women even had the audacity to sign a petition in defense of pasta (Marinetti, 98). The Futurists were not worried. Time, they believed, was on their side. As their movement triumphed, the kitchen would no longer be "the dominion of inept housewives" (Marinetti, 47).

Actually the kitchen would eventually not be the province of anyone but scientists. The old ghost of Professor Wogglebug was alive and well with the Futurists. Meat and wine would have to be accommodated, "until such time as chemistry creates synthetic substances which have the strengths of meat and wine" (Marinetti, 68). Science's hour of triumph, if not imminent, was inevitable. The present offered merely an intermediate stage. It was just a matter of waiting "for chemistry to complete its specific task, that is 'to give the body the calories it needs as quickly as possible, utilizing equivalent nutrients (provided free by the State) in the form of powder or pills'" (Marinetti, 73). All in all, cooking had to undergo a major transformation. The palate had to be prepared "for the foods of the Future," because "our whole way of life has changed" (Marinetti, 70, 69).

For all their bluster, the Futurist predictions have not come to pass. They were self-styled artistic promoters of the speed, efficiency, and power of the new (twentieth) century. Ironically enough, in philosophical terms, the Futurists were apostles of the old, at least apostles of the old, if my stomach-centered reconstruction of philosophy makes any sense. Although contemporaries of Ortega, James, Heidegger, and Dewey, they did not, as was the case with these latter, attempt to redirect the stream of ideas from the post-Renaissance, "Modern," channels that had guided thought for four hundred years. They continued to accept the spectator stance as fundamental, bought into the "let's start from scratch" scenario, accepted the bifurcation of mind from matter, and were anything but hospitable to strangers. Indeed, politically, they inclined toward Fascism.

Two of their phrases are especially important with regard to how, far from pointing to the future, they were rooted in the past. Both expressions also help weave together strands that have been prominent in this study's previous chapters. The first is the dramatic "our whole way of life has changed." Statements like this should immediately raise alarms. They are more in the line of propaganda than elaboration of fact. Those who make such pronouncements have a point of view they seek to impose on others. These others, they hope, will not notice that in spite of whatever changes have occurred, most of their everyday concerns, joys, activities, and interactions remain quite similar to what went before. The stomach, unlike the mind, is quite wary of utopian, totalizing reconstitutions of reality. "Modern" philosophy, was, unfortunately, prone to such dramatic pronouncements. This trend took shape with the Descartes we discussed in chapter 4, the thinker who wished to eliminate historical heritage, wipe the slate clean and start afresh. The "whole way of life has changed" impulse reached a sort of culmination in the nineteenth-century utopian dreams of a Charles Fourier or a Karl Marx. Mind, in its haughty isolation, can project "everything has changed" and "we can become the creators of ourselves" fantasies. Such pronouncements become much harder to defend once the stomach is included. Experience, ancestral wisdom, and inherited common sense are dismissed at one's peril. Moving forward can occur apart from a total break with the past. Despite the crystallization of Modern ideas in Freud's "Oedipus Complex," a new generation can get along quite well without killing off its fathers.

The second claim indicating how the Futurists extended rather than challenged older modes of thought is their dismissal of the stomach as a "crude materialist." Here they simply continue one great centerpiece of post-Renaissance thought, the dualism of mind and body. They have remained blind to the possibility of our condition being described as "stomach-gifted." In consequence, their understanding of "good" can only be conceived in terms of radical distancings from the material sphere. This distancing took various forms. Women in general and housewives in particular, mired in the material, had to be marginalized. When it came to "aesthetics" in relation to food, the Futurists meant, as their "banquets" clearly revealed, an activity divorced from ordinary experience. Their meals remained more spectatorial than gustatory. For them, the "aesthetic" still suggests something that, as we have seen, Dewey dismissed as the "beauty parlor of civilization."

For all their talk about new sensations and strange mixtures, the Futurists, above all, belonged to the "truest equals purest" school of thought. They targeted pasta, the food prized by ordinary folk, because they recognized it as a foreign import. To be precise, they treated it as "barbaric," telling a story about its origin with the Ostrogoths.

> I can just see them, those mustachioed Ostrogoths, setting themselves to gouge out great holes in the grass with their heavy daggers and then squatting round them, wiping their mouths on the ends of their moustaches in seraphic anticipation. Then their worthy consorts, worn and filthy, come and empty into these improvised bowls a slimy heap of worms called "macaroni" and their hairy arms plunge into the fuming hole up to the elbow and their mouths open wide—gobble gobble—and tears run down their grimy cheeks in an excess of bliss. (Marinetti, 51)

Such a snidely insulting story is revealing. It indicates how the Futurists' fascination with Italian Fascism was not an aberration, but rather a coherent outgrowth of their overall orientation. They even invented a term of scorn, "xenomane," for those who would befriend strangers. "Xenomane" and "xenomania" were epithets they applied to those who, engaging in a "cretinous ecstasy before all foreigners," would welcome these outsiders and their influences into Italian culture.[3]

EATING PAUSE:
3 GIFTS OF YEAST

Last chapter, last meal. The most famous final meal of the twentieth century was that engaged in by former French president François Mitterand. Knowing death from cancer was looming, he wanted to celebrate a last meal in style. His choice involved an elaborate ritual centered on the tiny bird called "ortolan." The bird itself is so endangered the French—how rare is this?—have forbidden its use for food. The poor little thing is caught live and left with lots of grains and fruit in a completely dark environment. This causes it to gorge itself. Subsequently it is drowned, I'm just repeating the process, not praising here, in Armagnac. Even though the gorging has fattened it up, it still fits, whole, in one's mouth. This is important, because after a quick baking, it is eaten whole, except for the head, which is bitten off. The process of eating, bones, innards, and all, takes place while the diner is draped beneath a large napkin. Let's face it, this is a bit much. The rest of Mitterand's last menu, which included foie gras and oysters, would have been plenty for any gourmet. As a counter-Mitterand suggestion, and certainly worlds away from the fantasies of the Futurists, I would propose a final meal that is simplicity itself. It celebrates one of the great intromitters we prize dearly: yeast. There is no recipe involved, only three separate components: red wine, good cheese, and bread. Any decent red will do. For the cheese, it would be one made of goat's milk—something with a definitive taste, a crottin de chevignol, *for example. The bread would be crusty with big airholes. Spread the cheese on a chunk of bread (torn off not cut), taste, and follow with a gulp of wine. Close one's eyes and imagine what great possibilities for combination have been provided by the cooperation of plants, animals, humans, and even single-celled fungi. Then, be grateful.*

MULTIPLICITY

The *Futurist Cookbook*, though its blend of art, culture, and cooking is hopeful, obviously stands opposed to the project I have attempted in this book. The purist circle drawn around themselves by the Futurists is inimical to the "hospitality" impetus (chapter 2) that is associated with taking food seriously. "Xenomane," in my context, identifies a praiseworthy attitude. Our stomachs are engines for driving us out of ourselves. By contrast, the Futurists tended to continue the "di" attitude, the splitting of life-experience that was discussed in the chapter on time. Di-remption, di-vision, di-vorce, splitting and separating are the themes of the day. Even the sensorial collage they referred to as "aerofood" was but a series of separate sensations layered over each other. The aesthetic is divorced from the ordinary, and the new is sharply divided from the old.

By contrast, a stomach-sensitive philosophy favors, as we have seen, a philosophical orientation emphasizing relations, or, stated grammatically, prepositions. Among the prepositions, one stands out as especially prominent, the universal accompanist "with." The stomach not only forces us to engage with our surroundings, with those who grow food, with those who store, transport, and prepare it. It also forces us to mix different foods with each other. Pre-Columbian societies in the Americas survived on corn as their staple crop. But experience (no fresh start from scratch here) had taught them to combine the corn *with* beans, *with* squash, and *with* a bit of ash (lime). Without this mixture, corn would have failed miserably as the staple food. Margaret Visser explains why:

> All this was sheer tradition: corn, beans, and squash, with a pinch of ash in every pot. Only very recently have scientists fully grasped the wisdom of the Indians' behaviour. Corn, we now know, is about 10 percent protein, but is deficient in the amino acids lysine and tryptophan, which people must get from food. In addition, although corn contains the vitamin niacin, almost all of it occurs in a "bound" form called niacytin, which makes it biologically unavail-

able to human beings. Corn, in other words, cannot feed people adequately if it is not supplemented by other foods, and beans and squash are excellent complements to corn. The holy threesome, in fact, enabled corn to be consumed as a staple. (Visser 1986, 32)

The fourth element, lime, usually in the form of some ash, was what released the bound niacin. Somehow, via tradition, experimentation, and inherited experience, the original Americans knew that it was only crucial for humans, for "when they offered their sacred grain to the gods they never added ash" (Visser 1986, 33).

One important way in which the stomach complements the mind-only approach to philosophy is in emphasizing the importance of combinations. Whereas abstract thinking encourages reduction to ultimate simples, stomach thoughtfulness is all about mixtures. The combinations with regard to cooking cannot be the sort of random concatenations fostered by the Futurists. Tastes have to blend well with each other, not in some arbitrary fashion, but in ways that will satisfy nutritional needs while appealing to diners. The cook in Nicole Mones *The Last Chinese Chef* explains what it means to be solicitous of mixture. There is a name for the art of mixing and matching, "*tiaowei*." Having grasped "ideal flavors and textures," the art involves, first, properly blending them. Next comes the appropriate matching of "dishes in their cycles. Then there is the meal as a whole—the menu—which is a sort of narrative of rhythms and meanings and moods" (Mones, 54).

Such emphasis on the pervasiveness of relations, expressed technically as a *philosophy of prepositions*, represents the most important change that emerges from my study. For a long time the guiding philosophical presupposition has been to envision mixture as derivative and defective. The unmixed source was thought to be purer, unitary. In an earlier book, I identified this as the Plotinian Temptation. Plotinus (205–270) was a thinker who, by influencing the thought of St. Augustine, shaped subsequent Western philosophy. What he bequeathed was a narrative built around an aboriginal One. First, simplicity, unmixed and good, then complexity, mixed and worse. Since mixture meant distance from the source, a particular kind of normative attitude accompanied this narrative. Good was associated with the unalloyed purity of the unmixed original. The multiple, on the other hand, signaled that which was contaminated.

Taking account of experiences associated with the stomach, we can now avoid this prejudice. Philosophically, our general theory of reality, what philosophers call "metaphysics," can retrieve a pre-Socratic position associated with Anaximander (610–547). His word *apeiron* (chapter 5) indicated an initial pell-mell of possibilities. Such an original synchresis offers opportunities for innumerable combinations. If we want to tell ourselves a story about a source out of which everything emerges, a stomach-centered approach inclines toward thinking in terms of an original multiplicity, "infinity" as Levinas referred to it (chapter 2). Each existent is a particular combination, a specific blend of elements from out of the original hurly-burly of possibilities. Existents can then be considered as mixtures (limited) out of the ultimate mixture (unlimited). They would also be understood as incomplete in a way that blocks finding fulfillment within themselves alone. Fostering affiliations via ligating objects (chapter 7) then becomes one way of responding to our condition. Multiplying ligatures (chapter 8) offers, in general, a mode of heeding the lure of the infinite.

NEEDINESS

The incompletion at the heart of our condition indicates another philosophical turn associated with taking the stomach seriously. Neediness and dependence, terms that are inherently pejorative within the mind-only approach, come to be reevaluated. Neither, in the new conceptual landscape, suggests a defective state. They are understood, rather, to be part and parcel of our condition. They represent occasions for enhancing good. A good life, as the chapters on hospitality, fraternity, and the parasite tried to indicate, is no longer defined by how closely one approximates the status of complete self-sufficiency ("autarchy" or "autonomy" in the more formal philosophical language). Freedom is now rescued from autonomy. A good life is defined in terms of having a healthy nexus of interdependencies. Recognizing and welcoming these dependencies becomes a defining ingredient in the religious dimension of life (chapter 8). Interdependencies and combinations are, at any rate, irreducible. Corn, beans, squash, and ash. We need their combination. And together, we and they need the geological, meteorological, and biological constituents that give rise to healthy, productive agricultural land.

When all works well together, the mixture blurs the old opposition between spirit and matter. Instead of denigrating the stomach as a "crude materialist," there is an emphasis on the sort of alchemy best represented in Isak Dinesen's story "Babette's Feast." There, despite the participants' official commitment to a dualistic spirit *versus* matter version of Christianity, it is the table, the eating and drinking, that moves old animosities to melt away. When the story begins, the neediness that forces people toward each other has worn thin. "Discord and dissention" had become prominent in the little community (Dinesen, 18). Old slanders, betrayals, and infidelities had once again surfaced. "The sins of old Brothers and Sisters came, with late piercing repentance like a toothache, and the sins of others against them came back with bitter resentment, like a poisoning of the blood" (Dinesen, 19). During the meal a kind of transformation takes place. The participants, usually taciturn, find it easy to speak. By the end of the meal, acknowledgement, forgiveness, and reconciliation have become widespread. "The vain illusions of this earth had dissolved before their eyes like smoke, and they had seen the universe as it really is. They had been given one hour of the millennium" (Dinesen, 42). "Time itself had merged into eternity" (Dinesen, 41). The nexus of interdependencies, indispensable in a world where "to be is to be needy" will inevitably occasion hurt, betrayal, misunderstanding, and general discord. Some glimpse of the concord that is also possible emerges every now and then. Babette's meal offered one of those instances. Through the sharing of food, eternity blended seamlessly with temporality.

PARASITES, THIRD PARTIES, GUEST-HOSTS

If "to be is to be needy," then one food plant stands out as prototypical. Maize, still a mainstay of North American diets,[4] falls into the category of plants called "cultigens." Cultigens have no wild varieties. They are the product of human intervention. Maize is even more special, in that it cannot propagate itself. An intermediary is required, one knowledgeable enough to store the ears and preserve the seeds from rot before the next planting season. This is a task well suited to humans. *Between* one generation of corn and the next, comes a third party, us.

The "needy cultigen" lesson for philosophy involves a move away from the stock scenario of subject and object. Mind-inspired philosophy envisioned a situation in which an inner self, the subject, received data from objects in the outer world. A philosophical perspective that includes stomach along with the mind tends not to envision the paradigmatic scenario as that of subjects confronting objects. Rather, it thinks in terms of participants constantly inserting themselves into ongoing situations. This shifts the bipolar, "stand over against one another" approach, into one that stresses intermediaries-in-action. Our basic relation to surroundings, as we saw in the first chapter, is that of individuals involved in dealings with things. Even when it comes to art, as we saw in chapter 5, ours is not the stance of detached spectators. For our dealings with things, we are forced to insert ourselves in the midst of goings-on around us. In a stomach-and-mind world, primacy goes neither to the subject (firsts) nor objects (seconds) but to intermediaries (thirds or, more colloquially, third parties).

The Greek-derived name for those who always place themselves into ongoing processes is "parasites." As we saw in chapter 3, that word had an initially innocuous connotation. Whether contemporary parasitologists can recover a more neutral connotation, only time will tell. Although I would prefer to speak positively of "parasite" or "para-site," its general negative associations make this impossible at present. As a result, it's probably best to stay with the less emotively charged "third party" or the Scottish "intromitter." In some way or another we are all, despite what we would like to think, "third parties." Once we recognize the "between" or the "intromitter" as prototypical, we begin to realize how this is not unusual at all. Its prominence is well attested in our narrative tradition. Oedipus is a third party, both as a child who enters into the world of his mother and father and as the adult who once again comes between them. Jane Eyre, orphan, moves from place to place. Odysseus constantly washes up on one shore after another. Tom Jones is inserted, uninvited, into the world of Squire Allworthy. Ilse comes back into Rick's life in *Casablanca*. Romeo wants to become part of the Capulet family. *E. T.* drops into a suburban American neighborhood. Film noirs get going when an unexpected visitor comes into a particular setting. Babette, force for reconciliation, arrives as a scruffy, worn-out exile. We have all been new kids in school, the most recently hired employees, travelers, people who have moved into a new neighborhood. The stranger, the exile, the wanderer, the "third party" is not an exception. It is rather the rule. As Barbara Kingsolver points out, two great archetypes dominate storytelling: "A stranger comes to town" and "I set out upon a journey" (Kingsolver et al., 335).

We are, in other words, both guests and hosts. As the chapter on hospitality pointed out, there is a richness in the Latin and French ambiguity that uses the same term for both. Philosophies typically work with concepts, but, since we are imaginative creatures, the concepts can be supplemented by representative figures. In a philosophical landscape that takes the stomach seriously, the pair "guest-host" comes to serve as a central metaphor for our dealing with things and with each other. Guest-host thinking acknowledges the primacy of mixing. "In the beginning was contact" could be its slogan. Contact is not embraced for manipulation, the imperialist approach. Rather the guest-host perspective urges contact for enhanced understanding and for the transformations that will result from the interpersonal commerce. One way to describe artists, chapter 5 argued, was as "hosts" inviting us into a participational activity. Building *communitas*, chapter 7 suggested, would only occur if we made an effort to welcome as guests, those who do not normally share our tables. One measure for the health of a multicultural democratic republic could then be identified: examine what sorts of generous or restrictive hosts are its citizens.

AUTONOMY AND SYMBIOSIS

If there are two words whose contrast summarizes the theme of this book, they would be "autonomy" and "symbiosis." Each came to prominence at a different time. Each signaled an important philosophical turn. Chapter 3 pointed out how "autonomy" emerged in the seventeenth century. The burgeoning philosophical orientation of that time, emphasizing self-sufficiency and release from old forms of bondage, made it a suitable label for the age's aspirations. By the end of the nineteenth century, things were changing. The rise of biological sciences along with fundamental alterations in the physical sciences occasioned a shift in perspective. This shift itself required a new guiding concept. That concept would no longer highlight the concatenation of ultimate simples ("atoms" of various sorts) that had provided the prime analogues of the earlier period. Instead the new word would indicate a nexus of intertwinings. "Symbiosis," literally, "living with" (there's that key preposition again), although coined earlier, gained traction only as the twentieth century dawned.

In a sense, the theme of this book could be summarized in the phrase "from autonomy to symbiosis." The mind-alone approach tended to emphasize isolation, reduction to ultimate simples, spectator epistemology, autarchy, separation of subject from object, and a quest for an "authentic" purity. When stomach is added to the mix, the kinds of conceptual transformations described in the previous chapters can all be categorized as changes rung on the theme of symbiosis. In fact, the philosophy embraced in this book could go by the Latin synonym for symbiosis, "convivialism."[5] That term, intimately associated with the table and weaving together biological, social, and gustatory dimensions, offers a less foreboding label than the Greek term.

In this regard Bo Diddley and his gumbo (from chapter 7) can serve as appropriate representative figures. We recall his self-evaluation as a mix and blend: "All my people are from New Orleans, the bayou country. French, African, Indian, all mixed up. I like gumbo, dig?" The mode in which the stomach urges us out of ourselves, together with the importance of mixtures and blends in cooking, occasions a renewed appreciation for such amalgamated individuals. It also carries with it a special kind of responsibility. Food, in its ordinary setting, cannot be merely spectatorial. As a biological necessity, it demands to be eaten. Food is for consumption, and consumption with others is something we seem naturally inclined to prefer. The ancient Greeks had many words we can translate as "banquet" or "meal." Only one, *deipnon*, specifically addresses the biological need. The others, as Pauline Pantel-Schmitt explains, involve the context in which the meal occurs, a context invariably associated with sharing (Pantel-Schmitt, 5).[6] The next question, one that has been a leitmotif throughout this book, has to do with the composition of those with whom we share. What kind of amalgamation or miscegenation (now a rehabilitated term) do we embrace? Too typically we follow the practices of ancient symposia and include those who are most like us. This is the hospitality to "one's circle" described by Elizabeth Telfer (chapter 2). Within this kind of hospitality, though, there is little room for the Bo Diddleys of the world.

Here is where the ideal of harmony, discussed in chapter 3, offers one fruition for the table ideal of sharing. Instead of unity or purity, a new guiding ideal takes center stage. It is one that must involve holding together disparate elements. This makes eminent sense when the highest reality, the "infinite," is considered as the combination of all possibilities. With the infinite as axiological lure, the moral impetus shifts toward cumulative rather than purificatory ideals. If we wish to approximate the infinite, then we must find ways to accommodate difference without splintering into chaos. Of course, this impetus can be ignored. The path of least resistance will always be the same: thinking that the way things are is the only way they can be. "Not much can be done" would then be the watchword. This is the attitude that restricts guests to people of "one's circle." Some individuals, though, stand as models for getting beyond the "not much can be done" attitude. Artists, as we saw, are those who experiment with ways to get beyond the apparent limitations of necessity. This is certainly true of culinary artists who must take into account, despite the Futurists' dismissal, the demands of the stomach.

During the Franco-Prussian War, for example, when food supplies were almost entirely used up, the legendary chef Auguste Escoffier rose to the occasion. Rejecting the "not much can be done" attitude, he managed ways to offer variety and a medley of tastes. Supplied mostly with the meat from dying or ill horses, Escoffier did not resign himself to the bland and repeatable. He strove for a variety that would please as well as nourish: "horse stew one day, braised horse meat the next, macaroni horse meat the next, horse meat with lentils, with beans, with peas, etc. I must say that if the meat of 'man's best conquest' was at that time not cooked with every possible sauce, then it was at least garnished with every possible kind of bean" (Escoffier, 38). Officers fared somewhat better. The meal described next might actually be considered excellent even outside of battle conditions: "Dinner menus were made up of a thick or thin soup followed by the main dish, a roasted fowl from my farmyard, salad, and fruit, and then coffee and cognac" (Escoffier, 38). Not bad for a setting in which cannon fire and smoke were all around. Perhaps, some of us may think, an army that has hardly any meat but has plenty of cognac does not exactly have its priorities straight. Indeed, surrender was soon the order of the day and the great future chef at the Ritz became a prisoner of war. Still, what counts for our philosophical purposes is how Escoffier, the artist, worked to push back the limits of necessity.

Here is where the intersection of the artistic, the moral and the political (chapters 5, 2, 7) comes into play. Artists, as we have seen, expand the horizons of possibility. What does not seem feasible for most of us actually comes to be enacted by those with the right combination of talent and training. In the realm of moral philosophy this attitude has been well formulated by William James. Eliminative purification, although an ongoing temptation, is not what is to be sought as a moral desideratum. The goal, rather, is to blend and harmonize in ever-increasing instantiations of multiplicity. The ultimate good, that which motivates by drawing us toward itself (the "divine" in traditional terminology) remains the "infinite." The "infinite," to repeat a common theme in this book, stands as the archetypal congregation of multiplicities. Seeking the good, etymology teaches us, is to engage in a project of gathering. Both "good" and "gather" go back to the Germanic root indicating a bringing together (Barnhart, s.v. "good"). Chaucer's poet, discussed in chapter 5, saw himself as a host who gathers others around him. Borobudur, the great Buddhist monument also discussed in chapter 5, has been described as akin to an "antenna," a source of gathering. When William James comes around to describing this moral end-in-view philosophically, he speaks of "the *best whole*." Let us seek, he urges, the victory of

> the more inclusive side,—of the side which even in the hour of triumph will to some degree do justice to the ideals in which the vanquished party's interests lay. The course of history is nothing but the story of men's struggles from generation to generation to find the more and more inclusive order. *Invent some manner* of realizing your own ideals which will also satisfy the alien demands,—that and that only is the path of peace! (James 19897, 205)

Substitute "stranger," "exile," "parasite," "alien," or "intromitter" for "vanquished party" in James's citation, and his plea overlaps with the understanding of "good" encouraged by "needy being" and "multiplicity goes all the way down" metaphysics. Politically, the impulse should urge effort toward ever-closer approximations of *communitas* (chapter 7). It is not a matter of blanket inclusion. Permitting and omitting, as chapter 5 suggested, are correlative. "Harmony," at any rate, as with a good meal, is not just a slapdash, Futurist-cookbook-style, "creative, innovative" agglomeration. Nor does harmony result from rigid exclusion. No contact and mixtures: no Bo Diddleys. What counts is an effort at achieving a concordant miscellany. Good chefs succeed in accomplishing such combinations. They do so, however, only as a result of sweat, effort, and experimentation. A great weakness to be avoided is to submit to the "not much can be done" approach. James thinks the key alternative words important enough that he highlights them: responsibility to *invent some manner* for fabricating the "best whole."

LIGATING OBJECTS AND UNFORGETTING

All of this takes us back to affiliating objects and symbols. They, more than anything, serve as physical manifestations of existing and potential linkages. Ancient Rome and Greece, with their communal hearths, had in them an obvious primary candidate for ligating instrument. There were others as well. One of the most significant is associated with the Greek symposium. Since "symposium" literally means "drink together," it is not surprising that wine would play the role of ligating device. Any symposium would have a leader, the symposiarch. His (it was always a he) task was to make certain initial determinations. First, how much water to mix with the wine in the *krater*, the central container. The ancient Greeks apparently drank a sweet wine better diluted. Second, what would be the topic of discussion. Both the wine and the conversation, circulating in common among the attendees, would serve as "thirds," as mediating instrumentalities, the ligating media helping foster and secure affiliations. In a late symposium, *The Dinner of the Seven Wise Men*, the wine is treated separately from the conversation. Plutarch's participants admit how the god of the vine, Dionysus, "softens and relaxes" the characters of participants with wine, thus providing "some means for beginning a union, and friendship with one another." Among more temperate individuals, however, instead of the *krater*, it is better to set "discourse" in the middle, "a non-intoxicating bowl as it were" (Plutarch, 156 d).

The topic of conversation, with or without wine, would also band participants together since it served as a theme in which they all shared. Its nexus-encouraging function was as real as that of a tangible object. Similarly, the wine drawn from the *krater* would ally those who imbibed. Since we are embodied creatures, linkages do not simply arise from acts of disembodied will. In a concrete, practical sense, they depend on common activities usually accompanied by some physical mediating device that touches all the participants. Michel Serres suggests that a central or circulating object is always present when there is "intersubjectivity" in the making (Serres 1980, 305). What counts is that the members of the budding *communitas* all come into contact with a liaison-encouraging medium.

An anthropological study provides a telling example from a different tradition. The book in question examines feasts. One of the people described are the Luo. They live in western Kenya. Central to their celebrations is a unique version of the *krater*. They call it a *thago*. It's just a large pot filled with beer. Senior males in the community are honored by being granted long straws. It's pretty obvious where this is headed. At the feast, the elder males sit around the pot and, making good use of the straws, sip the *thago*'s alcoholic elixir (Dietler and Hayden, 96–98).

Alcoholic connecting instruments are abundant in our culture, most prominently in religious observances. But alcohol is expendable. Some cultures prohibit it altogether. No culture, however, can prohibit all food. As a more general nexus object, the central serving dish can take on the "symbolic" function of the *krater* or the *thago*. Prior to the nineteenth century, even in Europe, food was served in a style called *à la française*. This continued the medieval tradition of placing platters of food on the table and having the eaters draw from them. Then came a change in manners inspired by Russian nobility. The new service, *service à la russe*, bypassed the serving vessels. Instead, food was plated individually. This habit never took hold in China.[7]

In that regard, Chinese culture remains more in line with the philosophy of convivialism. Cultures favoring individual platings tend to continue the Modern European emphases on autonomy and de-ligaturing. For us, who find ourselves in the "we plate" culture, the challenge is that which was identified in the first chapter, *anamnesis*. Something important has been forgotten. Bringing back the *krater*, the *thago*, or the central serving dish (see this book's cover) can move us toward an important kind of unforgetting.

NOTES

1. Translation by the author.
2. "Pastasciutta, however agreeable to the palate, is a passéist food because it makes people heavy, brutish, deludes them into thinking it is nutritious, makes them skeptical, slow, pessimistic" (Marinetti, 33). Futurist cooking would abolish pasta, this "absurd Italian gastronomic religion" (Marinetti, 37).
3. "Xenomanes and therefore guilty of anti-Italianism, are those young Italians who fall into a cretinous ecstasy before all foreigners, even now the world crisis is robbing these people of their wealth; they fall in love with them out of snobbishness and sometimes marry them, absolving them from all defects (arrogance, bad manner, anti-Italianism, or ugliness) simply because they don't speak the Italian language and come from distant countries about which little or nothing is known" (Marinetti, 58–59). The anti-xenomane rant comes to a sort of culmination in this passage: "Therefore, we Futurists, who twenty years ago cried at the top of our socially-democratically-communistically-clerically parliamentarily softened voices: 'The word Italy must rule over the word Liberty!', today proclaim:
   a) The word Italy must rule over the word genius.
   b) The word Italy must rule over the word intelligence.
   c) The word Italy must rule over the words culture and statistics.
   d) The word Italy must rule over the word truth" (Marinetti, 61).
4. Both Visser (1986) and Pollan indicate how corn touches just about everything we consume. See especially Visser's chapter 1 "Corn: Our Mother, Our life," and Pollan's section I "Industrial Corn."
5. See my "Convivialism: A Philosophical Manifesto."
6. Nicole Mones makes a similar point in her novel about Chinese cuisine: "When my master sent out his untouched dishes from the huge imperial repasts to the families of the princes and the chief bureaucrats, he would send them only as complete meals for eight people in stacked lacquerware. Never any other way. Always for eight. The high point of every meal was never the food itself, he taught us, but always the act of sharing it" (Mones, 266).
7. "One more. The most important one of all. It's community. Every meal eaten in China, whether the grandest banquet or the poorest lunch eaten by workers in an alley—all eating is shared by the group. . . . 'We don't plate. Almost all other cuisines do. Universally, in the West, they plate. Think about it'" (Mones, 37).

Bibliography

Ackermann, Robert John (1985). *Data, Instruments, and Theory: A Dialectical Approach to Understanding Science.* Princeton: Princeton University Press.
Addams, Jane (1910; 1981). *Twenty Years at Hull-House.* New York: Signet Classics.
Aeschylus (1938). *The Suppliants.* In Whitney Oates and Eugene O'Neill Jr., *The Complete Greek Drama.* New York: Random House.
Aiken, William, and LaFollette, Hugh (1996). *World Hunger and Morality.* Upper Saddle River, NJ: Prentice Hall.
Albanese, Catherine (1981). *America: Religions and Religion.* Belmont, CA: Wadsworth.Publishing Co.
Alcoff, Linda, ed. (1998). *Epistemology: The Big Questions.* Oxford: Blackwell.
Alexander, Thomas (2003). "Between Being and Emptiness: Toward and Eco-Ontology of Inhabitation." In William Gavin, *In Dewey's Wake: Unfinished Work in Pragmatic Reconstruction.* Albany: SUNY Press.
Allhof, Fritz, and Monroe, Dave, eds. (2007). *Food and Philosophy.* London: Wiley-Blackwell.
Amy, Michaël (2002). "The Body as Machine, Taken to Its Extreme," *New York Times,* January 20, 2002: Art/Architecture, 37.
Aquinas, Thomas (1952). *Truth.* Trans. Robert W. Mulligan, s.j. Chicago: Henry Regnery.
Aristotle (1995). *The Poetics.* In *Aristotle: Poetics; Longinus: On the Sublime; Demetrius: On Style.* Cambridge: Loeb Classical Library.
——— (1985). *Nicomachean Ethics.* Trans. Terence Irwin. Indianapolis: Hackett Publishing Co.
——— (1941). *The Politics.* In *The Basic Works of Aristotle.* Ed. Richard McKeon. New York: Random House.
Aron, Raymond (1953; 1997). *Introduction à la philosophie politique: Démocratie et révolution.* Paris: Livre de Poche.
Austin, John (1961). *Philosophical Papers.* Oxford: Clarendon Press.
Ayer, Alfred J. (1965). *The Problem of Knowledge.* London: Macmillan.
——— (1946; 1952). *Language, Truth and Logic.* New York: Dover Publications.
Ayto, John (1990). *Dictionary of Word Origins.* New York: Arcade Publishing.
Balthasar, Hans Urs von. (1958) "Man Creates Meaning in Encounter." In Roland Houde and Joseph Mullaly, eds. *Philosophy of Knowledge: Selected Readings.* New York: J. B. Lippincott.
Balzac, Honoré de (1845; 1925). "Le Chef-d'Oeuvre Inconnu." In *La Comédie Humaine, Études Philosophiques II.* Ed. Marcel Bouteron and Henri Longnon. Paris: Louis Conard.
Barnhart, Robert K. (1988). *The Barnhart Dictionary of Etymology.* n.p. The H. H. Wilson Co.
Barrett, William (1964). *What is Existentialism?* New York: Grove Press.

——— (1978). *The Illusion of Technique: A Search for Meaning in a Technological Civilization.* Garden City: Anchor Press/Doubleday.
Bates, Katherine Lee (1911). *America the Beautiful and Other Poems.* New York: Thomas Crowell Co.
Baum, L. Frank (1919; 1996). *The Magic of Oz.* Etext # 419. Project Gutenberg. www.gutenberg.org/dirs/etext96/magoz10.txt.
Becker, Carl (1931). *The Heavenly City of the Eighteenth Century Philosophers.* New Haven: Yale University Press.
Behar, Ruth (1996). *The Vulnerable Observer: Anthropology that Breaks Your Heart.* Boston: Beacon Press.
Belasco, Warren (2000). "Future Notes: The Meal-In-A-Pill." *Food and Foodways* 8 (4): 253–271.
Bellah, Robert, Madsen, Richard, Sullivan, William, Swidler, Ann, and Tipton Steven (1985). *Habits of the Heart: Individualism and Commitment in American Life.* New York: Harper Perennial.
Benedict, St. *The Rule of Benedict.* Retrieved from the World Wide Web: www.osb.org/rb/text/rbeaad1.html.
Bennett, Jane (2001). *The Enchantment of Modern Life: Attachments, Crossing, and Ethics.* Princeton: Princeton University Press.
Bergson, Henri (1932). *Les deux sources de la morale et de la religion.* Paris: Presses Universitaires de France.
Berkeley, George (1710; 1998). *A Treatise Concerning the Principles of Human Knowledge.* Ed. Jonathan Dancy. New York: Oxford University Press.
Berry, Wendell (2002). *The Art of the Commonplace: The Agrarian Essays of Wendell Berry.* Ed. Norman Wirzba. Washington, DC: Counterpoint.
Bible (1989). *The Harper Collins Study Bible.* New York: Harper Collins.
Bohr, Niels (1934; 1987). *Atomic Theory and the Description of Nature: The Philosophical Writings of Niels Bohr*, Vol. 1. Woodbridge, CT: OxBow Press.
Boisvert, Raymond (2010). "Convivialism: A Philosophical Manifesto," *The Pluralist* 5, no. 2: 57–68.
——— (2000). "Philosophy: Postmodern or Polytemporal," *International Philosophical Quarterly*, XL: 313–326.
——— (1998). *John Dewey: Rethinking Our Time.* Albany: SUNY Press.
Bordo, Susan (1993). *Unbearable Weight: Feminism, Western Culture and the Body.* Berkeley: University of California Press.
Brehier, Emile (1932; 1968). *The History of Philosophy, Volume VI: The Nineteenth Century: Period of Systems, 1800–1850.* Chicago: University of Chicago Press.
Brillat-Savarin, Jean-Anthelme (1923). *La Physiologie du goût.* Paris: A. Lemerre.
Buchler, Justus, ed. (1955). *Philosophical Writings of Peirce.* New York: Dover.
Bury, J. B. (1932; 1955). *The Idea of Progress; An Inquiry into Its Origin and Growth* New York: Dover Publications.
Caird, G. B. (1980). *The Language and Imagery of the Bible.* Philadelphia: Westminster Press.
Camus, Albert (1958). *Le Malentendu suivi de Caligula.* Paris: Gallimard.
——— (1957; 1991). *Exile and the Kingdom.* Trans. Justin O'Brien. New York: Vintage International.
——— (1948; 1991). *The Plague.* Trans. Stuart Gilbert. New York: Vintage.
Carruthers, Mary J. (1990). *The Book of Memory: A Study of Memory in Medieval Culture.* Cambridge: Cambridge University Press.
Chang, Kenneth (2006). "Explaining Ice: The Answers Are Slippery." *New York Times.* February 21, Section F 1, 4.
Chapman, H. Perry, Kloek, Wouter T., Wheelock, Arthur K. Jr. (1996). *Jan Steen: Painter and Storyteller.* New Haven: Yale University Press.
Chaucer, Geoffrey (ca. 1400; 1985). *The Canterbury Tales.* Trans. David Wright. Oxford: Oxford University Press.
Cherno, Melvin (1963). "Feuerbach's 'Man Is What He Eats': A Rectification." *Journal of the History of Ideas* 24: 397–406.

Chua, Amy (2003). *World on Fire: How Exporting Free Market Democracy Breeds Ethnic Hatred and Global Instability.* New York: Doubleday.
Cicero (1942). *De Fato.* In *De Oratore* Book III, together with *De Fato, Paradoxa Stoicorum, De Partitione Oratoria.* Cambridge: Loeb Classical Library.
Coleridge, Samuel Taylor (1817; 1994). 'The Rime of the Ancient Mariner." In Duncan Wu, ed. *Romanticism: An Anthology.* Oxford: Blackwell.
Collingwood, R. G. (1932; 1978). *The Principles of Art.* Oxford: Oxford University Press.
Coveney, Peter, and Highfield, Roger (1995). *Frontiers of Complexity: The Search for Order in a Chaotic World.* New York: Fawcett Columbine.
DaSilva, Cara, ed. (1996). *In Memory's Kitchen: A Legacy from the Women of Terezin.* Northvale, NJ: J. Aronson.
Davidson, James (1997). *Courtesans and Fishcakes: The Consuming Passions of Classical Athens.* New York: HarperCollins.
Davies, N. B. (2000). *Cuckoos, Cowbirds and Other Cheats.* London: T & A D Poyser.
Dawkins, Richard (2006). *The God Delusion.* New York: Houghton Mifflin.
——— (1989; 2006). *The Selfish Gene.* Oxford: Oxford University Press.
Delio, Ilia (2003). *A Franciscan View of Creation: Learning to Live in a Sacramental World.* The Franciscan Heritage Series, Vol. 2. St. Bonaventure, NY: Franciscan Institute.
Dennett, Daniel (2006). *Breaking the Spell: Religion as a Natural Phenomenon.* New York: Viking.
Derrida, Jacques, and Dufourmantelle, Anne (1997). *De l'hospitalité.* Paris: Calman-Lévy.
Derrida, Jacques (2001). *On Cosmopolitanism and Forgiveness.* Trans. Mark Dooley and Michael Hughes. London: Routledge.
——— (1999). *Adieu to Emmanuel Levinas.* Trans. Pascale-Anne Brault and Michael Naas. Stanford: Stanford University Press.
——— (1988). *Limited Inc.* Trans. Samuel Weber. Chicago: Northwestern University Press.
——— (1968; 1981). "Plato's Pharmacy" in *Dissemination.* Trans. Barbara Johnson. Chicago: University of Chicago Press.
——— (1976). *Of Grammatology.* Trans. Gayatri Chakravorty Spivak. Baltimore: Johns Hopkins Press.
Descartes, Rene (1644; 1985). "The Principles of Philosophy." In *The Philosophical Writings of Descartes*, Vol 1. Trans. John Cottingham, Robert Stoothoff, Dugald Murdoch. Cambridge: Cambridge University Press.
——— (1641; 1984). *Meditations on First Philosophy.* In John Cottingham, Robert Stoothoff, Dugald Murdoch, *The Philosophical Writings of Descartes*, Vol. 2. Cambridge: Cambridge University Press.
Desmond, William (1995). *Being and the Between.* Albany: SUNY Press.
Desowitz, Robert S. (1987). *New Guinea Tapeworms and Jewish Grandmothers: Tales of Parasites and People.* New York: W. W. Norton & Co.
Deval, Jacqueline (1993). *Reckless Appetites: A Culinary Romance.* Hopewell, NJ: Ecco Press.
Dewey, John (1939; 1988). *Freedom and Culture.* In *The Later Works*, Vol. 13. Carbondale: Southern Illinois University Press.
——— (1937; 1987). "Democracy and Educational Administration," in *The Later Works*, Vol. 11. Carbondale: Southern Illinois University Press.
——— (1934; 1987). *Art as Experience.* In *The Later Works*, Vol. 10. Carbondale: Southern Illinois University Press.
——— (1986). *The Later Works, Volume 9: 1933–1934.* Ed. Jo Ann Boydston. Carbondale: Southern Illinois University Press.
——— (1929; 1984). *The Quest for Certainty.* In *The Later Works*, Vol. 4. Carbondale: Southern Illinois University Press.
——— (1927; 1984). *The Public and Its Problems.* In *The Later Works*, Vol. 2. Carbondale: Southern Illinois University Press.
——— (1925; 1981). *Experience and Nature.* In *The Later Works*, Vol. 1. Carbondale: Southern Illinois University Press.
——— (1922; 1983). *Human Nature and Conduct.* In *The Middle Works*, Vol. 14. Carbondale: Southern Illinois University Press.

——— (1919; 1982). "Philosophy and Democracy." In *The Middle Works*, Vol. 11. Carbondale: Southern Illinois University Press.
——— (1916a; 1980). *Democracy and Education*. In *The Middle Works*, Vol. 9. Carbondale: Southern Illinois University Press.
——— (1916b; 1983). "Nationalizing Education." In *The Middle Works*, Vol. 10. Carbondale: Southern Illinois University Press.
——— (1972). *The Early Works, Volume 5: 1895–1898*. Ed. Jo Ann Boydston. Carbondale: Southern Illinois University Press.
Dietler, Michael, and Hayden, Brian, eds. (2001). *Feasts: Archaeological and Ethnographic Perspectives on Food, Politics, and Power*. Washington, DC: Smithsonian Institution Press.
Dinesen, Isak (1953; 1993). "Babette's Feast." In *Anecdotes of Destiny*. New York: Vintage International.
Dostoevsky, Feodor (1880; 1950). *The Brothers Karamazov*. Trans. Constance Garnett. New York: Modern Library.
Dufourmantelle, Anne (2000). *Of Hospitality: Anne Dufourmantelle Invites Jacques Derrida to Respond*. Trans. Rachel Bowlby. Stanford: Stanford University Press.
Eco, Umberto (1986). *Art and Beauty in the Middle Ages*. Trans. Hugh Bredin. New Haven: Yale University Press.
Edman, Irwin (1928; 1967). *Arts and the Man: A Short Introduction to Aesthetics*. New York: W. W. Norton & Co.
Eldridge, Michael (1998). *Transforming Experience: John Dewey's Cultural Instrumentalism*. Nashville: Vanderbilt University Press.
Elshtain, Jean Bethke (1995). *Democracy on Trial*. New York: Basic Books.
Encyclopedia of Islam (1960). Ed. H. A. R. Gibb, J. H. Kramers, E. Lévi-Provençal, J. Schacht. Leiden: E. J. Brill.
Encyclopaedia of Religion and Ethics (1913). Ed. James Hastings. Edinburgh: T & T Clark.
Escoffier, Auguste (1997). *Memories of My Life*. Trans. Lawrence Escoffier. New York: Van Nostrand Reinhold.
Euripides (1938). *Ion*. In *The Complete Greek Drama*. Ed. Whitney J. Oates and Eugene O'Neill Jr. New York: Random House.
Fagles, Robert, trans. (1996). *Homer: The Odyssey*. New York: Penguin Books.
Faulkner, Robert K. (1993). *Francis Bacon and the Project of Progress*. Lanham, MD: Rowman & Littlefield.
Feder, Barnaby J. (1997). "Defining Fast Food: Between 55 Seconds and 30 Minutes." *New York Times*, Sunday, June 22, section E.
Feigl, Herbert, and Sellars, Wilfrid (1949). *Readings in Philosophical Analysis*. New York: Appleton-Century-Crofts.
Fesmire, Steve (2003). *John Dewey and Moral Imagination: Pragmatism in Ethics*. Bloomington: Indiana University Press.
Fielding, Henry (1749; 1973). *Tom Jones*. Ed. Sheridan Baker. New York: W. W. Norton & Company.
Fingarette, Herbert (1972). *Confucius—The Secular as Sacred*. New York: Harper Torchbooks.
Fish, Stanley (1980). *Is There a Text in this Class? The Authority of Interpretive Communities*. Cambridge: Harvard University Press.
Fischler, Claude (2001). *L'Homnivore*. Paris: Odile Jacob.
Fisher, M. F. K. (1976). *The Art of Eating*. New York: Vintage Books.
Focillon, Henri (1948). *The Life of Forms in Art*. Trans. Charles Beecher Hogan and George Kubler. New Haven: Yale University Press.
Food and Nutrition Needs in Emergencies (n.d.). Geneva: World Health Organization.
France, Anatole (1921). *Le jardin d'Épicure*. Paris: Calmann-Lévy.
Frederic, Louis, and Nou, Jean-Louis (1966). *Borobudur*. New York: Abbeville Press.
Freeman, Kathleen (1953). *The Pre-Socratic Philosophers*. Oxford: Blackwell.
Freud, Sigmund (1930; 1961). *Civilization and Its Discontents*. Trans. James Strachey. New York: W. W. Norton & Co.
Gaarder, Jostein (1996). *Sophie's World: A Novel about the History of Philosophy*. Trans. Paulette Miller. New York: Berkley Books.

Galison, Peter (2003). *Einstein's Clocks, Poincaré's Maps: Empires of Time*. New York: W. W. Norton & Co.

Gasset, Jose Ortega y (1966; 1969). *Some Lessons in Metaphysics*. Trans. Mildred Adams. New York: W. W. Norton & Co.

——— (1960). *What is Philosophy?* Trans. Mildred Adams. New York: W. W. Norton & Co.

——— (1958; 1962). *Man and Crisis*. Trans. Mildred Adams. New York: W. W. Norton & Co.

——— (1930; 1957). *The Revolt of the Masses*. Trans. anonymous. New York: W. W. Norton & Co.

Geertz, Clifford (1973). *The Interpretation of Cultures*. New York: Basic Books.

Gilson, Etienne (1965). *The Arts of the Beautiful*. New York: Charles Scribner's Sons.

——— (1952). *Being and Some Philosophers*. 2nd ed. Toronto: Pontifical Institute of Medieval Studies Press.

Gleick, James (1999). *Faster: The Acceleration of Just About Everything*. New York: Pantheon Books.

Goethals, Gregory (1981). *The TV Ritual: Worship at the Video Altar*. Boston: Beacon Press.

Gratzer, Walter (2005). *Terrors of the Table: The Curious History of Nutrition*. New York: Oxford University Press.

Greene, Brian (2004). *The Fabric of the Cosmos: Space, Time and the Texture of Reality*. New York: Alfred A. Knopf.

Guignon, Charles (1991). "Pragmatism or Hermeneutics? Epistemology after Foundationalism." In *The Interpretive Turn: Philosophy, Science, Culture*. Ed. David Hiley, James F. Bohman, Richard Shusterman. Ithaca: Cornell University Press.

Hadot, Pierre (1995). *Philosophy as a Way of Life: Spiritual Exercises from Socrates to Foucault*. Ed. Arnold Davidson. Trans. Michael Chase. Oxford: Blackwell.

Halliwell, Stephen (1995). "Introduction." In Aristotle (1995). *The Poetics*. In *Aristotle: Poetics; Longinus: On the Sublime; Demetrius: On Style*. Cambridge: Loeb Classical Library.

Hamady, Samia (1960). *Temperament and Character of the Arabs*. New York: Twayne Publishers.

Harris, Sam (2007). *Letter to a Christian Nation*. New York: Alfred A. Knopf.

——— (2004). *The End of Faith: Religion, Terror, and the Future of Reason*. New York: W. W. Norton & Co.

Harrison, G. B. ed. (1948). *Shakespeare: The Complete Works*. New York: Harcourt Brace & World.

Hegel, Georg W. H. (1835; 1975). *Aesthetics: Lectures on Fine Art*. Vol. 1. Trans. T. M. Knox. Oxford: Clarendon Press.

Heidegger, Martin (1971). *Poetry, Language, Thought*. Trans. Albert Hofstadter. New York: Harper & Row.

——— (1947; 1962). "Plato's Doctrine of Truth." In *Philosophy in the Twentieth Century*. Vol. 3. Ed. William Barrett and Henry Aiken. New York: Random House.

——— (1926; 1962). *Being and Time*. Trans. John Macquarrie and Edward Robinson. New York: Random House.

Heldke, Lisa, and Curtin, Deane, eds. (1992). *Cooking, Eating, Thinking*. Indianapolis: Indiana University Press.

Heldke, Lisa M. (2003). *Exotic Appetites: Ruminations of a Food Adventurer*. New York: Routledge.

Heldke, Lisa, Mommer, Kerri, and Pineo, Cynthia (2005). *The Atkins Diet and Philosophy*. Peru, IL: Open Court.

Heldke, Lisa (2006). "The Unexamined Meal Is Not Worth Eating, or, Why and How Philosophers (Might/Could/Do) Study Food." *Food, Culture and Society* 9, 201–219.

Henig, Robin Marantz (1993). *A Dancing Matrix: Voyages Along the Viral Frontier*. New York: Alfred A. Knopf.

Hiley, David, Bohman, James, and Shusterman, Richard, eds. (1991). *The Interpretive Turn*. Ithaca: Cornell University Press.

Hilgartner, Stephen (2000). *Science on State: Expert Advice as Public Drama*. Stanford: Stanford University Press.

Hitchens, Christopher (2007). *God Is Not Great: How Religion Poisons Everything.* New York: Hachette Book Group.

Hofstadter, Douglas (1997). *Le Ton beau de Marot: In Praise of the Music of Language.* New York: Basic Books.

Hollinger, David (1995). *Postethnic America.* New York: Basic Books.

Homer (ca. 700 bce/1996). *The Odyssey.* Trans. Robert Fagles. New York: Penguin Books.

Horgan, John (1996). *The End of Science: Facing the Limits of Knowledge in the Twilight of the Scientific Age.* New York: Helix Books.

Horne, Alistair (2003). *Seven Ages of Paris.* New York: Alfred A. Knopf.

Howell, Martha, and Prevenier, Walter (2001). *From Reliable Sources: An Introduction to Historical Methods.* Ithaca: Cornell University Press.

Hume, David (1739; 1992). *A Treatise of Human Nature.* Amherst, NY: Prometheus Books.

Huxley, Thomas H. (1896). *Evolution and Ethics and Other Essays.* New York: D. Appleton & Co.

Jackson, Michael (1989). *Paths Toward a Clearing: Radical Empiricism and Ethnographic Inquiry.* Indianapolis: University of Indiana Press.

James, William (1907; 1981). *Pragmatism.* Indianapolis: Hackett Publishing Co.

——— (1902; 1994). *The Varieties of Religious Experience.* New York: Modern Library.

——— (1899, 1958). *Talks to Teachers on Psychology; and to Students on Some of Life's Ideals.* New York: W. W. Norton & Co.

——— (1897; 1956). *The Will to Believe and Other Essays in Popular Philosophy.* New York: Dover Publications, Inc.

——— (1890; 1950). *The Principles of Psychology.* Vol. 1. New York: Dover Publications.

——— (1882; 1956). "The Sentiment of Rationality." In *The Will to Believe and Other Essays.* New York: Dover Publications.

Jaspers, Karl (1967). *Philosophical Faith and Revelation.* Trans. E. B. Ashton. New York: Harper & Row.

Johnson, Mark (1987). *The Body in the Mind: The Bodily Basis of Meaning, Imagination, and Reason.* Chicago: University of Chicago Press.

Johnson, Mark, and Lakoff, George (1980). *Metaphors We Live By.* Chicago: University of Chicago Press.

Johnson, Mark, ed. (1981). *Philosophical Perspectives on Metaphor.* Minneapolis: University of Minnesota Press.

Jordan-Smith, Paul (1990). "The Hostage and the Parasite." *Parabola* 15: 24–31.

Jullien, François (2001). *Du "Temps," Éléments d'une philosophie du rire.* Paris: Grasset.

Kandinsky, Wassily (1912). "On the Spiritual in Art." In *Kandinsky: Complete Writings on Art.* Ed. Kenneth C. Lindsay and Peter Vergo. N.p.: Da Capo Press.

Kant, Immanuel (1795; 1983). *Perpetual Peace, and other essays on politics, history, and morals.* Trans. Ted Humphrey. Indianapolis: Hackett Publishing Co.

——— (1790; 2000). *Critique of the Power of Judgment.* Trans. Paul Guyer and Eric Matthews. Cambridge: Cambridge University Press.

——— (1784; 1963). "What Is Enlightenment?" In *On History.* Ed. Lewis White Beck. Indianapolis: Library of Liberal Arts.

Kaplan, David, ed. (2012). *The Philosophy of Food.* Berkeley: University of California Press.

Kass, Leon (1994). *The Hungry Soul.* New York: Free Press.

Kasulis, Thomas P. (2002). *Intimacy or Integrity: Philosophy and Cultural Difference.* Honolulu: University of Hawaii Press.

——— (1981). *Zen Action, Zen Person.* Honolulu: University of Hawaii Press.

Kawabata, Yasunari (1951; 1989). *Thousand Cranes.* Trans. Edward Seigensticker. New York: Perigee Books.

Keller, Evelyn Fox (1985). *Reflections on Gender and Science.* New Haven: Yale University Press.

——— (1983). *A Feeling for the Organism: The Life and Work of Barbara McClintock.* New York: W. H. Freeman and Co.

Kingsolver, Barbara, Hopp, Steven, and Kingsolver, Camille (2007). *Animal, Vegetable, Mineral: A Year of Food Life.* New York: HarperCollins.

Kirk, G. S. and J. E. Raven (1969). *The Presocratic Philosophers: A Critical History with a Selection of Texts*. Cambridge: Cambridge University Press.

Klein, Ernest (1966; 1967). *A Comprehensive Etymological Dictionary of the English Language*. London: Elsevier Publishing Co.

Kohák, Erazim (1984). *The Embers and the Stars: A Philosophical Inquiry into the Moral Sense of Nature*. Chicago: University of Chicago Press.

Korsmeyer, Carolyn (2005). *The Taste Culture Reader: Experiencing Food and Drink*. New York: Berg.

——— (1999). *Making Sense of Taste*. Ithaca: Cornell University Press.

Korthals, Michiel (2004). *Before Dinner: Philosophy and Ethics of Food*. Trans. Frans Kooymans. Dordrecht: Springer.

Krieger, Leonard (1977). *Ranke: The Meaning of History*. Chicago: University of Chicago Press.

Lachs, John (2004). "The Future of Philosophy" retrieved from www.politicaltheory.info/essays/lachs.htm on May 2, 2006, originally in *The Proceedings and Addresses of the American Philosophical Association* 78, no. 2: 5–14.

Landes, Joan (1988). *Women in the Public Sphere in the Age of the French Revolution*. Ithaca: Cornell University Press.

Langer, Susanne (1951; 1978). *Philosophy in a New Key*. 2nd ed. Cambridge: Harvard University Press.

Latour, Bruno (2004). *Politics of Nature: How to Bring the Sciences into Democracy*. Trans. Catherine Porter. Cambridge: Harvard University Press.

——— (1999). *Pandora's Hope: Essays on the Reality of Science Studies*. Cambridge: Harvard University Press.

Laue, Theodore H. von (1950). *Leopold Ranke: The Formative Years*. Princeton: Princeton University Press.

Lawrence, William J. (1927; 1968). *The Physical Conditions of the Elizabethan Public Playhouse*. New York: Cooper Square Publishers.

Leibniz, Gottfried. W. (1714; 1991). *The Monadology*. In *Discourse on Metaphysics and Other Essays*. Trans. Daniel Garber and Roger Ariew. Indianapolis: Hackett Publishing Co.

Lenardon, Robert, and Morford, Mark (2003). *Classical Mythology*, 7th ed. New York: Oxford University Press.

Levinas, Emmanuel (1969). *Totality and Infinity*. Trans. Alphonso Lingis. Pittsburgh: Duquesne University Press.

Lewontin, Richard (2000). *The Triple Helix: Gene, Organism, and Environment*. Cambridge, MA: Harvard University Press.

Lin, Yutang (1937). *The Importance of Living*. New York: Reynal & Hitchcock.

Locke, John (1690; 1980). *Second Treatise on Government*. Indianapolis: Hackett Publishing Co.

——— (1690a; 1961). *An Essay Concerning Human Understanding*. 2 vols. New York: Everyman's Library.

Lovegren, Sylvia (1995). *Fashionable Food: Seven Decades of Food Fads*. New York: Macmillan.

Lucas, George (1997). "Philosophy's Recovery of Its History: A Tribute to John E. Smith." In Thomas P. Kasulis and Robert Cummings Neville, *The Recovery of Philosophy in America*. Albany: SUNY Press.

Lucian (2nd century; 1927). "The Carousal or the Lapiths." In *Lucian with an English Translation*. Vol. 1. Trans. A. M. Harmon. London: Wm. Heinemann.

Macquarrie, John (1983). *In Search of Humanity: A Theological and Philosophical Approach*. New York: Crossroad.

Mahdi, Muhsin (1964). *Ibn Khaldûn's Philosophy of History: A Study in the Philosophic Foundation of the Science of Culture*. Chicago: University of Chicago Press.

Marcel, Gabriel (1951). *Homo Viator: Introduction to a Metaphysic of Hope*. Trans. Emma Craufurd. Chicago: Henry Regnery and Co.

Margulis, Lynn, and Fester, René (1991). *Symbiosis as a Source of Evolutionary Innovation: Speciation and Morphogenesis*. Cambridge: MIT Press.

Marias, Julian (1969). "Les Genres Littéraires en Philosophie." *Revue Internationale de Philosophie* 23, no. 90.
Marinetti, F. T. (1932; 1989). *The Futurist Cookbook*. Trans. Suzanne Brill. San Francisco: Bedford Arts, Publishers.
Martin, Janet, and Nelson, Suzann (1995). *They Glorified Mary . . . We Glorified Rice: A Catholic-Lutheran Lexicon*. Hastings MN: Martin House Publications.
Mbiti, John (1990). *African Religions and Philosophy*. 2nd ed. London: Heinemann.
McKenna, Erin, and Light, Andrew (2004). *Animal Pragmatism: Rethinking Human-Nonhuman Relationships*. Bloomington: Indiana University Press.
McKeon, Richard, ed. (1941). *The Basic Works of Aristotle*. New York: Random House.
Melville, Herman (1851; 1956). *Moby Dick or, The Whale*. Boston: Houghton Mifflin.
Menand, Louis (2001). *The Metaphysical Club*. New York: Farrar, Straus and Giroux.
Mepham, Ben (1996). *Food Ethics*. London: Routledge.
Midgley, Mary (1997). *Beast and Man: The Roots of Human Nature*. New York: Meridian.
——— (1989). *Wisdom, Information, and Wonder*. London: Routledge.
——— (1984). *Animals and Why They Matter*. Athens, GA: University of Georgia Press.
Milton, John (1667; 1997). *Paradise Lost*. Ed. Roy Flannagan. New York: Macmillan.
Molière, Jean-Baptiste (1669; 1967). *Tartuffe and Other Plays by Molière*. Translated Donald M. Frame. New York: Signet Classics.
Mones, Nicole (2007). *The Last Chinese Chef*. Boston: Houghton Mifflin.
Monk, Ray (1990). *Ludwig Wittgenstein*. New York: Free Press.
Mossner, Ernest Campbell (1954). *The Life of David Hume*. London: Nelson.
Mounier, Emmanuel (1949). *Le personnalisme*. Paris: Presses Universitaires de France.
Myers, Allen, ed. (1987). *The Eerdmans Bible Dictionary*. Grand Rapids: William B. Eerdmans Publishing Co.
Nagel, Thomas (1987). *What Does it All Mean?: A Very Short Introduction to Philosophy*. New York: Oxford University Press.
Norris, Kathleen (1996). *The Cloister Walk*. New York: Riverhead Books.
——— (1993). *Dakota: A Spiritual Geography*. New York: Ticknor & Fields.
Nussbaum, Martha (2001). *Upheavals of Thought*. Cambridge: Cambridge University Press.
Oates, Whitney J. ed. (1940). *The Stoic and Epicurean Philosophers*. New York: Random House.
Onfray, Michel (1995). *La Raison Gourmande*. Paris: Bernard Grasset.
——— (1989). *Le Ventre des Philosophes*. Paris: Bernard Grasset.
Ortega y Gasset, Jose (1966; 1969). *Some Lessons in Metaphysics*. Trans. Mildred Adams, New York: W. W. Norton & Co.
——— (1960). *What Is Philosophy?* Trans. Mildred Adams. New York: W. W. Norton & Co.
——— (1958; 2000). *Man and Crisis*. Trans. Mildred Adams. New York: W. W. Norton & Co.
Osborne, Kenan B. (2003). *The Franciscan Intellectual Tradition: Tracing Its Origins and Identifying Its Central Components*. The Franciscan Heritage Series, Vol. 1. St. Bonaventure, NY: The Franciscan Institute.
Owens, Joseph (1951). *The Doctrine of Being in the Aristotelian Metaphysics: A Study in the Greek Background of Mediaeval Thought*. Toronto: Pontifical Institute of Medieval Studies Press.
Parsons, June Jamrich, and Dan Oja (1995). *New Perspectives on Computer Concepts*. Cambridge, MA: Course Technology, Inc.
Partridge, Eric (1958). *Origins: A Short Etymological Dictionary of Modern English*. New York: Macmillan Co.
Pasternak, Boris (1958). *Dr. Zhivago*. Trans. Max Hayward and Manya Harari. New York: Signet Books.
Pateman, Carol (1988). *The Sexual Contract*. Stanford: Stanford University Press.
Patočka, Jan (1993). *Liberté et sacrifice*. Trans. E. Abrams. Paris: Jerome Millon.
Peirce, Charles (1897; 1955). "Logic as Semiotic: The Theory of Signs." In *Philosophical Writings of Peirce*. Ed. Justus Buchler. New York: Dover Publications, Inc.

―――― (1868; 1984). "Some Consequences of Four Incapacities." In *Writings of Charles Sanders Peirce: A Chronological Edition*, Vol. 2. Ed. Edward C. Moore. Bloomington: Indiana University Press.

Pepper, Stephen (1942). *World Hypotheses.* Berkeley: University of California Press.

Phillips, Adam (2000). *Darwin's Earthworms: On Life Stories and Death Stories.* New York: Basic Books.

Phillips, D. Z. (1996). *Introducing Philosophy: The Challenge of Scepticism.* Oxford: Blackwell.

Pinker, Steven (1994). *The Language Instinct.* New York: William Morrow and Co.

Plato (2010). *The Apology, in Plato: The Last Days of Socrates.* Trans. Christopher Rowe. London: Penguin.

―――― (1998). *Phaedrus.* Trans. James H. Nichols Jr. Ithaca: Cornell University Press.

―――― (1997). "Apology." In *Plato: Complete Works.* Ed. John M. Cooper. Indianapolis: Hackett Publishing Co.

―――― (1977). *Plato's Phaedo.* Trans. G. M. A. Grube. Indianapolis: Hackett Publishing Co.

―――― (1974). *The Republic.* Trans. G. M. A. Grube. Indianapolis: Hackett Publishing Co.

―――― (1961). *Phaedrus.* In *The Collected Dialogues of Plato.* Ed. Edith Hamilton and Huntington Cairns. New York: Bollingen Foundation.

―――― (1961). *The Laws.* In *The Collected Dialogues of Plato.* Ed. Huntington Cairns and Edith Hamilton. New York: Bollingen Foundation.

Pleij, Herman (2001). *Dreaming of Cockaigne: Medieval Fantasies of the Perfect Life.* Trans. Diane Webb. New York: Columbia University Press.

Pliny (1952). Book XXXV. In *Natural History*, Vol. ix. Trans. H. Rackam. London: Loeb Classical Library.

Plotinus (1946). *Enneads.* 6 vols. Trans. A. H. Armstrong. Cambridge: Loeb Classical Library.

Plutarch (1928 ed.). "Dinner of the Seven Wise Men." In *Plutarch's Moralia II.* Trans. Frank Babbitt. Cambridge, MA: Loeb Classical Library.

Polanyi, Michael (1969). *Knowing and Being.* Ed. Marjorie Grene. Chicago: University of Chicago Press.

―――― (1966; 1983). *The Tacit Dimension.* Gloucester: Peter Smith.

―――― (1959). *The Study of Man.* Chicago: University of Chicago Press.

―――― (1958). *Personal Knowledge: Towards a Post-Critical Philosophy.* Chicago: University of Chicago Press.

Pollan, Michael (2006). *The Omnivore's Dilemma: A Natural History of Four Meals.* New York: Penguin Press.

Popper, Karl (1968; 1972). "Epistemology Without a Knowing Subject." In *Objective Knowledge: An Evolutionary Approach.* Oxford: Clarendon.

Proctor, Robert (1988). *Racial Hygiene: Medicine Under the Nazis.* Cambridge: Harvard University Press.

Putnam, Robert (2007). "*E Pluribus Unum*: Diversity and Community in the Twenty-First Century: The 2006 Johan Skytte Prize Lecture." *Scandinavian Political Studies* 30, no. 2: 137–174.

Putnam, Robert (2000). *Bowling Alone: The Collapse and Revival of American Community.* New York: Touchstone.

Rahula, Walpola (1974). *What the Buddha Taught.* 2nd ed. New York: Grove Press.

Rammel, Hal (1990). *Nowhere in America: The Big Rock Candy Mountain and Other Comic Utopias.* Urbana and Chicago: University of Illinois Press.

Randall, John Herman Jr. (1968). *The Meaning of Religion for Man.* New York: Harper Torchbooks.

―――― (1940). "Dean Woodbridge." *Columbia University Quarterly* 32 (1940): 324–331.

―――― (1926). *The Making of the Modern Mind: A Survey of the Intellectual Background of the Present Age.* New York: Houghton Mifflin.

Reece, Steve (1993). *The Stranger's Welcome: Oral Theory and the Aesthetics of the Homeric Hospitality Scene.* Ann Arbor: University of Michigan Press.

Regan, Tom (1983). *The Case for Animal Rights.* Berkeley: University of California Press.

Rennie, John (1992, January). "Trends in Parasitology: Living Together," *Scientific American* 266.1: 122–23, 126–33.
Rescher, Nicholas (1995). *Essays in the History of Philosophy*. Brookfield: Avebury.
Revel, Jean-François and Matthieu Ricard (1999). *The Monk and the Philosopher: A Father and Son Discuss the Meaning of Life*. New York: Shocken Books.
Riccardi, Victoria Abbott (2003). *Untangling My Chopsticks: A Culinary Sojourn in Tokyo*. New York: Broadway Books.
Rockefeller, Steven (1991). *John Dewey: Religious Faith and Democratic Humanism*. New York: Columbia University Press.
Rorty, Richard, Vattimo, Gianni, and Zabala, Santiago (2005). *The Future of Religion*. New York: Columbia University Press.
Rorty, Richard (1998). *Achieving Our Country: Leftist Thought in Twentieth-Century America*. Cambridge: Harvard University Press.
——— (1997). "Religious faith, intellectual responsibility, and romance." In Ruth Anna Putnam, ed. *The Cambridge Companion to William James*. Cambridge: Cambridge University Press.
——— (1994) "Tales of Two Disciplines." *Calalloo* 17, no. 2: 575–585.
——— (1989). *Contingency, Irony, and Solidarity*. Cambridge: Cambridge University Press.
——— (1982). *Consequences of Pragmatism*. Minneapolis: University of Minnesota Press.
——— (1979). *Philosophy and the Mirror of Nature*. Princeton: Princeton University Press.
Rosenberg, Jay (1978). *The Practice of Philosophy: A Handbook for Beginners*. Englewood Cliffs: Prentice Hall.
Rousseau, Jean-Jacques (1755; 1992). *Discourse on the Origin of Inequality*. Trans. Donald A. Cress. Indianapolis: Hackett Publishing Co.
——— (1762; 1979). *Emile*. Trans. Allan Bloom. New York: Harper Books.
Royce, Josiah (1982). *The Philosophy of Josiah Royce*. Ed. John K. Roth. Indianapolis: Hackett Publishing Co.
Rule of St. Benedict, rule.kansasmonks.org.
Russell, Bertrand (1912; 1959). *The Problems of Philosophy*. New York: Oxford University Press.
Ryan, Alan (1995). *John Dewey and the High Tide of American Liberalism*. New York: W. W. Norton & Co.
Ryle, Gilbert (1949). *The Concept of Mind*. London: Hutchinson & Co.
Sack, Daniel (2000). *Whitebread Protestants: Food and Religion in American Culture*. New York: St. Martin's Press.
Santayana, George (1931; 1968). "The Genteel Tradition at Bay." In *Santayana on America: Essays, Notes, and Letters on American Life, Literature, and Philosophy*. New York: Harcourt Brace & World, Inc.
——— (1913; 1968). "The Genteel Tradition in American Philosophy." In *Santayana on America*. Ed. Richard Colton Lyon. New York: Harcourt, Brace & World.
Sartre, Jean-Paul (1938; 1964). *Nausea*. Trans. Lloyd Alexander: New York: New Directions.
Schaefer, Jack (1949). *Shane*. Boston: Houghton Mifflin Co.
Schmitt-Pantel, Pauline (2000). *La Cité au Banquet: histoire des repas publics dans les cités grecques*. Rome: École Française de Rome.
Schopenhauer, Arthur (1818; 1819; 1969), *The World as Will and Representation*, Vols. 1 & 2. Trans. E. F. J. Payne. New York: Dover Publications.
Scruton, Roger (2010). *I Drink Therefore I Am*. London: Bloomsbury Academic.
Searle, John (1998). *Mind, Language, and Society*. New York: Basic Books.
Seeskin, Kenneth R. (1979/1980). "Never Speculate, Never Explain: The State of Contemporary Philosophy." *The American Scholar* 49.
Sen, Soshitsu (1971). "Host and Guest," *Chanoyu Quarterly* II, no. 2: 1–2.
Serres, Michel (2002a). *Revue Jules Verne: Conversations Avec Michel Serres*. La Revue Jules Verne, no. 13–14.
——— (2002b). *En Amour sommes-nous des bêtes?* Paris: Le Pommier.
——— (2001). *Hominescence*. Paris: Le pommier.
——— (1992). *Éclaircissements: Cinq Entretiens Avec Bruno Latour*. Paris: François Bourin.

Bibliography

——— (1990). *Le contrat naturel*. Paris: François Bourin.
——— (1985). *Les Cinq Sens*. Paris: Bernard Grasset.
——— (1980). *Le Parasite*. Paris: Bernard Grasset.
——— (1974). *Hermes III: La traduction*. Paris: Éditions du minuit.
Severson, Kim (2006). "On the Soup Line, Endive and Octopus." www.nytimes.com/2006/12/20/dining/20soup.html?ex=1324270800&en=076fb98b0da565d0&ei=5088&partner=rssnyt&emc=rss, retrieved April 4, 2007.
Shakespeare, William (1948). *Shakespeare, The Complete Works*. Ed. G. B. Harrison. New York: Harcourt Brace & World.
Sherringham, Marc (1992). *Introduction à la philosophie esthétique*. Paris: Editions Payot.
Shusterman, Richard (1997). *Practicing Philosophy*. New York: Routledge.
Siegfried, Tom (2000). *The Bit and the Pendulum: From Quantum Computing to M Theory—The New Physics of Information*. New York: John Wiley & Sons.
Singer, Peter (1990). *Animal Liberation*. New York: Avon Books.
Skinner, B. F. (1953). *Science and Human Behavior*. New York: Free Press.
——— (1938). *The Behavior of Organisms: an Experimental Analysis*. Englewood Cliffs, NJ: Prentice-Hall.
Smith, Alexander McCall (2005). *Friends, Lovers, Chocolate*. New York: Pantheon Books.
Smith, Dennis E. (2003). *From Symposium to Eucharist: The Banquet in the Early Christian World*. Minneapolis: Fortress Press.
Smith, Tom (2004). "Humanitarian Daily Rations." retrieved April 9, 2007.
Smoot, George and Davidson, Keay (1993). *Wrinkles in Time*. New York: William Morrow and Co, Inc.
Spence, Gregory, ed. (2001). *The Ethics of Food*. London: Rowman & Littlefield.
Stephen, James Fitzjames (1873; 1991). *Liberty, Equality, Fraternity, and Three Brief Essays*. Chicago: University of Chicago Press.
Stoller, Paul (1997). *Sensuous Scholarship*. Philadelphia: University of Pennsylvania Press.
——— (1989). *The Taste of Ethnographic Things: The Sense in Anthropology*. Philadelphia: University of Pennsylvania Press.
Suetonius (ad 121; 1989). *The Twelve Caesars*. Trans. Robert Graves. New York: Penguin.
Suzuki, Daisetz T. (1959; 1970). *Zen and Japanese Culture*. Princeton: Bollingen Foundation.
Swift, Jonathan (1726; 1981). *Gulliver's Travels and Other Writings by Jonathan Swift*. Ed. Miriam Kosh Starkman. New York: Bantam Books.
Symons, Michael (1998). *A History of Cooks and Cooking*. Urbana: University of Illinois Press.
Taylor, Charles (2007). *A Secular Age*. Cambridge: Harvard University Press.
——— (1995). *Philosophical Arguments*. Cambridge: Harvard University Press.
——— (1991). "The Dialogical Self." In Hiley, Bohman, and Shusterman.
Dennis and Barbara Tedlock, eds. (1975). *Teachings from the American Earth: Indian Religion and Philosophy*. New York: Liveright.
Telfer, Elizabeth (1996). *Food for Thought: Philosophy and Food*. London: Routledge.
Thackeray, William Makepeace (1904). *Letters of Thackeray to Mrs. Brookfield; Miscellaneous Essays, Sketches and Reviews*. New York: Brentano's.
The Interpreter's Dictionary of the Bible: An Illustrated Encyclopedia (1962). Nashville: Abingdon Press.
Thompson, Paul (1995). *The Spirit of the Soil: Agriculture and Environmental Ethics*. New York: Routledge.
Thuan, Trinh Xuan (1995). *The Secret Melody: And Man Created the Universe*. Trans. Storm Dunlop. New York: Oxford University Press.
Tilley, Christopher (1993). "Introduction." In *Interpretative Archaeology*. Ed. C. Tilley. Oxford: Berg.
Tolstoy, Leo (1898; 1975). *What Is Art? And Essays on Art*. Trans. Aylmer Maude. London: Oxford University Press.
Toulmin, Stephen (2001). *Return to Reason*. Cambridge MA: Harvard University Press.
Trager, William (1970). *Symbiosis*. New York: Van Nostrand Reihnold Co.
Truffault, François (1985). *Hitchcock*. New York: Simon and Schuster.

Turner, Victor (1969; 1995). *The Ritual Process: Structure and Anti-Structure.* New York: Aldine de Gruyter.

Van Ness, Peter, ed. (1996). *Spirituality and the Secular Quest.* Vol. 22 of *World Spirituality: An Encyclopedic History of the Religious Quest.* New York: Crossroad.

Visser, Margaret (1991). *The Rituals of Dinner: The Origins, Evolution, Eccentricities, and Meaning of Table Manners.* New York: Penguin.

——— (1986). *Much Depends on Dinner.* NY: Collier Books.

Vonnegut, Kurt (1961; 1988). "Harrison Bergeron." In *Welcome to the Monkey House.* NY: Dell.

Walters, Kerry and Portmess, Lisa (1999). *Ethical Vegetarianism: From Pythagoras to Peter Singer.* Albany: SUNY Press.

Walzer, Michael (1977). *Just and Unjust Wars: A Moral Argument with Historical Illustrations.* New York: Harper Torchbooks.

Watson, John B. (1925). *Behaviorism.* New York: W. W. Norton & Co.

Whitehead, Alfred North (1926). *Science and the Modern World.* New York: Macmillan Co.

Wilson, Edward O. (1994a). *Naturalist.* Washington D.C.: Island Press.

——— and Bert Hölldobler (1994b). *Journey to the Ants.* Cambridge: Harvard University Press.

Winthrop, John (1630; 1956). "A Model of Christian Charity." In *The American Puritans: Their Prose and Poetry.* Ed. Perry Miller. New York: Anchor Books.

Woodbridge, Frederick J. E. (1965). *Nature and Mind.* New York: Russell & Russell.

World Food Program. "Rapid Response." www.wfp.org/operations/introduction/emergencies_operations.asp?section=5&sub_section=1, retrieved April 9, 2007.

Yanagi, Soetsu (1972). *The Unknown Craftsman: A Japanese Insight into Beauty.* Adapted by Bernard Leach. Kodansha International Ltd.

Zaidman, Louise Bruit (1995). "Ritual Eating in Archaic Greece: Parasites and *Paredroi.*" In John Wilkins, David Harvey, and Mike Dobson, *Food in Antiquity.* Exeter: University of Exeter Press.

Zakaria, Fareed (2003). *The Future of Freedom: Illiberal Democracy at Home and Abroad.* New York: Norton.

Zeilinger, Anton (2006). "Spooky Action and Beyond." Interview in *Die Weltwoche*, January 3. Made available at the *SignandSight* website: www.signandsight.com/features/614.html.

Zimmer, Carl (2000). *Parasite Rex: Inside the Bizarre World of Nature's Most Dangerous Creatures.* New York: Free Press.

Ziolkowski, Theodore (1997). "Philosophy into Fiction," *The American Scholar* 66.

Index

Addams, Jane, 21, 33, 67
Aeschylus, 26
agape, 119, 120
agriculture, 9, 18, 27, 127
Alexander, Thomas, 88, 92n22
anamnesis, 2, 148
Aquinas, Thomas, 85, 92n17
Aristippus, 13, 20n3
Aristotle, 10, 11, 27, 41, 52n4, 52n7, 76, 78, 83, 90n3, 100, 108, 109, 109–110, 111, 112, 114, 116, 117
Augustine, St., 58, 140
autonomous, 30, 31, 44, 80, 100, 101, 102, 103, 104
autonomy, 40, 43, 46, 79, 93, 95, 96, 97, 98, 102, 103, 143–144, 148

Balzac, Honoré de, 87
Barrett, William, 15, 16, 87
Baum, L. Frank, 3–4
Belasco, Warren, 114
Bergson, Henri, 6, 10, 37, 52n1
Berkeley, Bishop, 10, 17, 20n5
Bordo, Susan, 4, 8n4, 14
Borobudur, 81, 86, 89, 146
Buddhism, 80, 81, 124, 129

Camus, Albert, 22–23, 25, 31, 33, 34, 37–38, 47, 55, 129–130
Ceres, 9, 9–10, 15, 16, 18–19, 24
Chaucer, 82, 91n14, 146

China/Chinese, 10, 13, 68, 75, 90n2, 94, 95, 96, 97, 99, 104, 140, 148, 148n6
chronomania, 7, 96, 102–103
Cloaca, 74
Collingwood, R. G., 77–78, 83, 91n8
colonialism, 23–24
communitas, 111, 112, 114, 116–117, 143, 146, 147
convive, 5, 18, 19, 69n1
cultigen, 142
Curtin, Deane, 14

Darwin, Charles, 43, 44, 70n15, 80, 95
Delvoye, Wim, 74, 78
Demeter, 9, 10
dependence, 6, 43, 46, 70n14, 93, 97, 127, 129, 130, 131, 141
Derrida, Jacques, 29, 31–33, 34, 40, 48, 61
Descartes, Rene, 2, 9, 10, 15, 16, 17, 18, 40, 42, 52n8, 97, 137
Dewey, John, x, 6, 7, 13, 14, 15, 30, 52n5, 73, 80, 81, 82, 84, 85, 86, 89, 90, 90n1, 91n11, 91n12, 94, 95, 96, 99, 109, 114, 116, 129, 130, 137, 138
diabolical, 126, 132
diet, 1, 14, 70n19, 109, 116, 117, 142
Dinesen, Isak, 53n25, 141–142

Eco, Umberto, 83, 91n12
Enlightenment, The, 10, 23, 59, 69n6, 93, 94, 95, 102, 124, 127

Eros, 96, 97
Escoffier, 145
ethics, chapter 2 *passim*, 24, 28, 35n2
expression (art as), 77

factivity, 86
faith, 69n5, 120, 121–122, 122, 123, 124, 129, 130, 133n4
fast food, 21, 103, 108
Feuerbach, Ludwig, 13
Fielding, Henry, 9, 38, 70n17, 91n14, 92n15, 99
Forster, E. M., 40, 73, 74
Fourier, Charles, 137
fraternity, ix, 7, 26, 105, 106, 107, 108, 110, 111, 111–112, 115–116, 117n6, 141
freedom, 2, 44, 57, 90n1, 97, 102, 106, 107, 108, 141
Freud, Sigmund, 107, 111, 117n1, 137
friendship, chapter 7 *passim*, 107, 108, 109, 110, 111, 112, 114, 117, 117n2, 117n7
futurists, 136, 137, 138, 139, 140, 145, 146, 148n3

Gasset, Jose Ortega, 41, 44, 50, 94
gaster, 18, 19, 97, 97–98, 101, 104
Gemeinschaft, 109–110
Gesellschaft, 109–110
Gödel, Kurt, 12
Gospels, 120; Gospel of Matthew, 26; Gospel parable, 38
Greene, Brian, 94
guest, 5, 9, 10, 22–23, 25, 26, 27, 28, 33, 35n2, 37–38, 40, 45, 47, 51, 66, 68, 81, 82, 91n13, 106, 113, 142, 143, 145
Gulliver, 3

Hadot, Pierre, 2, 8, 8n3, 16, 19
Heidegger, Martin, 6, 32, 41, 63, 80, 84, 85, 86, 87, 92n20, 94, 137
Heldke, Lisa, ix, 4–5, 8n4, 14
Hitchcock, Alfred, 74
Hollinger, David, 23, 24, 31
Homer, 27, 39, 113
Hopper, Edward, 98, 101, 102, 103, 104
hospitality, chapter 2 *passim*, 21, 23, 24–25, 25, 25–27, 27–28, 29–30, 30–31, 32, 33, 34, 35, 35n2
host, 5, 22, 23, 27, 29, 33, 37, 38, 40, 45, 52n2, 53n14, 53n15, 66, 68, 81, 82, 91n13, 92n15, 120, 142, 143, 146
humanitarian daily ration (HDR), 21–22, 23, 31
Hume, David, 10, 13, 43, 46, 95

imitation (art as), 75–76, 77, 78, 81, 82, 89, 90n3, 90n4
infinite, 68, 69n8, 92n18, 98, 115, 141, 145, 146
intromitter, 48, 49, 51, 53n17, 56, 61, 66, 139, 143, 146
Islam, 26

James, William, 2, 6, 10, 15, 34, 69n4, 85, 121, 137, 145–146
Jaspers, Karl, 124
Jullien, François, 94, 95, 96, 104

Kingsolver, Barbara, 143
Korsmeyer, Carolyn, 4, 14
Korthals, Michiel, 4, 8n4, 14

Langer, Susan, 14, 15
Leibniz, Gottfried Wilhelm, 9, 10, 42–43, 46, 100
Levinas, Emmanuel, 26, 32–33, 34, 40, 41, 48, 68, 115, 141
ligature line, 122, 127, 128, 130, 131
Light, Andrew, 4, 8n4
Lucian, 20n3, 105, 113
Luo, the, 147

Marcel, Gabriel, 10, 15, 31, 35n4, 80, 104n1
Marinetti, Filippo, 135–136, 138, 148n2, 148n3
Marx, Karl, 124, 137
McKenna, Erin, 4, 8n4
Melville, Herman, 1, 3
metaphysics, 40, 41, 42, 43, 44, 45, 46, 47, 48, 49, 50, 52n4, 52n5, 52n7, 63, 140, 146
Midgley, Mary, 4, 8n4, 65
Millet, Jean-François, 98, 100, 101–102, 104
mimesis, 76, 82, 89

mingei, 6, 80
Mones, Nicole, 75, 90n2, 140, 148n6
Moses, 31
Mounier, Emmanuel, 33–34, 68

negligence, 119, 125, 126

object, 5, 6, 11, 18, 19, 34, 46, 47, 49, 58, 59, 62, 63, 64, 65, 68, 69n8, 70n14, 70n15, 74, 77, 78, 89, 91n6, 91n9, 91n11, 96, 99, 110, 141, 142, 144, 146–147, 147
The Odyssey, 26, 35n3, 38
Onfray, Michel, 9, 10, 12, 14

Parrhasius, 75, 76
Pasternak, Boris, 1, 3, 14
Patočka, Jan, 87, 92n21
Pears, David, 16, 20
Peirce, Charles, 10, 15
Phillips, D. Z., 17, 43
philosophy, nature of, chapter 1 *passim*, 9, 10, 11, 14–15, 16–17, 18–20
Plato, 1–2, 8n2, 10, 11, 12, 27, 40, 69n2, 76, 77, 78, 83, 86, 88, 89, 90, 90n3–91n5, 92n22, 103, 105, 109, 113
Pliny the Elder, 75
Plotinian temptation, 140
Plotinus, 69n2, 83, 140
pluralism, 29, 115, 122
Plutarch, 106, 112–113, 114, 147
practices, 4, 7, 16, 19, 24, 49, 58, 63, 64, 65, 79, 83, 96, 97, 99, 100, 108–109, 113, 114, 117, 119, 120, 121, 122, 123, 124, 125, 126–127, 128, 129, 131, 132, 144
pragmatism, pragmatist, x, 15, 52n6, 85, 88, 95, 96, 114, 122
praxis, 122, 123
prepositions, 49, 53n18, 64, 66, 85, 139, 140, 144
Prytaneum, 45, 110, 114
psyche, 18, 20, 96, 97, 97–98, 100, 104
Putnam, Robert, 115, 116, 117n3

rallier, 110, 112, 126
Randall, John Herman, 69n5, 73, 130
recipes, 3, 8, 12, 51, 59, 84, 101, 111, 119, 124, 125, 126, 127, 131, 132, 139

Regan, Tom, 4, 8n4
religion, x, 7, 16, 24–25, 34, 35n2, 52n1, 58, 107, 112
religion, chapter 8, *passim*, 119, 120–122, 123, 124, 125, 126, 127, 128, 128–129, 130, 132, 133n4, 148n2
Revel, Jean-François, 123–124, 133n5
Ricard, Matthieu, 123, 133n5
Rodin, Auguste, 11, 20n1
Russell, Bertrand, 10, 60, 61, 62
Ryan, Alan, 130

Saint Francis, 34, 35n6
Santayana, George, 13, 15–16, 19, 31–32
Sartre, Jean-Paul, 10, 12, 103
Schopenhauer, Arthur, 10, 11, 92n15
Searle, John, 15, 16, 121, 122, 123, 127, 128, 129, 130
Serres, Michel, 10, 14, 44, 46, 47, 50–51, 53n18, 53n19, 97, 120, 126, 127, 147
Shakespeare, William, 52n2, 74, 79
Singer, Peter, 4, 8n4
situatedness, 124
Smith, Alexander McCall, 8, 22, 49, 53n17
Sodom, 25
Soetsu, Yanagi, 6, 80, 81
spectator, 6, 8, 19, 65, 68, 69n8, 78–79, 79, 80, 81, 83, 85, 91n11, 92n15, 96, 103, 104, 110, 137, 142, 144
spirit, 13, 19, 58, 100, 124, 125, 141
Spoerri, Daniel, 9
Strawson, Peter, 113, 118n8
subject, 3, 5, 15, 18–19, 20n2, 27, 32, 46, 49, 52n2, 58, 59, 61, 62, 63, 64, 65, 68, 69n3, 70n14, 77, 78, 92n16, 96, 104, 142, 144
substantive goods, 107, 108
symbal, 122, 125, 126, 146
symbiosis, 53n15, 131, 143–144
symposium, 11, 105, 106, 108, 112, 119, 120, 146, 147

Taylor, Charles, 18–19, 133n3
tea, 6, 12, 38, 55, 80, 80–82, 83, 90, 91n13, 93, 94
Telfer, Elizabeth, 14, 28–30, 30, 31, 32, 144
Terezin, 124–125, 125, 127
Thackeray, William Makepeace, 74

theoxeny, 26, 28
time, chapter 6 *passim*, 93, 93–96, 97, 98–100, 101–102, 102–103, 103, 104, 104n3, 104n4
Tolstoy, Leo, 77, 78, 83, 91n6, 91n7
Torah, 26
truth, 1, 6, 11, 13, 40, 43, 44, 49, 62, 63, 76, 78, 82, 83, 84–85, 85–86, 87–88, 88, 90, 90n4, 92n17, 92n20, 108, 130, 148n3

Voltaire, 10, 112
Vonnegut, Kurt, 2

Wahl, Jean, 15
Whitehead, Alfred North, 6, 15, 70n13
Winthrop, John, 110
Wittgenstein, Ludwig, 11, 80
Woodbridge, Frederick J. E., 19, 73

Yutang, Lin, 13, 97

Zeno, 98, 99
Zeus, 26, 35n3
Zeuxis, 75, 76

About the Author

Raymond D. Boisvert is a specialist in American philosophy. He has written two books on John Dewey and many articles on Pragmatism. Lately, an interest in the philosophy of culture helped him contribute to developing the new field "food and philosophy." He has been Fulbright professor of American Studies at the Université de Lyon, a scholar in residence at the Institut Protestant de Théologie in Montpellier, France, and an officer in the Society for the Advancement of American Philosophy. He teaches philosophy at Siena College.